WE THE BACTERIA

WE THE BACTERIA

Notes Toward
Biotic Architecture

by

Beatriz Colomina
Mark Wigley

Lars Müller Publishers

1 Cover of first *Whole Earth Catalog*, 1968, edited by the biologist Stewart Brand, who had long campaigned for NASA to release this photo of Earth from space

If you don't like bacteria,
you're on the wrong planet[1]

—Stewart Brand, after J. Craig Venter, 2010

This book is covered with microbes. There are countless bacteria, viruses, and fungi on each page. Some were added just now by your hands and breath. Some descended in the dust swirling around you. Others were on the table when you picked the book up, arrived when a friend took a quick look, were already in the bookstore or at the printing house. They are not just on the surface of the pages but within the recesses of the binding and the cellulose of the paper. They flourish if the book becomes moist, forming a visible pattern as one cell quickly replicates itself to become millions. Many more microbes float in the air between you and the book, and even swim in the moist surface of your eye. You are literally looking through layers and clouds of microbes.

The hundreds of species of bacteria living on your eyes, along with their viral and fungal companions, interact with the vast microbial communities living in your gut via the recently discovered gut–eye axis. Those communities in turn communicate back and forth with the brain via the better-known gut–brain axis. In fact, our eyes are electrically and microbially part of the brain, as is the rest of the body. We see, think, and feel with and through microbes. We are microbial, as is the room around us: the air; the surfaces and internal layers of floors, walls, and ceiling; countertops, cabinets, handles, switches, furniture, carpets, and curtains; the air, water, and waste systems; appliances and electronic equipment; every crevice, and the very substance of most building materials.

Nothing could seem more different than microbes and buildings. One is a kaleidoscopic, pulsating variety of tiny organisms that might each have a life span of twenty minutes. The other are large, seemingly inert objects that sit still for decades, sometimes for hundreds, or even thousands of years. Yet nothing is straightforward about either microbes or buildings. Microbes have been around for billions of years and buildings have been permanently inhabited for just ten thousand years. Microbes are the smallest organisms of all, yet they constructed the whole planetary biosphere in which every organism lives, including humans.

A microbe is a mobile room, an interior divided from its exterior, a cell. To think about sheltering humans, the construction of spaces for human life, we have to think about the microorganisms that invented interior space more than four billion years ago – and in so doing eventually made us possible.

Microbes invented architecture. Yet the fear of unseen microorganisms shapes how we interact with each other and other species; our relationship to the ground, water, and air. It shapes our spaces and the ways we move through them. Cities, buildings, rooms, furniture, and devices are molded by this fear. Much of everyday life is devoted to killing microbes, with an ever-growing range of techniques and products to decimate the enemy. Exteriors and interiors of buildings are increasingly assembled out of antimicrobial materials or coated in a thin layer of plastic to avoid becoming a home for microbes and facilitate regular disinfection.

At the same time, there is a growing understanding of the beneficial role of microbes. Newspapers, magazines, books, and social media keep reporting on the importance of the microbiome – the community of microbes that live on and within us that is completely unique to each person and responsible for our health. The best defense against the microbes that cause disease turns out to be other microbes. Probiotics to replenish microbiomes are sold alongside products to kill microbes. Less known is that our personal microbiomes are intimately connected with the microbiomes of buildings. All buildings have specific human-associated communities of microbes, as does the air we breathe and what we eat and drink. Buildings and bodies are constantly exchanging microbes. In fact, we use buildings to store and share microbes. Buildings are part of us, as are all our companions, human and otherwise. To live together is to exchange microbes in a space. In the end, a space is just that: a pattern of microbial exchange.

We inhabit and digest a microbial world. More precisely, and uncannily, microbes continuously make us by digesting the world. We are an effect of microbes. We are never more than microbes. To look at these strange creatures is to look in a mirror.

The more we look in this mirror and become familiar with bacteria, viruses, and fungi, the stranger architecture becomes. Microbes turn out to be architectural and architecture turns out to be microbial. Despite all the obsessive antimicrobial warfare, microbes make and inhabit most building materials, the spaces that buildings make, the environment they are constructed in, and all the inhabitants – human and more-than-human. Buildings and bodies remain suspended within microbes rather than microbes within them.

To see architecture in terms of microbes is to see it through the highest resolution lens. On the one hand, it dissolves buildings into clouds of microorganisms that infuse every space, material, and system. On the other hand, it expands buildings, seeing how the human-built environment infuses the whole planet, from deep in the earth's crust to outer space – transforming the microbial world. Buildings entangle scales and species.

This book offers an alternative history of architecture from the point of view of microbes. The human-built environment was shaped by microbes for thousands of years before they were first seen at the end of the seventeenth century. Disease is the real designer of cities. Nineteenth-century cities were completely transformed in response to devasting waves of cholera, typhoid fever, and tuberculosis. Modern architecture was explicitly formulated as an antimicrobial project – with the most influential architects and historians even identifying themselves as bacteriologists.

This rethinking of the history and theory of architecture in terms of microbes draws on the evolving field of microbiology, not because it is an expert knowledge that needs to be applied to improve architecture, but because it is already a reflection on architecture – a theory about how spaces, organisms, and relationships are mutually formed. Microbiologists, architects, artists, and philosophers inevitably find themselves drawn into a new conversation and collaboration.

The point is not that nature is remarkable and humans are not, that buildings need to learn from the beautiful intelligence of the natural world. Buildings are actually part of the natural world. They are complex ecosystems built by creatures that are themselves ecosystems. Yet they recently arrived and are having radical effects on ecosystems at every scale, including humans themselves and the planet. To think about the relationship between microbes and architecture – even in just one building, room, or piece of furniture – is immediately to think of the future of humans and countless other species.

1 Stewart Brand, *Whole Earth Discipline: Why Dense Cities, Nuclear Power, Transgenic Crops, Restored Wildlands, and Geoengineering Are Necessary* (New York: Penguin, 2010), 187. Citing J. Craig Venter, interviewed in "Seeing Earth's Future in a Petri Dish," *Los Angeles Times*, November 24, 2007.

1 Computer-generated image of a group of extended-spectrum beta-lactamase-producing *E. coli* based on scanning electron microscopic imagery

1 WE ARE NEVER ALONE

Every one of us of every species is surrounded and inhabited by countless others. We are all both small and immense. Every individual is multiple, variable, and vertiginous. Every human – just one of the estimated trillion species currently inhabiting this planet – is a meta-organism, a continuous dynamic collaboration with a colossal number and diversity of invisible more-than-human others. We are portable ecosystems – trans-species alliances of seemingly infinite complexity and plasticity.

THE COMMUNITY

A human organism is an assemblage of around thirty trillion cells of different interlocking shapes and functions – a marvel of organization at the limits of comprehension. All these cells have the same unique DNA signature that persists from conception till after death, even as around 1 percent of them die and are replaced every day. The body is continually regenerating itself with copies of most of its cells. The singular human is not a static physical being, but a set of instructions guiding the operation and regeneration of countless cells.

To know this indelible genetic code – the human genome, which was only cracked in 2003 – is not yet to know an individual. **[2]** We are inhabited by many more microbes than human cells. This microbial community of around one hundred trillion includes around thirty-nine trillion bacteria in a combination of hundreds of species each with their own DNA, plus at least as many viruses with a similar amount of DNA, and a range of other single-celled organisms including fungi and archaea.

Each one of us has a personal combination of these microbes, and particular genetic variations of each. It fluctuates – especially during stress, illness, lack of sleep or exercise, change of diet or environment, exposure to toxins, antibiotic treatment, and older age – yet is remarkably stable given all the other microbes we constantly encounter, and the fact that

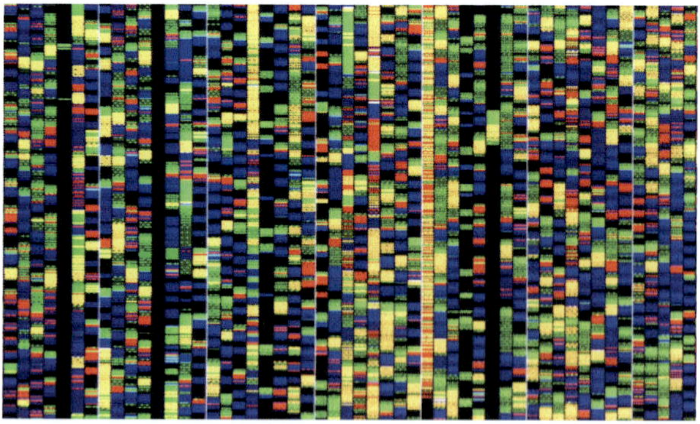

2 Colored bands on a computer screen representing the various building blocks of DNA that make up just a small portion of the human genome

the average life of a microbe is around twelve hours. The vastly intricate and complex microbial community of the human keeps rebuilding itself in the face of the ever-changing environment. It is the human's means of survival and the most unique thing about each individual – much more unique than a finger print. 99 percent of our DNA is in these microbes. They are not just guests of the human creature but its very possibility.

We are our microbiome, this vast personal community of continually interacting tiny organisms that occupy every surface between our body and the environment. If you zoom in on any place where humans touch and are touched by the world, there are highly organized colonies of different microbes collaborating to make that exchange. Touch itself is microbial.

There are more than 150 species of bacteria covering the palm of a human hand, a set that is unique to each human and even to the left hand versus the right.[1] Some of these micro-organisms are "transients" constantly picked up from the world, like the soil-related *Bacillus subtilis* in the bottom right of the palmprint that microbiologist Tasha Sturm made by lightly pressing her eight-year-old son's hand into a petri dish after playing outside. **[3]** Given the generous supply of nutrients in the dish, the bacillus exponentially multiplied over two days into a visible intricately organized circular colony of billions taking advantage of its new home. Many of the other colonies in different colors

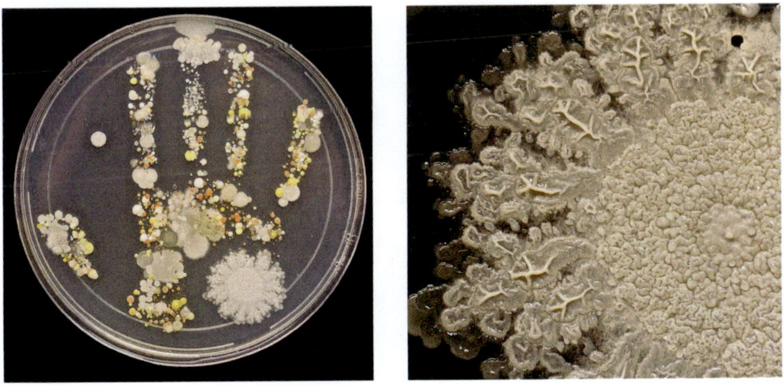

3 Bacterial handprint of eight-year-old child after playing outside and closeup of one of the colonies

are "resident" bacteria that remain on the palm (along with fungi and viruses) even after scrubbing with soap. Those live on the skin's surface in what microbiologists call a "biofilm" – an elaborate highly structured cooperative multi-species community held together in a stable matrix made of a sticky substance that its members produce. More precisely, they form that surface, both protecting the body and acting as its outer limit – with very different resident communities forming the outer skin of different parts of the body and lining every deep pore.

Microbiologists Paula Watnick and Roberto Kolter have likened biofilms to bustling cities with stable neighborhoods, where each individual and species collaboratively benefits from the presence of the others and constantly communicates with them.[2] This urbanization allows the microbes to survive, which allows the humans they colonize to survive. It is our real skin.

Likewise, around seven hundred species of bacteria inhabit the interior of the mouth and many of them actually form that interior. The surface of the tongue has a dense urbanism of microbial "skyscrapers" built around each of the outermost human cells, with particular species of bacteria at the core, the exterior, and in-between.[3] **[4]** Around two dozen species of bacteria attach themselves to each other to form these complex stable buildings, which act as a crucial part of the environment for all the other microbes permanently occupying the mouth, as well

4 Tongue-dwelling bacteria (different types marked by different colors) form a thick, highly structured film around human tongue surface cells (gray structure in the middle)

as those just passing through. The lips, teeth, gums, and inner cheeks have their own equally structured collaborative biofilms of different species.

The mouth – a transitional space between the inside and the outside of the body – is not a single environment but a series of interdependent micro-environments that sustain a dense ecology of interacting bacteria, viruses, and fungi. Every breath, sip, taste, kiss, and gulp engage this complex oral urbanism. In a sense, we only touch and are touched through such organized microbial architecture. No human cell is nakedly in the world. We wear a coat of microbes, or more precisely, we are woven and worn by them.

All aspects of life involve these microorganisms. The resilience of each human and the species, the capacity to survive change – whether the fluctuations of any day, injury, illness, trauma, or permanent environmental transformations – is based on the diversity of their microbial community. Conversely, any threat to the diversity and balance of that community is a threat to our well-being and survival. Humans are fed by microbes, maintained by microbes, live within microbes, live microbial lives, and are ultimately microbial creatures. To think about humans and the worlds they occupy, to think about architecture and the built environment, is to think about microbes.

THE GUT

97.5 percent of the one hundred trillion or so microbes that form the human are in the gut, the around seven-meter-long moist tube coiled up between mouth and anus, with the rest living in the skin, mouth, lungs, and genitals.[4] **[5]** Strangely, this slippery, pulsating intestinal tube is strictly speaking not inside us. Rather, it manufactures our inside. **[6]** The gut is the part of the outside world that flows through us. Its mucus-covered surface forms the real line between our inside and the outside, a line that is only one cell deep; a dotted line through which vital molecules (nutrients, minerals, vitamins, water, and electrolytes) are admitted and others are blocked. **[7]** The human cells that stand side-by-side to form this all-important "epithelial" surface are replaced every

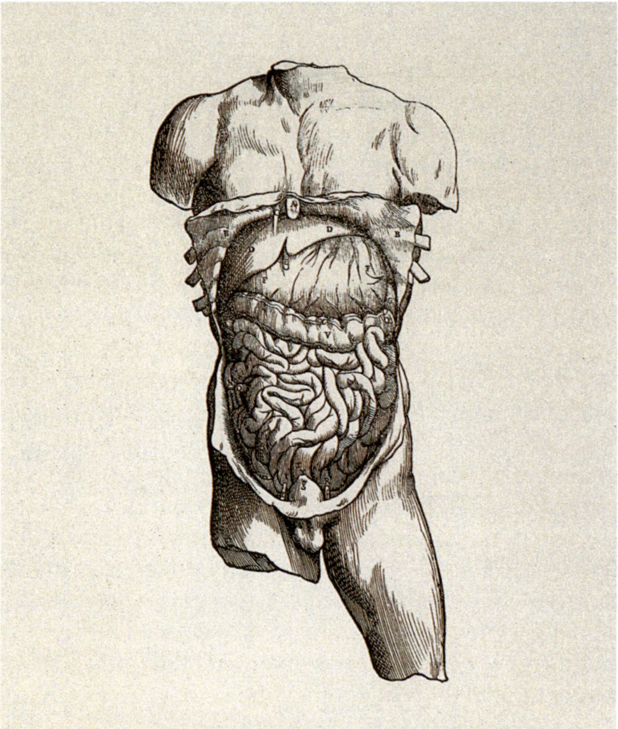

5 Andreas Vesalius, Dissected torso, from *De humani corporis fabrica libri septem*, 1543

6 Martin Oeggerli, scanning electron microscope (SEM) image of human excrement with intestinal bacteria and a plant fiber

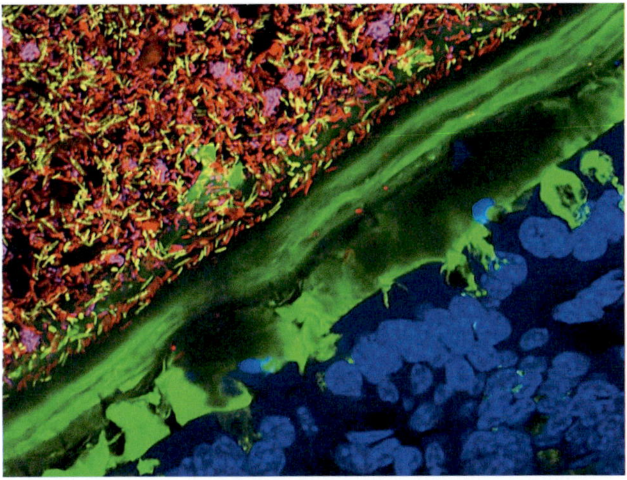

three to five days, so the limit of the human is being continuously redrawn.

The personal community of gut microbes play a major role in constructing and maintaining that line – preserving the protective layers of mucous secreted by it, giving energy to it, regulating the development and operation of its immune system, resisting pathogens near it, and constantly communicating with the host organism. They stimulate the production of the fine blood vessels that absorb nutrients and fluids, they regulate what is absorbed, and they produce much of it. The human is literally manufactured on this microbial front line. We are wrapped around our intestines. We don't simply have intestines – intestines have us. We are not simply inhabited by microbes – we inhabit microbes. We are the fragile effects of microbes

To say it another way, the human organism is never simply in the world but is a certain way of folding the world into an interior, a folding that begins with microbes. Microbes are the first and smallest form of life on this planet, which is to say that microbes initiated architecture. Life is the construction and maintenance of an interior. Life is architecture. Microbes never simply occupy

7 Gut microbes and debris separated from the lining of the colon (stained blue) by a layer of mucus (stained green)

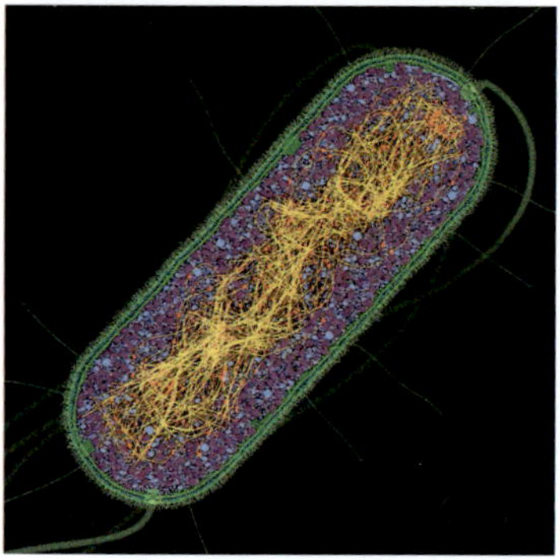

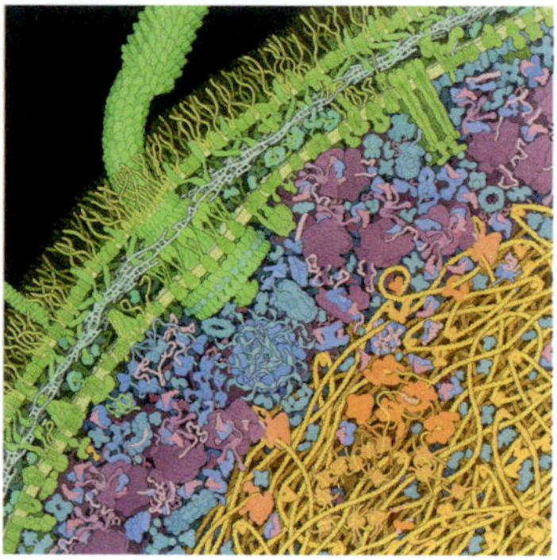

8 Cross-section of an *E. coli* bacteria

9 Detail of cross-section through the two-membrane cell wall of an *E. coli* bacteria, including flagella (tail) motor

space – microbes make space. A bacteria is a single-celled organism, a few thousandths of a millimeter long, usually with a tail – or several tails – to move through the world. **[8]** It is not a mobile living organism with cells, but a cell that lives like us by maintaining a membrane that divides its interior from the world around it. Each bacteria is a room, a tiny single-room building that only allows certain molecules to enter or leave through its membrane. It manufactures its own interior environment out of its exterior and in so doing ultimately transforms the exterior. Like us, microbes produce and maintain themselves by digesting the world, ingesting some things and excreting others. The line between inside and outside that seems so clear in an electron microscope image is not simply a division but an active processing. To zoom in on that line is to encounter an extraordinarily intricate mechanism that reaches outward to the surrounding environment and inward to the organism, transforming one into the other. **[9]** A microbe is not a thing but a verb, the unceasing action of constructing an interior. Architecture is always a verb.

The real work of digestion that forms and maintains the human is carried out by our trillions of bacteria – some of which are only found in humans but none of which are found in every human. Our unique sets are drawn from a pool of five thousand or so species, many of which have been around for millions of years; nomads that become residents of our gut without whom

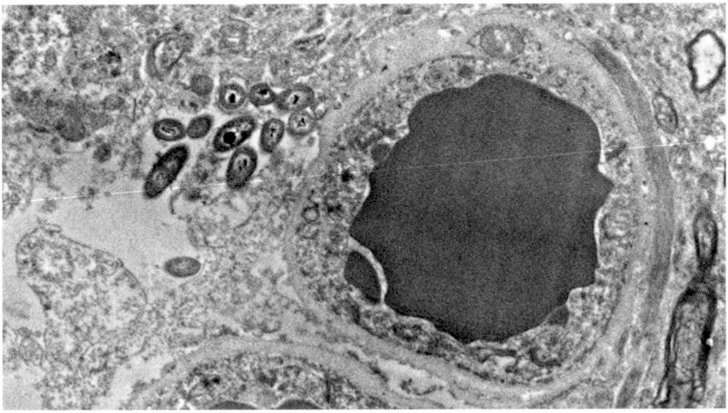

we could not be ourselves. The strange sense that we are made by these others echoes the strange architecture of each and every microbe. Just as we are never alone, no microbe is thinkable without countless other microbes, countless different types of microbes, and countless variations of each type, with unending new variations and hybridities. The seemingly stable architecture of any organism depends on a radical heterogeneity and plasticity, a constant mixing and morphing, which has been the very engine of architecture for billions of years, long before the human species appeared and eventually made a building. That is, microbes eventually excreted a creature that would eventually be capable of excreting buildings.

These microscopic outsiders are the ultimate insiders, responsible for feeding and defending us. They are essential to every aspect of well-being, including emotions and thought. Their lives are directly connected to the brain. Signals travel continuously back and forth along the multiple pathways of the so-called gut–brain axis. Signals from the brain rapidly affect the combination of microbes in different parts of the gut, just as signals from the gut affect the brain – shaping mood and thinking via the vast network of nerves in the intestinal surface.[5] The human brain is therefore ultimately part of the digestive system, even a bacteriological effect. The early development of the brain is regulated by the personal set of gut microbes that is assembled in parallel

10 Electron microscope image of gut bacteria near a blood cell inside human brain, 2018

11 The unfolded size of the gut, installation photograph, *We the Bacteria: Notes Toward Biotic Architecture* exhibition, 24th Milan Triennale International Exhibition *Inequalities*, 2025

to the brain during the first three years of a child's life. Brain and gut remain inseparable. Imbalances in the gut microbiome disrupt the development of the brain, its ability to form new neural connections, psychological and emotional states, moods, and behaviors. Psychological and neurological disorders are tied to gut disorders.

Thinking itself is microbial. The act which the human species considers most uniquely human – as marked by its very name for itself, *Homo sapiens sapiens*, the most thoughtful of the apes – is made by microbes. Gut microbes even inhabit the brain. **[10]** The diversity of this recently discovered brain microbiome turns out to be a large subset, around 20 percent, of the species in an individual's gut microbiome of bacteria, viruses, and fungi, distributed in distinct combinations within different niches of the brain.[6] The gut infuses the brain. Imbalances in this brain community are associated with neurological disorders like Alzheimer's.

The human creature is not just wrapped around the gut that feeds it or manufactured by it. It is ultimately an extension of the gut. There is no point at which the gut gives way to the human. In other words, the human is a particular way of digesting the world.

UNFOLDING THE HUMAN

The surface of the human gut would have on average thirty-two square meters if unfolded.[7] **[11]** It is bigger than the surface of most rooms we occupy, bigger than the twenty square meters that is the average built living space of a human on the planet – with the majority having substantially less. Human surfaces are actually bigger than the surfaces we inhabit. There is inevitably a constant intimate exchange between the microbe-rich surfaces that define the human body–gut–brain and the surfaces of buildings. Each human releases a cloud of around eighty million microbes an hour, colonizing any space and any other occupants.[8] The surfaces of bodies and buildings become a single microbial landscape with its own microbially dense atmosphere that passes through rooms and lungs. Architecture inhabits humans just as much as humans inhabit architecture.

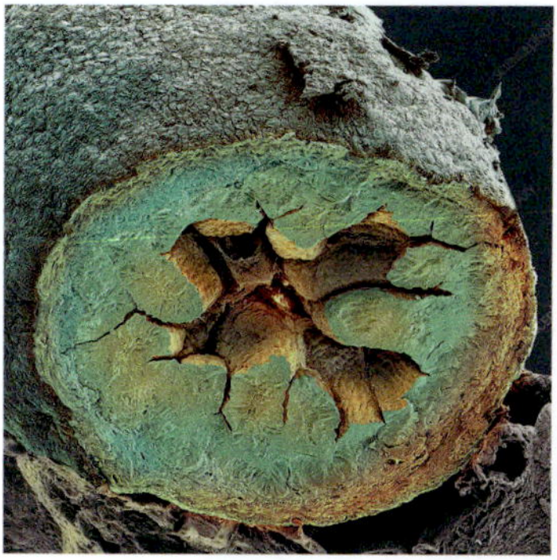

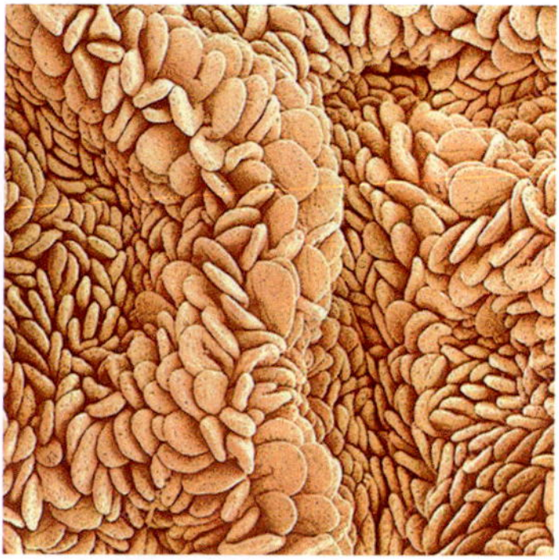

Like the mouth at its entrance, the portable intestinal surface that interacts so intimately with buildings has its own architecture. The moist microbe-covered inner surface of the intestines is densely folded, refolded, and refolded yet again. The pulsating tube is a twisting knot whose inner lining is a continuous landscape of deep ravines and peaks. [12] This landscape forms, as it were, the river bank surrounding the flowing fecal matter and all the microbes digesting it. Its folds maximize the amount of surface contact and therefore the possibly of exchange. The folds are themselves folded again into a landscape of peaks and ravines at a smaller scale. [13] It twists and turns as an ambiguous territory that is neither human or non-human, like marshy wetlands that are neither land nor water yet define the limit of both. [14] Its surface is the single line of epithelial cells that side-by-side form the border between inside and outside. [15] Each of them is covered with a kind of carpet of microscopically thin threads. [16] This deeply labyrinthine carpet is the real façade of the human. [17]

Different combinations of species of microbes occupy different layers of different neighborhoods down the length of the implausibly long, twisted, and internally convoluted tube – multiplying, competing, collaborating, and dying in specific niches and micro-niches produced by different combinations of nutrients, oxygen, acidity, chemicals, antimicrobials, and even the microbes

12 Colored SEM image of a cross-section through a fetal small intestine

13 SEM image of villi lining small intestine

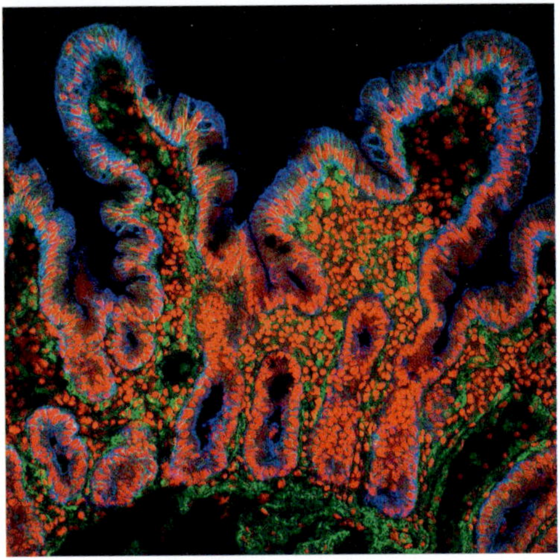

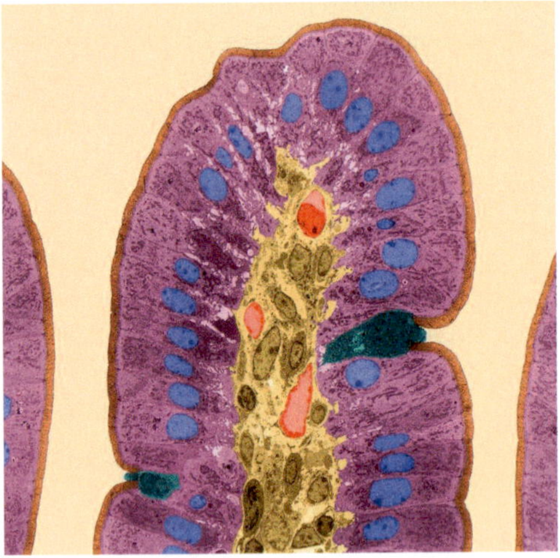

14 Fluorescence light micrograph of cross-section through human small intestine lining showing folded landscape of villi and the deep crypts between them

15 Small intestine villus showing side-by-side epithelial cells forming outer limit of human

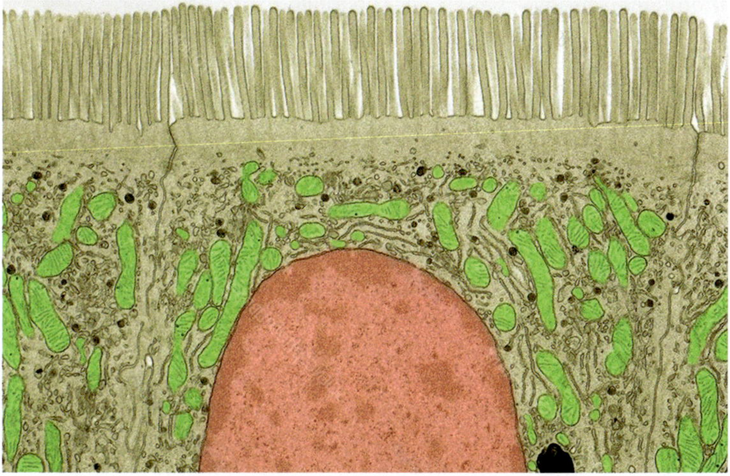

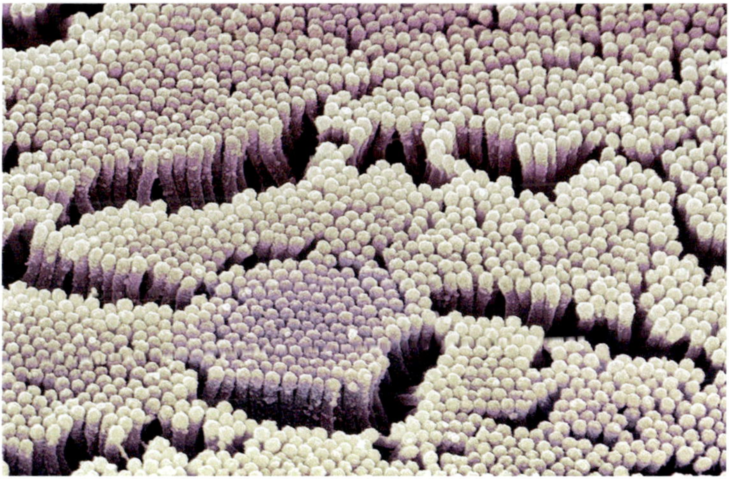

16 Transmission electron micrograph of an intestinal epithelial cell showing microvilli

17 SEM image of carpet of intestinal microvilli

themselves. Some spaces, like the millions of deep ravines, are withdrawn from the fecal stream and only accessible to particular microbes that establish multi-layered collaborative communities producing unique micro-environments with their own internal conditions. The outer mucus layers of the intestine form the environment for other bacterial communities, as does the stream itself at the center of the tube.[9]

The nutrients in this stratified biogeography don't simply come from decomposing what humans eat and drink. The waste of one species of microbe is the nutrient for another that in turn supports another in a dense chain of interdependencies, with each niche supporting adjacent niches. Microbes are not just residents of the intestinal environment. They manufacture that environment in all its liquid yet highly specific and stable zones. They maintain the architecture that maintains us.

What gurgles through and builds the human body is a complex spatial system, a vast, well-organized city that microbes both inhabit and produce. This city is so much bigger than all the human cities on earth; it is a dynamic architecture on which we depend for energy, health, thoughts, emotions, and life itself. And this hidden architecture inhabiting humans is intimately related to the architecture of buildings and cities we inhabit. Exploring the intestinal architecture of microbes allows the human-built environment to be seen differently, as if for the first time. The idea of "human-built" changes, along with the idea of inhabitation. The supposedly familiar, seemingly static world of architecture becomes strange, riddled with unexpected complications and alternative futures. Architecture literally comes to life.

1 Noah Fierer, Micah Hamady, Christian L. Lauber, and Rob Knight, "The influence of sex, handedness, and washing on the diversity of hand surface bacteria," *PNAS* 105, no. 46 (November 18, 2008): 17994–99. The study measured species-level "phylotypes" in the genetic data to account for those microbial species that cannot be individually cultured. The differences between the hands of different individuals, and between the hands of each individual, was much greater than predicted, and the total number of species represented on the fifty-one people that were sampled was 4742. A follow-up study demonstrated that the uniqueness of each palm microbiome enables an object that has been touched up to two weeks earlier to be forensically traced to the individual who touched it. Noah Fierer, Christian L. Lauber, Nick Zhou, and Rob Knight, "Forensic identification using skin bacterial communities," *PNAS* 107, no. 14 (March 15, 2010): 6477–81.

2 Paula Watnick and Roberto Kolter "Biofilm, City of Microbes," *Journal of Bacteriology* 182, no. 10 (2000): 2675–79. More recent studies have reinforced this association with urbanization in the way biofilms develop through the merging of "settlers" into ever=larger "villages" into "cities" that merge into "megacities." Amauri J. Paula, Geelsu Hwang, and Hyun Koo, "Dynamics of bacterial population growth in biofilms resemble spatial and structural aspects of urbanization," *Nature Communication* 11, (2020): 1354.

3 Steven A. Wilbert, Jessica L. Mark Welch, and Gary G. Borisy, "Spatial Ecology of the Human Tongue Dorsum Microbiome," *Cell Reports* 30, no. 12 (2020): 4003–15.

4 Gut length varies widely but the gut of babies is already three meters at birth, and women typically have a thirty-centimeter-longer gut than men.

5 Wuling Zhong, Karen Wang, and Amir Zarrinpar, "Mind over microbiota: neurons call the shots in the gut," *Nature Metabolism* 7, no. 6 (2025): 1–3.

6 Xinyue Hu, Chris-Anne Mckenzie, Colin Smith, Juergen G. Haas, and Richard Lathe, "The Remarkable Complexity of the Brain Microbiome in Health and Disease," *bioRxiv* (February 6, 2023). Gut microbes are paradoxically involved in forming and maintaining the blood–gut barrier that supposedly prevents their entry into the body, co-producing the line they are not meant to cross. But blood has its own microbiome. Likewise, microbes are involved in the formation and maintenance of the blood–brain barrier that lines the blood vessels passing through the brain to prevent the entry of large molecules and most cells, but many microbes cross over into the brain.

7 Herbert F. Helander and Lars Fändriks, "Surface Area of the Digestive Tract – Revisited," *Scandinavian Journal of Gastroenterology* 49, no. 6 (June 2014): 681–89.

8 James F. Meadow, Adam E. Altrichter, Ashley C. Bateman, et. al., "Humans Differ in their Personal Microbial Cloud," *PeerJ* 3, no. 1258 (September 22, 2015), e1258.

9 Gregory P. Donaldson, S. Melanie Lee, and Sarkis K. Mazmanian, "Gut Biogeography of the Bacterial Microbiota," *National Review of Microbiology* 14, no. 1 (January 2016): 20–32.

1 Joseph Picotti, Herophilus dissecting a corpse in ancient Alexandria, engraving, from Leopoldo Marco Antonio Caldani and Floriano Caldani, *Icones anatomicae*, 1801

2 MICROBES IN SPACE

Microbes flourish everywhere in the biosphere, the space of all living things and their sediments, reaching deep down into the planet and far up into the atmosphere. For more than four billion years, tiny microorganisms have transformed the crust of Earth so that it could be inhabited by other organisms and genetically engineered those organisms. Microbes are the architects, builders, maintenance workers, and inhabitants of the biosphere and every form of life within it – including humans.

SOIL AND SHIT

Humans are very recently arrived guests in a microbial world. Our species lives on the soil, surrounded by the greatest density and diversity of life. The highest density of microbes anywhere in the biosphere is in the eight-centimeter-wide colons of humans at the end of their digestive tract. **[1]** Just a gram of human feces contains up to a hundred billion microbes in up to a thousand species, a set unique to each human. The second greatest density of microbial life – a tenth as dense but with ten times the diversity of species – is in the topsoil, the ten-centimeter-thin layer of earth that contains a quarter of all microbes in the planetary biosphere. A gram of topsoil contains up to ten billion microbes from up to ten thousand species, a set unique to each location.

Humans live on this bio-rich soil. They are portable packages of microbes suspended within a colossal number and variety of other microbes, continuously nurtured by them. A large proportion of the millions of species of multicellular organisms on Earth is always nearby: in the ground, water, and air. Yet the human-built environment of buildings and cities separates humans from the soil and most other species – plants, insects, and animals. This self and environmentally destructive gesture disconnects humans from the soil that nurtured them. Buildings thereby cultivate a narrow set of companions – which means a narrow set of microbes. Buildings are an exercise in local biodiversity reduction, which has ultimately had a devastating impact on the biodiversity of the planet. The arrival of anatomically modern humans just 230,000 years ago was made possible by the arrival of soil four hundred million years earlier, when the first trees rapidly formed forests along with an ever-thicker layer of loose organic and inorganic material hospitable to their bacterial and fungal partners.[1] **[2]** Humans grew from the soil as much as any plant.

The microbiome of the human gut and that of soil co-evolved.[2] But around ten thousand years ago, buildings separated soil and gut, dramatically reshaping humans and eventually the microbial world they are part of.[3] They lifted humans off the ground into an isolated interior and restricted the transfer of microbes across its limits. This disconnection is a kind of unconscious experiment in biological engineering, a genetic experiment to modify humans

and other species that started with the first permanently occupied buildings in the so-called Neolithic transition from nomadic hunter-gatherers to permanent settlements. Architecture protected humans from exposure to multiple threats, but shelter itself immediately became a new threat.

As the doctor Benjamin Ward Richardson put it in *Our Homes and How to Make them Healthy*, a compendium of texts written by doctors and architects for the 1884 International Health Exhibition in London – which was attended by four million visitors just after bacteria had finally been confirmed as the cause of epidemic disease:

> Man, by a knowledge and skill not possessed by the inferior animals, in building cities, villages, houses, for his protection from the external elements, has produced for himself a series of fatal diseases, which are so closely associated with the productions of his knowledge and skill in building as to stand in the position of effect from cause. *Man in constructing protections from exposure has constructed conditions of disease.*[4]

There is no architecture without disease. Ancient bacterial diseases like tuberculosis that had already affected bands of hunter-gatherers became epidemic with the move indoors, and buildings

2 Soil, the birthplace of the human

incubated new diseases. Buildings are ultimately toxic to their inhabitants, and had a toxic effect on the biosphere as they spread across the planet. To rethink architecture out of concern for all species, including the human, means to rethink architecture's relationship to microbes.

Architecture is never simply a static inanimate object on a solid ground. From the perspective of microbes, the very distinction between ground and air, stillness and movement, gives way. The soil is inseparable from the rock below and the air above. It is a kind of confusion of them. Not only does it sustain countless biochemical circuits passing between solidity and atmosphere, but rocks are alive and the air is filled with material. Likewise, no human-built wall, floor, or roof is as still or sealed as it might appear. Buildings are alive. They can never simply exclude microbes. Rather, they cultivate particular microbial communities within spaces, surfaces, materials, and systems. Microbes are the real environment, raw material, and occupants of buildings. Architecture is suspended in a cloud of microbes stretching deep into the earth and deep into the atmosphere.

THE MICROBIAL CLOUD

Microbes are the most abundant, diverse, and ancient cells on earth. Imagine a core sample cut through the whole biosphere that shows only microbes. It would reveal a stratified cloud of different densities of over a trillion microbial species, only a thousandth of 1 percent of which have currently been identified. The cloud is densest near the earth's surface and thins out exponentially above and below, reaching five kilometers down into the earth's crust and fifty kilometers up into the stratosphere.

This fifty-five-kilometer band of biosphere wrapping the planet seems immeasurably vast from within, but it is actually a narrow film of life, a fragile biofilm that Earth scientist Jérôme Gaillardet calls "the thin coat of varnish on which humanity has established itself."[5] The varnish barely seeps into the planet's outer crust and centers on the gossamer-thin topsoil that hosts 25 percent of all microbes. Going deeper down into the earth, pressure and temperature increase and microbial density declines exponentially. Yet 70 percent of all microbes in the biosphere are below the topsoil in vast interlinked communities. Going farther up into the atmosphere, pressure and temperature decrease, and microbial density again declines exponentially. Only 5 percent of all microbes are floating in the atmosphere, but those are highly mobile and their presence at ever-higher altitudes enables them to travel across cities, regions, continents, and oceans – feeding and interconnecting the microbial life of the surface.

This invisible microbial cloud suspended in rock, soil, water, and air is the home of multicellular life, from worms to whales, that is likewise concentrated near the surface but goes as deep as 3.2 kilometers below, where nematode worms wriggle in rock crevices, **[3]** and as high as eleven kilometers above, where African vultures hover. **[4]** Microbes, which extend even further down and up, engineer the space of multicellular life, including the humans that inhabit the densest part of the cloud and are themselves the very densest points of the cloud, yet constitute only 0.01 percent of planetary biomass. Plants constitute 82.4 percent of all biomass, bacteria 12.8 percent, other microbes 4.2 percent, and animals just 0.47 percent.[6] The human is infinitesimal. Yet from 2020 onward, the human-built environment – the currently used buildings and infrastructural networks that are exponentially growing across the planet – weighs more than the total weight of all organic life.[7] The human experiment of separating

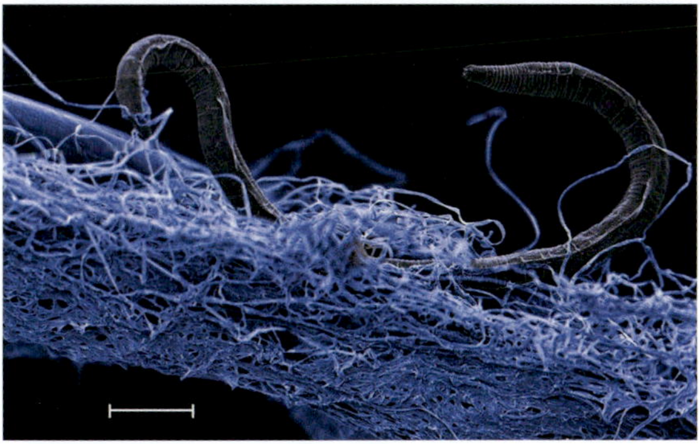

3 Nematode worm, *Poikilolaimus oxycercus*, in a biofilm of microorganisms in Kopanang gold mine, South Africa, 1.4 kilometers below the surface

itself from the soil has provoked a planetary-scale geological and biological transformation. Architecture has redesigned the microbial home of rock, soil, water, and air.

Within the band of life filled and maintained by microbes, humans construct their shelters right on the earth's surface, within the greatest concentration of life. These built structures on average reach less than a meter below the ground and around six meters above, yet can extend up to 275 meters deep, in Q'anat water systems that have supported cities in Persia for three thousand years, [5] and 828 meters high, in the recent Burj Khalifa skyscraper in Dubai. Humans live almost everywhere on the planet's surface, but mainly occupy a surprisingly narrow

4 African vulture

5 Aerial view of the vertical shafts of a Q'anat system in Jupar, Iran band of the climate envelope.[8] Humans have thrived for millennia where environmental conditions are moderate compared with most of the planet's surface, and extremely mild compared with the deep earth and atmosphere. They use buildings as environmental control devices to further moderate the already moderate condition around them, as their fragile metabolism cannot tolerate much deviation from a steady internal temperature between 36 and 37 degrees Celsius. They survive in architecturally manufactured microclimates that disconnect them from the wider world, yet dramatically impact the world they isolate themselves from and are utterly reliant on.

Paradoxically, the moderate environment where humans live is produced by extremophiles, microbes that flourish in extremes of heat, pressure, acidity, salinity, radiation, dryness, heavy metals, oxygen, sugar, sulphur, etc. Extremophiles live in the deepest subsurface and the highest atmosphere, but also in extreme conditions on the surface, in thermal vents, deserts, ice caps, and acid lakes, along with kitchen appliances like microwaves and the very extreme conditions inside the human gut. **[6–7]**

Extremophiles deep in the Earth's crust at very high pressure and temperatures with little water, oxygen, and organic carbon, have a very slow metabolic rate. A typical microbe on the surface replicates itself every twenty minutes, but deep subsurface microbes replicate in hundreds of years, and sometimes millions.[9]

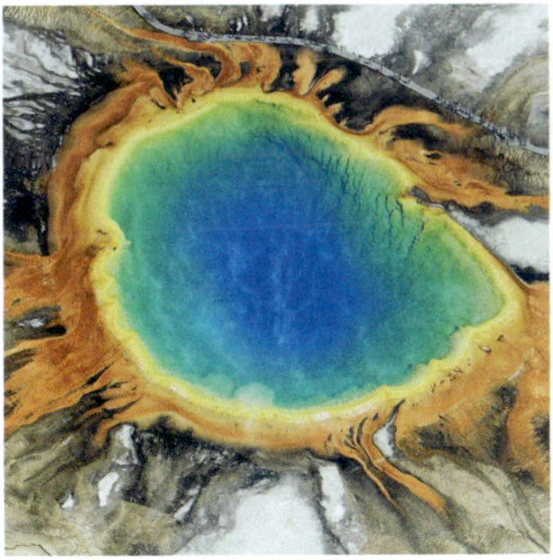

6 Bright colors of heat-loving extremophiles in Yellowstone National Park

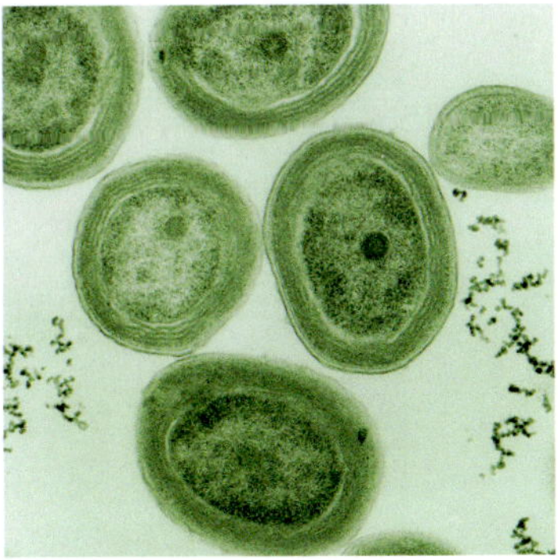

7 Extreme-cold-loving *Prochlorococcus marinus*

One recently discovered colony of yet-to-be-classified microbes 2.5-kilometers-deep replicates itself so slowly that it was able to live off of the clay minerals present within completely enclosed fractures of two-billion-year-old rock.[10] The scientists who opened this rock met the oldest living inhabitants of the planet.

The deepest microbe yet discovered, *Candidatus Desulforudis audaxviator*, evolved very little over the last hundred million years, surviving by digesting minerals released by the radioactive decay of uranium in the surrounding rocks.[11] **[8]** Its home is the least diverse ecosystem on the planet, having only one species – itself.[12] Other deep subsurface ecosystems feature diverse communities of microbes living in dispersed mutually reinforcing biofilms – digesting methane, radiation, rocks, and each other's metabolites.

The lower limit of microbial life is thought to be five kilometers deep, where temperatures are higher than 125 degrees Celsius. Communities are vertically stratified between that limit and the surface depending on temperature, oxygen, methane, pressure, radiation, etc. Yet these communities are ultimately all interconnected and play a crucial role in planetary bio-geo-chemical cycling. They don't simply inhabit the earth but continuously reconstruct it, making life at the surface possible.

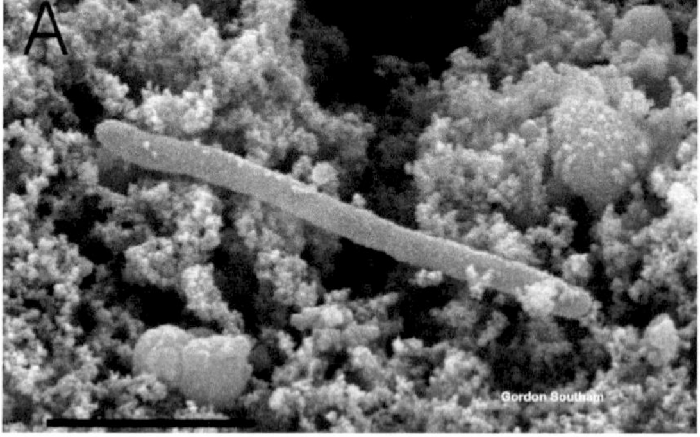

8 *Candidatus Desulforudis audaxviator* found at 3.2 kilometers depth in Driefontein Mine, South Africa

THE GROUND IN THE AIR

To occupy a building sitting on top of five kilometers of life is not just to disconnect from the teeming life nurtured in the topsoil cocooned in some human-specific space insulated from the fluctuations of temperature, humidity, rain, and wind immediately outside. It is to disconnect from life itself. Or, it is to fantasize such an impossible disconnection as the mark of supposed human exceptionalism. Buildings are not just made and maintained by materials taken from deep within the earth – they are built within the earth. Which is to say, with and within microbes. Microbes are the very ground of architecture.

Strangely, this ground includes the air. The atmosphere is as vertically stratified and maintained by interconnected microbial communities as the earth's crust, and is ultimately part of that crust. The highest density of microbes in the atmosphere is in the air immediately above the soil and around plants and animals – especially in the "laminar" zone that flows across every surface, ranging from a few millimeters thick during the day to a few meters on a calm night. Each surface, including human skin, has such a microclimate.

Bacteria, fungi, and viruses move small distances within this layer of air, attached to dust or organic particles. Those that escape this layer in a gust of wind enter a more turbulent zone, reaching up to a thousand meters above the ground during the day and much lower at night, in which they can travel across fields, forests, cities, regions, continents, and oceans. Microbes in the regular dust storms of topsoil from Asia and Africa, for example, reach the Americas in a few days via relatively predictable "highways" between 1.5 and 6 kilometers above the ground, with microbes multiplying and picking up additional microbial companions along the way.[13] **[9]**

The more dynamic the structure of air mass, the more efficient microbial movement is in a continuous daily cycle driven by temperature: emission up into the air, dispersal, and deposit back down. It has recently been calculated that eight hundred million viruses descend onto each square meter of the planet every day along with a smaller number of bacteria.[14] The specific forms of microbial life in this turbulent layer of air depend on the land or water below, the season, moisture levels, fog, clouds, etc. The

average density of microbial life here is nothing like that on the surface, but there are at least nineteen thousand bacteria, twenty-four thousand fungi, and a similar number of viruses per cubic millimeter. To look across a street or a field, or up to the clouds, is always to look through microbes. To breathe is to take in millions of microbes from thousands of species.

These flying microbes can be suspended for a long time, even for years, but eventually descend with gravity or inside rain, hail, or snow. Every seemingly pure raindrop is filled with microbes. When it rains, it rains microbes that become part of the microbiome of plants and soil. Raindrops are not just filled with microorganisms but induced by them.[15] Plant-associated microbes such as the bacteria *Pseudomonas syringae* are released in aerosols that rise up into the clouds and cause water to freeze at higher temperatures than usual, which provokes rain, playing a key role in geochemical cycling. Clouds even form in response to microbes, sometimes those coming from other continents.[16]

It is thought that bacteria might have developed the ability to provoke rain in order to disperse themselves.[17] Furthermore, each raindrop hitting the ground, plants, or buildings lifts more microbes into the air inside hundreds of tiny droplets. These bioaerosols potentially travel for kilometers in the wind. **[10]** It is estimated that annual global rainfall lifts a quarter of all of the

9 Dust carrying microbes across Atlantic as seen from the International Space Station

soil's bacteria into the air.[18] The topsoil is formed by the air above it just as much as it forms the air. One is not thinkable without the other. No building ever simply sits on the ground because no ground is simply ground.

The movement of microbes always generates more movement of microbes in continuous ripples reaching across all horizons. The microbiome of any creature or place constantly interacts with microbes from distant organisms and enviroments. Just as marine-associated microorganisms rise into the air and get deposited on land, terrestrial microorganisms get deposited on water. The microbes from one creature land on another, pass from one house to another, from one hemisphere to another. As within any creature, there is a very specific microbiome in the air of any space, but this distinctive set of species always includes microbes from elsewhere. And what sustains a local microbiome is the way it accommodates these others, the way it keeps curating itself within the microbial flux – diminishing or modifying the active role of others to form itself.

Above the turbulent mixing layer that wraps the planet and redistributes microbes is a less turbulent layer of air that has fewer

10 Micro-droplets containing soil bacteria released by impact of single raindrop microbes, but those that survive adapt themselves to the more extreme temperatures, oxygen levels, dryness, UV radiation, and lack of nutrients. Even at eleven kilometers up, more than three hundred types of bacteria are known to be actively growing and reproducing, including those that affect cloud formation and condensation. Fewer and fewer survive in the next layer again, the "stratosphere" from twelve to fifty kilometers up. Living microbes have been found clumped together at forty-one kilometers, presumably driven up there by strong upward winds, volcanoes, thunderstorms, and electrostatic levitation. They include novel strains found nowhere else and species that are more prevalent up there than on the ground, along with soil-associated species like *Bacillus simplex*. But fifty kilometers is considered the hypothetical upper limit of life, just as five kilometers into the earth is the hypothetical lower limit.

Extremophiles live everywhere between these limits of the biosphere. Every environmental variable, or combination of variables, when taken to an extreme, acts as a microbial niche. *Deinococcus radiodurans*, for example, a bacteria at home in many different kinds of extremes, thrives inside nuclear reactors, digesting radiation just as it does in radioactive rocks. **[11]** It survives by having multiple copies of its DNA and the ability to continuously rebuild these strands as they are dissolved by intense waves of radioactive energy. Yet there is nothing

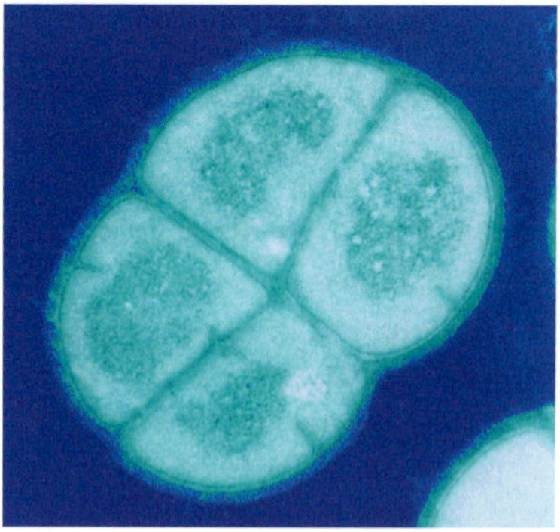

11 Radiation-loving *Deinococcus radiodurans*

extreme about radioactivity for this microbe. On the contrary, radioactivity is one of its homes, along with dryness, cold, vacuum, and acidity.

The very idea of the extreme is anthropocentric – even if the human is made possible by the extremophiles that live within it, relishing the acidity and lack of oxygen in the gut that the human itself cannot tolerate. No organism thinks of its everyday environment as extreme, or even as an environment. There is never a strict line between organism and environment. More precisely, all life is nothing other than the ingestion and transformation of its surroundings – a digesting of the environment that changes it. What is digested has been produced by other acts of digestion by other organisms. And so on. Ultimately, the biosphere is continuously made by the microbes that inhabit it. The material conditions of the planet are manufactured by its occupants, from sedimentary rocks to the air.

Oxygen, which was first produced by microbes billions of years ago, initially wiped out 95 percent of species on the planet. The first organisms able to digest oxygen, of which we are descendants, were extremophiles. All norms were once extremes.

THE EXPANDED BIOSPHERE

The human is the opposite of an extremophile. Not only does it construct interiors to shelter itself from extremes and most species, but it now spends 90 percent of its time indoors, and moves between interiors in portable architectures – cars, trains, ships, and planes – that enable it to survive immoderate conditions. The mobility of these protective bubbles has the paradoxical effect of expanding the biosphere. Human-associated microbes now occupy environments that humans cannot without architecture – whether it be the ice caps, mountaintops, the oceans, or the air. Every one of the more than twenty thousand planes that are in the upper atmosphere at any moment takes additional communities of microbes up with them, shedding microbes or moving them from place to place, continent to continent.

Even outer space has been colonized by human-associated microbes. Spacecraft 411 kilometers above the ground are filled and covered with bacteria, despite intense sterilization before launch. Like any architectural interior, the International Space Station, the most distant human house, is dominated by micro-organisms associated with human skin, mouth, and gut. **[12]** The excessive cleaning and lack of micro-biodiversity provided by companion species – plants, animals, and insects – contributes to the immune-related poor health of astronauts. Some microbes up there are mutating under the stressful conditions of low gravity, high radiation, and carbon dioxide, forming pathogenic strains different from those on Earth. These include the anti-microbial resistant intestinal *Enterobacter bugandensis*, raising the question of whether the station will soon become uninhabitable by humans.[19] Bacteria associated with land and marine environments are even found on cosmic dust around spacecraft.[20] The estimated 170 million pieces of human-built space junk above Earth could likewise be a habitat for extremophiles, and the two Voyager I and II satellites, launched in 1977, are taking billions of human-associated microbes ever deeper into interstellar space. But microbes have always been astronauts. They are the first astronauts.

12 International Space Station

PANSPERMIA

In 1864 Louis Pasteur tested the theory that life arrived on Earth from outer space in the form of microorganisms. He drilled into a fragment of a meteorite that had just landed in the South of France to look – unsuccessfully – for for evidence of microbial life. [13] When making the first classification of microbes in 1872, botanist Ferdinand Cohn noted the ability of bacteria to drift high into the atmosphere and survive extreme conditions before descending, arguing that they didn't need meteorites to seed life on Earth since they could be swept into the atmosphere of any planet and from there into outer space and travel to Earth.[21] [14] This theory of microbial astronauts was renamed "panspermia" by the physicist and chemist Svante Arrhenius in 1908 and has yet to be disproved.[22] Since 1903, the year he received the Nobel Prize for his work on electrolytes, Arrhenius had argued that extraterrestrial bacteria could survive a three-thousand-year trip

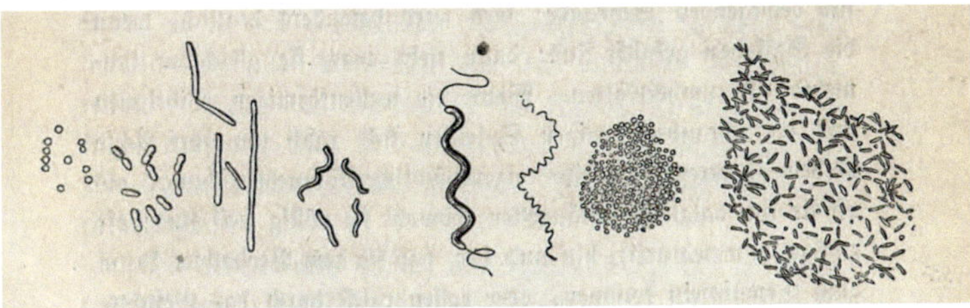

13 Orgueil meteorite, Muséum National d'Histoire Naturelle, Paris

14 First classification of microbes, from Ferdinand Cohn, *Über Bakterien, die kleinsten lebenden Wesen*, 1872

through space to seed life on Earth.[23] In his view, electrical energy is constantly launching microorganisms into outer space where they can attach to cosmic dust and move at high speed from planet to planet, from solar system to solar system.

With the launch of the first satellites in the late 1950s came the fear of seeding new life in outer space, or at least confusing potential evidence of other forms of life. The Sputnik launch in 1957 immediately provoked Joshua Lederberg – the molecular biologist who would receive the Nobel Prize in 1958 for showing that bacteria can mate and exchange genes – to write to colleagues expressing concern that contaminating the moon or other planets with microbes would prevent the ability to test the panspermia hypothesis about the origin of life on Earth. His follow-up speech and article mobilized the international community toward "planetary protection."[24] The first agreements to sterilize all spacecraft of microorganisms were made the following year, and eventually became the basis of the United Nations Outer Space Treaty of 1967.

The Apollo program to land on the moon raised the triple fear of depositing microbes in space, bringing back bacteria from space, and the microbes of astronauts mutating and returning to Earth in deadly form. There was a highly publicized project of sterilizing both the craft and the astronauts, and quarantining them and their samples on their return. Special housing was designed for the samples and astronauts – sealed spaces within sealed spaces within sealed spaces. Yet it was already understood at the time that techniques of sterilization and isolation were inadequate.

A huge microbial community was launched with Apollo 11 in 1969. Bags of urine, excrement, vomit, and food waste were simply left on the moon, and any surviving microbes on the returning spacecraft would simply have entered the nutrient-rich ocean on splashdown. **[15]** Sterilization was even less thorough with the two unmanned Voyager satellites in 1977, when there was no attempt to sterilize the rocket boosters – which, like the satellites, are still flying through interstellar space around twenty-five billion kilometers from Earth. The biosphere has been extended into outer, and now interstellar space.

As with any other species, the human modifies its surroundings, but the scale of human modification is more than planetary. Starting with buildings on the ground and continuing with buildings in space, the human paradoxically became an extremophile using architecture to survive in toxic conditions. But it has also managed to produce an environment that is toxic to itself and many of its companion species. It is unclear if it can survive what it has made. Yet it remains a question of whether this is a suicidal human project, or the project of the microbes that inhabit and made the human possible. It could be that the recently arrived human is already about to leave. But it is also possible that the real human, a less extractive and more collaborative creature, is about to arrive.

15 Jettisoned waste bag beneath the Apollo Lunar Module in 1969

1 The earliest fossil record of a mixture of archaic and anatomically modern *Homo sapiens* is in 300,000-year-old fragments of five individuals found in Jebel Irhoud in Morocco, and the first fully modern *Homo sapiens* was found in 230,000-year-old fragments in Omo Kibish in southern Ethiopia.
2 Winfried E. H. Blum, Sophie Zechmeister-Boltenstern, and Katharina M. Keiblinger, "Does Soil Contribute to the Human Gut Microbiome?," *Microorganisms* 7, no. 9 (August 23, 2019): 287.
3 The human separation from the soil paradoxically transformed the soil. Anthropogenic soil, soil deeply modified by humans, began with the first buildings and the emergence of agriculture, which has ultimately eroded, polluted, and depleted the microbial diversity of the soil worldwide.
4 Benjamin Ward Richardson, "Health in the Home," introduction to *Our Homes and How to Make Them Healthy*, ed. Shirley Forster Murphy (London: Cassell & Company, 1883), 5. Italics in original. Richardson goes on to list all the major diseases caused by humans' "self-invented and self-constructed protections from external influences" and details which architectural features actively promote each of them. He had written extensively on all aspects of medicine and in 1876 published a manifesto for the architectural design of "Hygeia," a model city devoted to the health of its inhabitants in which "disease would find no possible home." Benjamin Ward Richardson, *Hygeia: A City of Health*, (London: Macmillan & Co., 1876), 45. The text focuses on fresh air and water, light, and sanitation, with detailed prescriptions for building height and materials, smooth easy-to-clean finishes, lack of ornament, ventilation, plumbing, almost flat roofs with gardens on them, shafts to remove dust, subways for sewage, water and gas, street layouts, paving, planting, etc., along with a grid of small hospitals with glass walls and roofs. Richardson remained skeptical of the bacterial origin of disease, attacking it in the 1860s and 1870s, and still referring to it as but a "hypothesis" in 1888.
5 Jérôme Gaillardet, "The Critical Zone, a Buffer Zone, the Human Habitat," in *Critical Zones, The Science and Politics of Landing on Earth*, eds. Bruno Latour and Peter Weibel (Cambridge: MIT Press, 2020), 122. When the mineralogist and geochemist Vladimir Verdansky published his long-overlooked book *Biosfera* in 1926 – arguing that life is the real crust of the planet – he emphasized that even this expanded sphere that includes sedimentary rock/soil, water, and air is still but the "thin outer layer" of the planet. Verdansky described this crust as a single "living organism" sustained by countless interacting organisms, all of which derive from microbes. His calculations show that the combined weight of all the life continuously made, decomposing, and recomposing actually exceeds that of the inert matter in the outer sixteen kilometers of the planet. Verdansky's demonstration of the force of life is that just one of the smallest and most ancient organisms, such as a *Vibrio cholera* or *E. coli* bacteria, has the capacity to produce that weight in just a few days. He calculated that a single bacteria replicating every twenty-two minutes, with unlimited resources and space, would take only thirty-six hours to cover the earth, and effectively be moving at the speed of sound. Vladimir Verdansky, *The Biosphere*, trans. David B. Langmuir (New York: Corpenicus, 1998): 68.
6 Yinon M. Bar-On, Rob Phillips, and Ron Milo, "The biomass distribution on Earth," *Proceedings of the National Academy of Sciences* 115, no. 25 (2018): 6506–11.
7 Emily Elhacham, Liad Ben-Uri, Jonathan Grozovski, et al., "Global Human-Made Mass Exceeds All Living Biomass," *Nature* 588 (2020): 442–44. It is crucial to note that this calculation of the weight of human-made mass is extremely conservative because it does not include the mass no longer inhabited by humans. A substantial proportion of the built environment is demolished and discarded every year and it is estimated that 30 percent of all construction materials delivered to building sites are ultimately not used.
8 The greatest population densities are where the mean is 13 degrees Celsius, yet half of all humans on Earth live in stress with the mean higher than 20 degrees Celsius and climate change is steadily increasing that stress. Chi Xu, Timothy A. Kohler, Timothy M. Lenton, et al., "Future of the Human Climate Niche," *Proceedings of the National Academy of Science* 117 (2020): 11350–55.
9 Rachel C. Beaver and Josh D. Neufeld, "Microbial Ecology of the Deep Terrestrial Subsurface," *ISME Journal* 18, no. 1 (January 8, 2024).
10 Yohey Suzuki, Susan J. Webb, Mariko Kouduka, et al., "Subsurface Microbial Colonization at Mineral-Filled Veins in 2-Billion-Year-Old Mafic Rock from the Bushveld Igneous Complex, South Africa," *Microbial Ecology* 87, no. 116 (2024).

11 Eric D. Becraft, Maggie C. Y. Lau Vetter, Oliver K. I. Bezuidt, et al., "Evolutionary Stasis of a Deep Subsurface Microbial Lineage," *ISME Journal* 15 (2021): 2830–42.

12 Dylan Chivian, Eoin L. Brodie, Eric J. Alm, et al., "Environmental Genomics Reveals a Single-Species Ecosystem Deep Within Earth," *Science* 322 (2008): 275–78.

13 Xavier Rodó, Sofya Pozdniakova, Sílvia Borràs, et. al., "Microbial Richness and Air Chemistry in Aerosols above the PBL Confirm 2,000-km Long-distance Transport of Potential Human Pathogens," *PNAS* 121, no. 38 (September 9, 2024).

14 The difference in numbers is correlated to the smaller size of organic aerosol needed by viruses because they are smaller than bacteria. Isabel Reche, Gaetano D'Orta, Natalie Mladenov, et al., "Deposition Rates of Viruses and Bacteria above the Atmospheric Boundary Layer," *International Society of Microbial Ecology* 12 (2018): 1154–62.

15 Eva Mayol, Jesús M. Arrieta, Maria A. Jiménez, et al., "Long-range Transport of Airborne Microbes Over the Global Tropical and Subtropical Ocean," *Nature Communication* 8, no. 1 (August 4, 2017): 201.

16 Jessie M. Creamean, Kaitlyn J. Suski, Daniel Rosenfeld, et al., "Dust and Biological Aerosols from the Sahara and Asia Influence Precipitation in the Western U.S.," *Science* 339, no. 6127 (March 2013): 1572–78.

17 Recent research has built on the observation that: "The concept that biologically-catalyzed ice formation in the atmosphere could serve as a microbial dissemination strategy warrants more detailed investigation." Brent C. Christner, Rongman Cai, Cindy E. Morris, et al., "Geographic, seasonal, and precipitation chemistry influence on the abundance and activity of biological ice nucleators in rain and snow," *PNAS* 105, no. 48 (2008): 18858. The potential evolutionary advantages to microbes are summarized in: Steven Lindow, "History of Discovery and Environmental Role of Ice Nucleating Bacteria," *Phytopathology Review* 113 (2023): 605–15.

18 Young Soo Joung, Zhifei Ge, and Cullen R. Buie, "Bioaerosol Generation by Raindrops on Soil," *Nature Communication* 8, no. 14668 (2017).

19 Pratyay Sengupta, Shobhan Karthick Muthamilselvi Sivabalan, Nitin Kumar Singh, et al., "Genomic, functional, and metabolic enhancements in multidrug-resistant *Enterobacter bugandensis* facilitating its persistence and succession in the International Space Station," *Microbiome* 12, no. 62 (2024).

20 T. V. Grebennikova, A. V. Syroeshkin, E. V. Shubralova, et al., "The DNA of Bacteria of the World Ocean and the Earth in Cosmic Dust at the International Space Station," *The Scientific World Journal* (April 18, 2018).

21 "It is not impossible that a bacterium that has risen from the earth floats around in space for a while, then enters the atmosphere of another heavenly body, and if it finds the appropriate living conditions on it, continues to multiply there. Conversely, it is also conceivable that the germs of a bacterium or a similar extremely small and simple being are carried as dust into space from some life-sustaining heavenly body, and that such a germ finally enters the atmosphere of the earth and settles on its surface." Ferdinand Cohn, *Über Bakterien, die kleinsten lebenden Wesen* (Berlin: Lüderitz, 1872), 33.

22 Svante Arrhenius, *Worlds in the Making; The Evolution of the Universe* (London: Harper, 1908), 217.

23 Svante Arrhenius, "Die Verbreitung des Lebens im Weltenraum," *Umschau* 7 (June 13, 1903): 481–85.

24 Joshua Lederberg and Dean B. Cowie, "Moondust: The Study of this Covering Layer by Space Vehicles May Offer Clues to the Biochemical Origin of Life," *Science* 127, no. 3313 (1958): 1473–75.

1 Patrick Geddes, 1879

Life is entanglement. We live within microbes and microbes within us. Nothing lives before or beyond the ever-convoluting geometry of microbes. The very concept of environment – that which surrounds, supports, and shapes life – is microbial, whether the natural environment collaboratively built over billions of years by countless interdependent species, the recently arrived portable environment that is the human body, or the permanently occupied human-built environment that only emerged ten thousand years ago.

MICROBIAL URBANISM

The twenty-five-year-old Scottish evolutionary biologist Patrick Geddes, a specialist in the life cycles of bacteria whose research was appreciated by Charles Darwin, [1–2] was studying a curious phenomenon at the Zoological Station on the Naples waterfront in 1881. Some transparent marine organisms – from tiny Radiolarian to larger jellyfish and sea anemones – seemed to have a kind of plant living within them, as if one type of creature had been permanently invaded by a completely different one. [3] The invader appeared as distinct clusters of "yellow cells" scattered within the host, vividly seen in the drawings of Ernst Haeckel, who had coined the word "ecology" a decade earlier to describe the interplay between organisms and their environment. [4] In this case, Geddes thought the two creatures were acting as the environment for each other. He demonstrated that the smaller organisms were not parasites, as suggested by other scientists, but photosynthetic algae that produce oxygen for their hosts. He named them "philozoon" from *philo*, to love as a friend, and *zoon*, animal.[1] One species occupied the other in a relationship of mutual advantage to both. Each absorbed

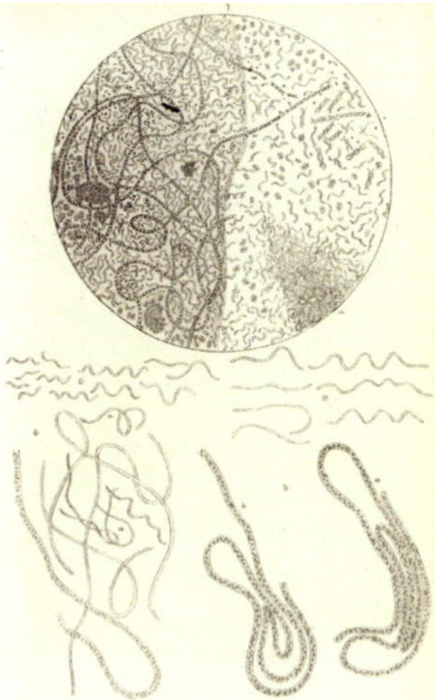

2 Patrick Geddes, illustration from "On the Life-History of Spirillum," 1878

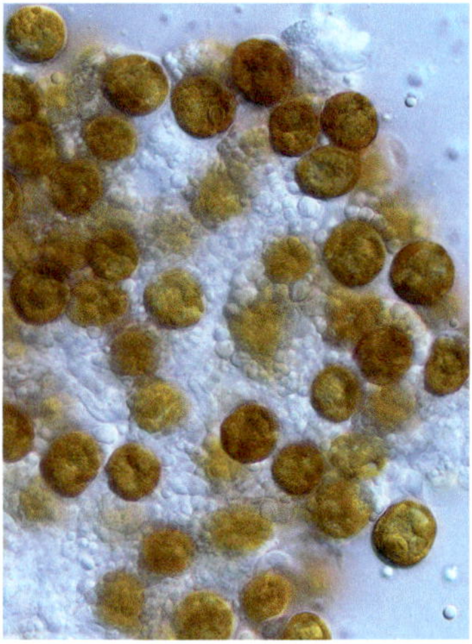

3 Yellow cells of the symbiotic algae *Philozoon colossum*

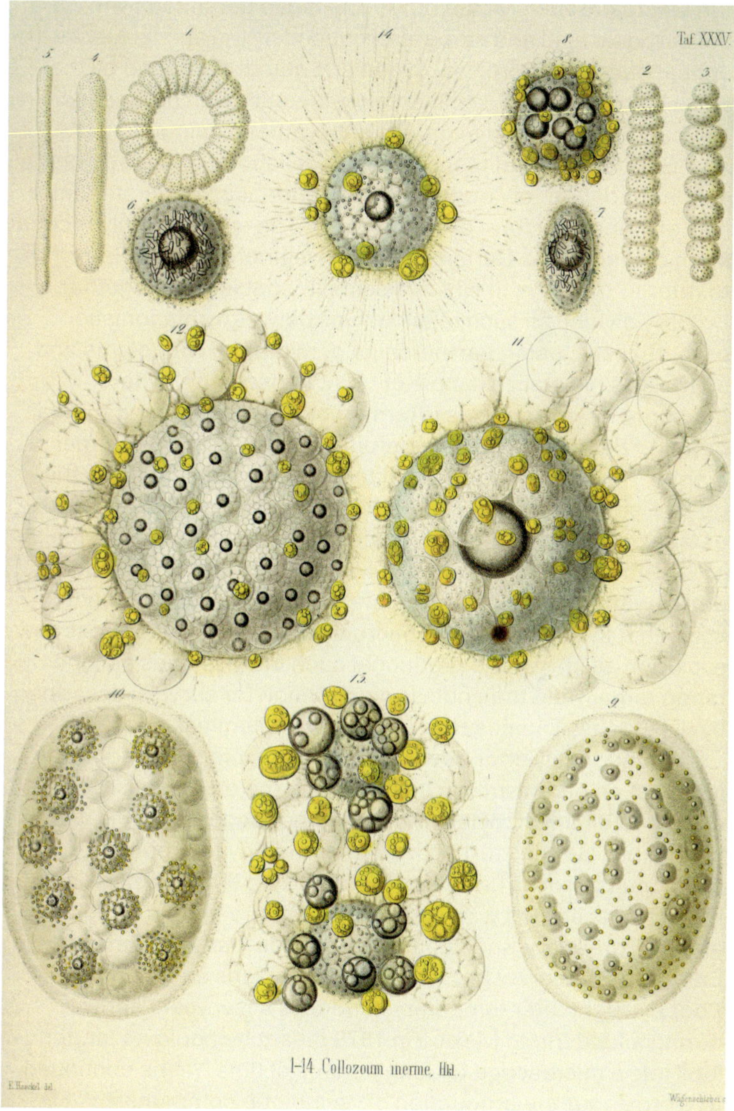

4 Ernst Haeckel, Plate XXXV, "Collozoum inerme," from *Die Radiolarien (Rhizopoda radiaria): eine Monographie*, 1862

the waste products of the other. The algae benefited from the carbonic acid and nitrogen produced by the animal just as the animal benefited from the oxygen and starch produced by the algae. The result was a collaborative creature with new capacities, a hybrid of animal and plant, a photosynthetic animal.[2]

Geddes referred to this intimate collaboration as "reciprocal accommodation" or "mutual interdependence," understanding it as an important form of "symbiosis."[3] The term had only recently been coined by the German botanist Heinrich Anton de Bary to refer to the ways in which dissimilar species live together. De Bary divided all such relationships between antagonistic or mutualistic, using partnerships of microbes with plants and animals as his main example of "joint households" where the home for one species is formed by the other to their mutual benefit.[4] But Geddes counterintuitively argued that the larger marine organisms, which seem to be the host, are actually the guests, since they cannot breathe without their lodgers. They paradoxically live within the space provided by the much smaller organism that is able to survive without them but does much better with them. The micro scale makes possible the macro scale that in turn allows the micro to flourish more.[5] Geddes saw evolution as mainly the product of such inter-species collaboration rather than the endless competition for survival described by his teacher Thomas Huxley, Darwin's relentless advocate.

Immediately after developing this seemingly paradoxical idea that an organism can be inhabiting the organisms that appear to inhabit it, where living together becomes living within each other, Geddes turned from bacteriology to urbanism, using mutualism as his model for rethinking the built environment. His projects started with acupunctural interventions bringing air, light, greenery, and community spaces into the slums of Edinburgh and grew to city and regional plans around the world. Poor eyesight after temporary blindness a few years earlier during a field trip to Mexico in 1879 meant he could no longer look into a microscope for long periods of time. Yet he continued to write about the production of "symbiotic community" through mutualism in encyclopedia entries and biology textbooks – treating the microbial scale as the basis for all other scales and their interdependencies.[6] His publications on city planning inevitably echoed those on biology since he understood cities as biological. They are both organisms and environments, depending on the scale. Geddes' 1901 *Chambers's Encyclopedia* entry on "Environment" rejected the idea of an organism as a distinct enclosure, a "rounded-off unity" separated from its environment. The environment is part of the organism and vice versa. Also, the environment always includes other organisms and is ultimately the largest organism.[7] Life is therefore not embodied in discrete creatures but in countless chemical, mechanical, and genetic interactions that all have an evolutionary history.

The implication of Geddes' argument is that the apparent line between organism and environment is actually forged and maintained by the interactions between them. Or, to say it the other way round, the apparent outer limit of an organism, marking what most properly belongs to it, is equally the skin of the living environment. As Geddes was still arguing in a 1931 textbook on "life," environments penetrate every layer of an organism, including the "germ cells" at its heart, and, in reverse, organisms penetrate all layers of environment.[8] **[5]** This is not to dissolve lines, but to see them differently: as the medium and evidence of interaction rather than isolation. A truly ecological city plan would be nothing but a set of lines treated as crossings, not divisions but intensities of engagement.

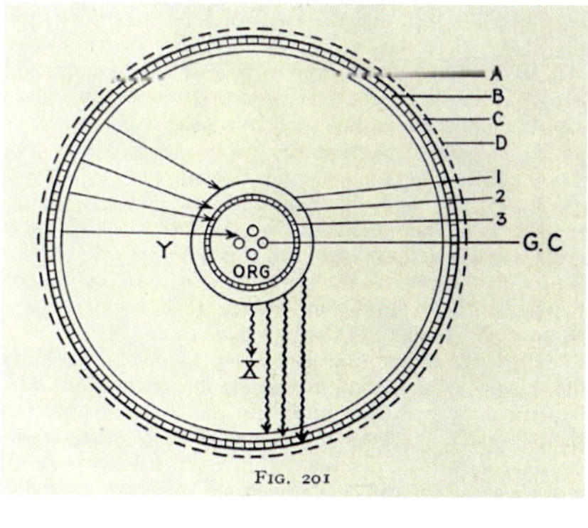

5 Patrick Geddes, diagram of action and reaction between all levels of organism and environment, 1931

Geddes' central argument as the founder of city and regional planning was that the nested relationships between human and building, building and city, city and wider conurbation, conurbation and region, built environment and nature should all take the form of mutualistic symbiosis.[9] Built spaces are living organisms interdependent with each other and with all other visible and invisible creatures. Buildings and cities are hosted and sustained by the smaller forms of life that seem to inhabit them. Design therefore has to be multi-scalar, biological, and ecological. No building can be thought independently of the bioregion it is both dependent on and transforms. The seemingly inanimate built environment is an evolving dance partner that both shapes and is shaped by endlessly overlapping and interacting entanglements of heterogeneous organisms living within each other. The real client for the design of a room, building, city, farm, or region is this expanded society of "inseparably interwoven" species reaching to every horizon. Microbial entanglements became the model for ever-wider and ultimately planetary entanglements. Each invisible community of microbes, and each co-evolving species within that community, is as important as the whole environment, and actively generates that environment.

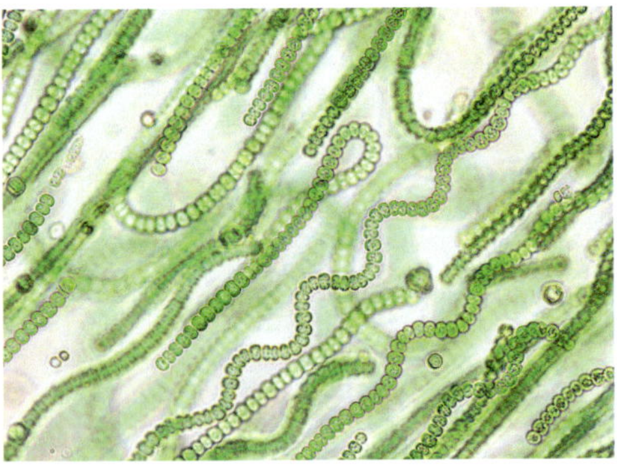

6 Microscopic view of cyanobacteria

MICROBIAL MATTER

Microbes are not just everywhere in the biosphere, maintaining all cycles of life. They manufactured the very material of the biosphere: all the solids, liquids gases, and lifeforms. Anything that breathes is connected to microbes, absorbing the oxygen excreted by cyanobacteria, the most numerous organisms on earth that are infused throughout the ocean and soil. **[6]** All multicellular life depends on the labor of this ancient lifeform whose gift is photosynthesis – the ability to use sunlight to turn hydrogen and carbon dioxide into energy. Cyanobacteria made plants possible, which made animals possible, which made humans possible, which made buildings possible. The human-built environment is unthinkable without this ubiquitous organism. The relationship between architecture and microbes is not just about the microbes inside and outside buildings, but the deep time in which microbes like cyanobacteria eventually made something like buildings possible, as living microbial artifacts.

The ancient ancestors of contemporary cyanobacteria developed the ability to generate oxygen about 3.4 billion years ago and are fossilized in rock formations called stromatolites as the oldest evidence of life on the planet.[10] **[7]** These laminated reefs were ecosystems made and occupied by diverse microbes living together collaboratively in thin mats. They grew around a centimeter a year in shallow waters over thousands of years as

7 3.4-billion-year-old stromatolite from Pilbara Craton, Western Australia

layers of calcium carbonate were excreted by countless trillions of cyanobacteria, trapping sediments of sand and minerals in the layers. The calcium carbonate formed around, on, and within the bacterial cells, dissolving any simple distinction between environment and organism, architecture and inhabitant, lifeform and fossil. These reefs could reach hundreds of meters high and thousands of meters long. Yet it was not for another billion years that the oxygen released by the cyanobacteria started to accumulate so rapidly that all the oceans and atmosphere became filled with it. This so-called "Great Oxidation Event" was a planetary revolution. The entire bio-geo-chemical system transformed, decimating 95 percent of the existing species for whom oxygen was toxic, yet triggering an exponential increase in biodiversity, which included the diversification of cyanobacteria themselves. The smallest organism had the largest possible impact, constructing a world, a planetary-scaled home.

If life is architecture, in the sense of the active production of internal environments distinct from their exterior – whether it be the internal space of a tiny microbe, the ecosystem of a reef, or the internal space of the whole biosphere generated by countless such organisms – how did this action of making interior begin? What made cyanobacteria possible?

Scientists forensically studying the genetic footprints of all known species have assembled a portrait of the microbe that

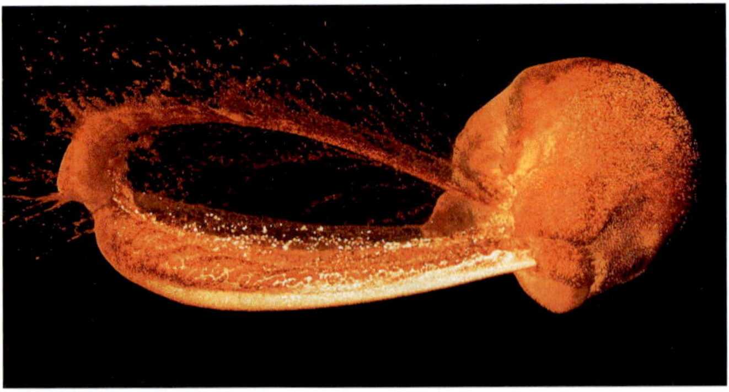

8 Still from computer simulation of the collision that formed Earth and Moon

is the "last universal common ancestor" (LUCA), its bacterium-like shape, membrane, tails, and proteins along with what it could do, when it lived, and its impact on the earth system. LUCA is estimated to have lived around 4.2 billion years ago in a world without oxygen just three hundred thousand years after Earth and its satellite moon were formed by a massive collision between two planetary bodies. The collision produced Earth as a molten sphere that still today has only cooled at its outermost crust.[11] **[8]** By LUCA's time, the crust was cool enough for water bodies to start forming below a growing atmosphere of thick gases expelled from volcanoes. LUCA, our shared ancestor, was an extremophile, likely living in hydrothermal vents – digesting the carbon dioxide and hydrogen gas bubbling up where the molten magma below met the water above.

The circuit diagram of the probable metabolism of this ancient little rod-shaped room with a tail is an intricate network of interacting processes, multiple metabolic circuits that process and exchange different things through its membrane. **[9]** The circuitry is as complex as that of a typical bacteria like *E. coli* today.[12] Life did not begin as a simple form that became

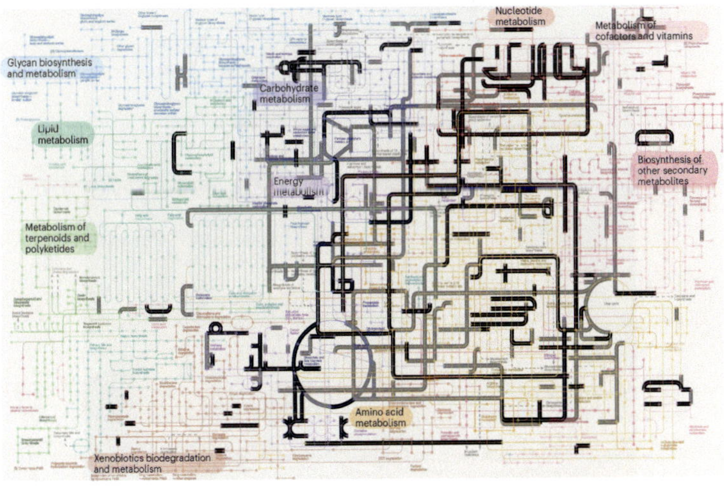

9 Likely metabolic pathways of LUCA, the last universal common ancestor

ever-more complex. Life is the opposite of simplicity. Each individual bacterial cell contains millions of proteins that are constantly on the move, all bumping into every other one at least once every second, resulting in trillions of molecular interactions.[13]

The real architecture of this tiny jostling room is not the seemingly stable line between inside and outside the cell, or even the internal circuitry that sustains that line, but a much wider set of entanglements. The metabolism of LUCA included, for example, means for sensing and communicating with other cells, along with an immune system against viruses. The ancestral living cell was already in an intimate relationship with other cells and much smaller, more numerous, parasitic microbes that cannibalized its operations to package their own genetic code.

Viruses, not discovered until 1892 and not seen until after electron microscopes exposed them in 1935, are particles one thousandth the size of bacteria that float randomly around in every ecosystem and reproduce by infecting bacteria they encounter. Technically, they are not living organisms but zombie-like packages of genetic information that dissolve the cells they hijack to reproduce and evolve. **[10]** Yet they are paradoxically

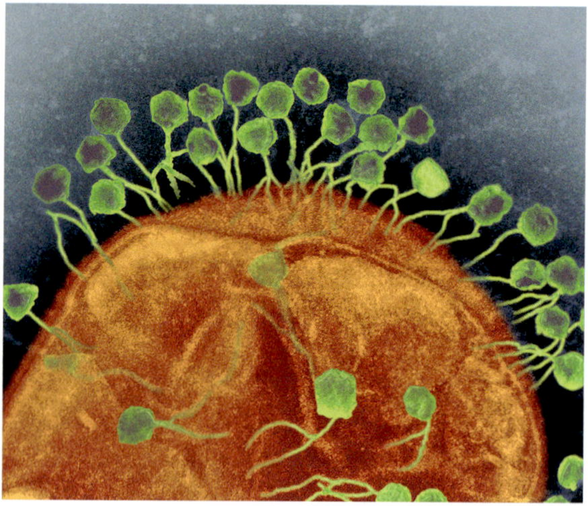

10 Bacteriophages attacking bacteria

crucial to the ability of those living cells to respond, adapt, and diversify. Many of an organism's crucial capacities come from genetic code that viruses permanently inserted into their DNA. It is estimated that 30 percent of adaptions in the human genetic code since diverging from other apes have been caused by viruses.[14]

Viruses have always been both a threat and a necessary companion. Or, to say it the other way around, viruses have been architectural collaborators throughout the billions of years of construction of the biosphere and its inhabitants. If microbes are the beginning of architecture, in the sense of constructing and maintaining an interior, then the parasitic viruses which seem so destructive of that interior are strangely integral to it.

Viruses are in turn dependent on even smaller so-called satellite viruses that hijack them without ever coming into contact with living cells. These satellites, unseen before 1962, take advantage of viruses that take advantage of cells that take advantage of each other in a chain of interdependencies that shapes life, and ultimately is life.[15] The vertiginous entanglement of microbes that is the very engine of life therefore uncannily includes entanglement with viruses that are neither living nor dead – zombies and the zombies that haunt them. Microbial life is strangely dependent on the galaxies of particles that threaten it. Life – and the spaces it builds, occupies, and maintains – is not just entanglement with other life but with the otherness of half-life. Living is permanently inhabited by that which doesn't live. It's an intimate example, perhaps the oldest example, of what Geddes would call "reciprocal accommodation." Despite the continual dissolving of living cells by viruses, literally bursting the membrane that seems to define an interior space, each acts as a house for the other. Living cells and viruses are completely interdependent and likely emerged together.[16] Bacteria and bacteriophages, the viruses that exploit them, are inseparable.

LUCA was not the first living cell, but the ancestor of all the organisms for which there is genetic evidence. It is, as it were, the end of the beginning of life. But LUCA was not alone. There were likely other organisms alongside for which there is no genetic trace because none of their descendants survived through billions of years – including the many mass extinction events that dramatically reduced planetary biodiversity. More than 99 percent of all living species ever have become extinct for multiple reasons. LUCA was already inseparable from a diverse ecosystem of other organisms and proto-organisms. These companions may have survived a long time and had a substantial impact on those that outlived them, since all organisms are shaped by the others they interact with, but finally they left no trace.

The point is that life is always life with multiple others, multiple complex interacting interdependencies that breed further complexity. There is no sharp line between no-life and life. Rather, life emerged in entanglements of living cells that are never fully autonomous with never-fully-living non-autonomous cells.

MUTUALISM

After a billion years of entangled coexistence with other microbes and their collective expansion from water onto land, LUCA diverged into bacteria and archaea, two very similar-looking but separate domains of organism with different membranes and constitutions.[17] Another billion years later, a remarkable thing happened. In a process called "endosymbiosis" – one species living within the cells of another – some cyanobacteria cells took up residence within some archaea cells to their mutual benefit, creating a whole new type of cell with internal divisions and enhanced capacities. The engulfed cell was able to produce the energy required by the one that engulfed it, and does so within every cell of every subsequent form of multicellular life, including the fungi that started appearing a billion years ago, plants 800 million years ago, animals 750 million years ago, insects 480 million years ago, birds 150 million years ago, flowers 140 million years ago, apes 25 million years ago, and modern humans just 230,000 years ago. Every human cell has the descendants of cyanobacteria replicating within it with their own genetic information. There is no non-bacterial human cell. Each contains an average of one hundred domesticated bacteria that are vital to its operation.[18] Like all other animals, we don't just breathe what these microorganisms excrete. We are made of them.

The possibility that all multicellular life is the product of different types of microbes taking up permanent residence within each other – that the kind of mutualism that Geddes described between the cells of very different species is the very basis of every plant and animal cell – was controversially raised in the late 1960s by the evolutionary biologist Lynn Margulis, who revived the repeatedly discredited propositions of some earlier scientists. **[11]** The Russian botanist Konstantin Mereschkowski, for example, had argued in 1905 that the green chloroplasts in plant cells that carry out photosynthesis are permanently internalized cyanobacteria – a suggestion first made in an 1883 footnote by the German botanist Andreas Schimper.[19] Mereschkowski coined the term "symbiogenesis" to describe how this incorporation of bacteria produced a more complex lifeform. He visualized two such transformative moments when separate lines in the tree of life fused to create new capacities. **[12]** In the 1920s, the American biologist Ivan Wallin was likewise heavily criticized for arguing that all plant and animal cells contain vital elements that were once independent bacteria. These "intimate microsymbiotic complexes" can be hard to recognize as the

11 Lynn Margulis in her lab in Boston University, late 1960s

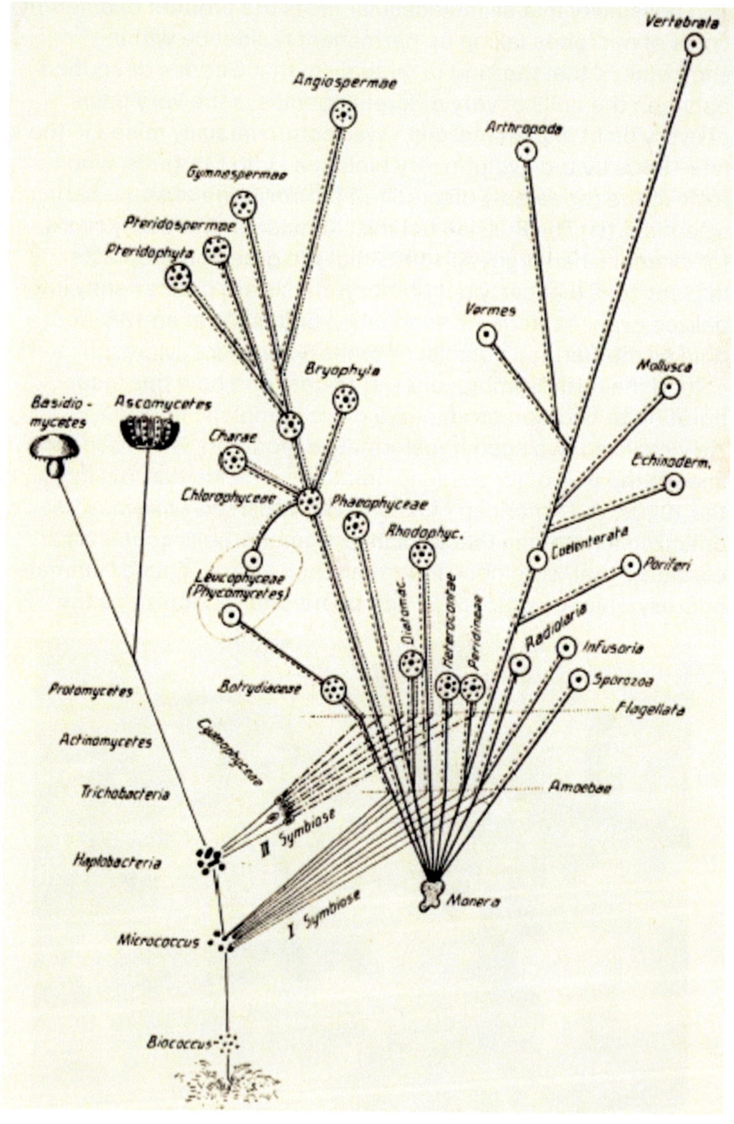

12 Konstantin Mereschkowski, 1910 diagram of symbiogenesis in tree of life embedded foreigner and its new home adapt to each other. The once freely swimming bacteria that generate energy for their host no longer need their tails, so appear as an organ of the host – even if on closer observation it keeps replicating independently and has its own DNA.[20]

Margulis went further than her predecessors in explaining the emergence of all forms of multicellular life though four successive internalizations of different types of bacteria, challenging the very idea of individual cells and species. Each seemingly individual cell, each living interior delimited by an enclosing wall, each microscopic home, is actually a permanent community of once independent creatures. **[13]** Individuality is the paradoxical effect of entangled heterogeneity, "individuality by incorporation," which is to say the loss of prior individualities:

> All organisms large enough for us to see are composed of once-independent microbes, teamed up to become larger wholes. As they merged, many lost what we in retrospect recognize as their former individuality.[21]

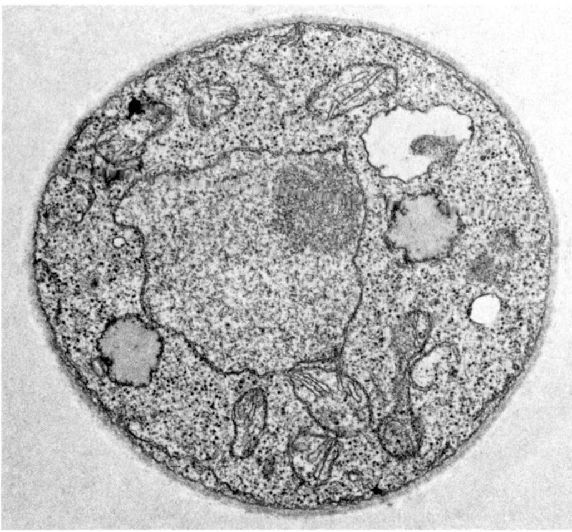

13 Lynn Margulis, microscope image of single *Cryptococcus neoformans* cell as a community

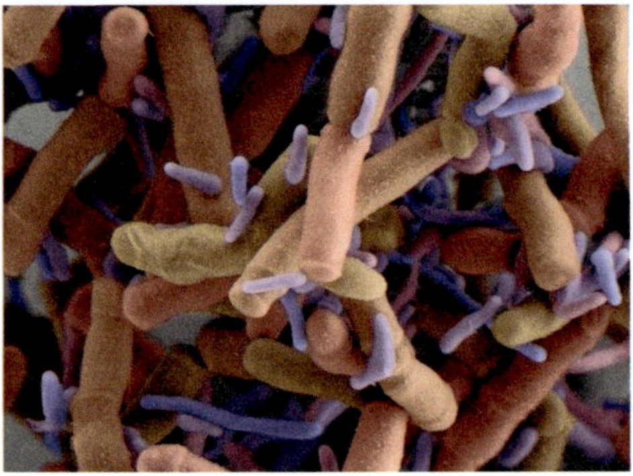

After years of dismissal, most of Margulis' theory of evolution through successive endosymbiosis events has eventually become accepted. Mutualism within and between cells rather than competition is the primary engine of evolutionary invention in what she calls the "symbiotic planet." Each form of life is nested within others, suspended within vertiginous circuits in and between microbes. No line between individuals is as secure as it seems. On the contrary, it is an effect of their collaboration. In the end, Margulis allows all lines to be thought differently, which allows architecture to be thought differently. Interiors don't simply contain heterogeneous life. They are formed by that life and are part of that life.

If this sense of the cosmopolitan density and mutually supportive entanglements of the diversity of life was not enough, the known biodiversity of microbes increased fivefold with the recent discovery of a whole range of ultra-small bacteria and ultra-small archaea in almost every environment from extreme hydrothermal vents to raindrops, the human mouth, and gut. [14] They are now thought to have as many species as all other microbes and reach even further back in time. Having a small amount of DNA and metabolic capacity, these smallest living organisms yet discovered, with their own tiny feelers, attach themselves to larger microbes in a range of symbiotic relationships and play a vital role in biochemical cycling through so-

14 A scanning electron micrograph shows ultra-small bacteria cells on the surface of much larger bacteria called "metabolic handoffs," in which something being processed by a larger microbe is modified in one phase by these more limited ones.

The fact that these ultra-small microbes, the smallest interiors yet discovered, are as ancient or even more so than the larger ones suggests that this even denser trans-species collaboration is not just at the beginning of life, but its very possibility. Life was never the production of independent interiors sustained by discrete metabolisms. On the contrary, it is the vertiginous entanglements of diverse interiors at different scales. The very idea of the interior, as a stable line between inside and outside, is mistaken. "Interior" is not just an activity, a verb; the continuous redrawing of a porous line that creates a space. Every such line is always interdependent with the active drawing of untold other lines at different scales. Every space is entangled with a myriad of other spaces. Every inside is made of multiple outsides.

COSMOPOLITICS

The mutualism between species that organizes the biosphere and its evolution offers an alternative paradigm for architecture – as it did for Geddes. All design involves a society of countless species living within and through each other as a complex form of community. All ecology from this point of view is political ecology – and vice versa. Geddes' 1888 entry on "Variation and Selection" in *Encyclopaedia Britannica* repeated his view that evolution is driven more by "co-operative adaption" between species than competition. Individuals subordinate themselves to the social. Geddes even presents evolution in ethical terms, going as far as to conclude that "love" for others is the "final law":

> Each of the greater steps of progress is definitely associated with an increased measure of subordination of individual competition to reproductive or social ends, and of interspecific competition to co-operative adaptation. The idea of evolution is thus an Eden; and although competition can never be wholly eliminated, and progress must be asymptotic, it is much for our pure natural history

> to see no longer struggle, but love, as "creation's final law." ... [We] make the transition from the self-regarding to the other-regarding (in ethical language, from the egotistic to the altruistic).[22]

Microbes were the basis of the political philosophy of mutualism. The anarchist socialist Peter Kropotkin, who was in regular dialog with Geddes, understood microbes as social beings and channeled the argument that cooperation organized all forms of life. Socialism inevitably begins with microbes. As Kropotkin put it in 1890: "we must be prepared to learn some day, from the students of microscopical pond-life, facts of unconscious mutual support, even from the life of microorganisms."[23] He readily embraced the just-published theory of the prominent German pathologist Richard Altmann that each cell is a "co-operative colony" produced by the collaboration of many once independent microbes carrying out metabolic tasks.[24] **[15]** This controversial theory was so heavily criticized that Altmann became a recluse in his office and was nicknamed "the ghost." It was elaborated by several scientists at the turn of the century and repeatedly discarded, only to be revived by Margulis and belatedly accepted. For Kropotkin, echoing Altmann, seemingly permanent parts of animal and plant cells were once "independent" and "separate organisms," and still need be treated as such to understand the collaborative agreements organizing life:

> At the present time, we know that no animal or plant, with the exception of the lowest unicellular beings, can be considered as *one* being – that each of them is a colony of multitude of micro-organisms.[25]

Kropotkin argued that just as plants are completely dependent on a "symbiotic association" with an "agglomeration" of micro-organisms attached to their roots, each cell of the plant itself, as with any animal, contains its own internal collaborating microbes. He concluded that the latest research on symbiosis dramatically changes the meaning of life.

Lewis Mumford, another long-term correspondent with Geddes and close reader of Kropotkin, invoked symbiosis in his

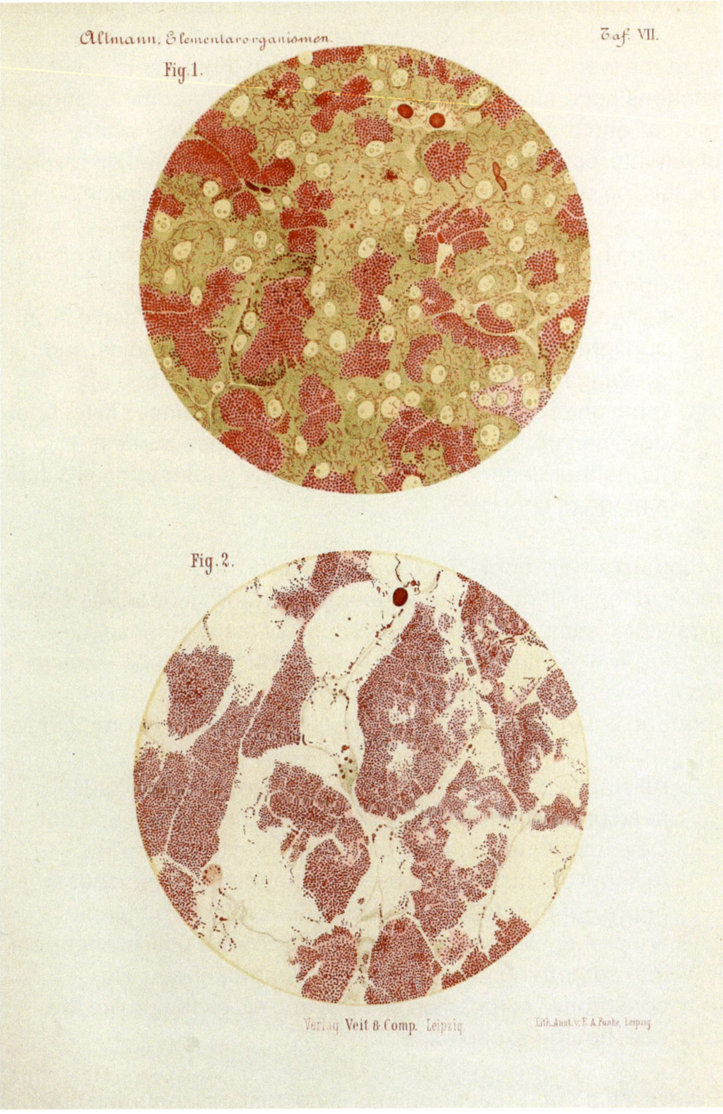

15 Robert Altmann, red-stained "bioplasts" (mitochondria) form organized patterns within a pancreas cell above, that match the patterns bacteria make on a plant root below, 1890

1962 critique of modern architecture. He condemned the aspiration of buildings to be hygienic machines disconnected both from the world around them and their own inhabitants – with kitchens becoming "laboratories," bathrooms becoming "surgical rooms," and the other parts of the house becoming "white, cleanable, empty of human contact." Mumford called on respect for the "organic interdependence" of microbial multiplicity:

> Man himself is an organism whose existence is dependent upon his maintaining the delicate balance that exists between all the forces of nature, physical and organic, from sunlight and air and the soil, the bacteria, the molds, and growing plants right up to the complex interaction of thousands of species. Despite the great advances in technology, man controls only a small part of these processes: for neither destruction nor mechanical substitution is in fact a mode of control.[26]

Mumford's 1951 book *The Conduct of Life* argued that the more independent a creature seems, the more it depends on the symbiotic "companionship and support of many other species," starting with bacteria and mold.[27] The biologist Donna Haraway's *Companion Species Manifesto* of 2003 echoes this line of thought, again drawing on late nineteenth-century microbiology:

> All stages of the life histories of evolving animals had to adapt to eager bacteria colonizing them inside and out. Developmental patterns of complex life forms are likely to show the history of these adaptations, once scientists figure out how to look for the evidence. Earth's beings are prehensile, opportunistic, ready to yoke unlikely partners into something new, something symbiogenetic. Co-constitutive companion species and co-evolution are the rule, not the exception.[28]

Haraway's point is that symbiosis is not just collaboration but collaboration between heterogeneous others, others that remain irreducibly other, even when incorporated. Otherness itself is finally what is hosted. **[16]**

More recently, the philosopher Isabelle Stengers' concept of "cosmopolitics" extends the decentering of humans and of individuality itself with a radically symbiotic view in which no line is drawn between microbes and all forms of living together. Stengers embraces the formulation of the whole biosphere itself as a living organism, named "Gaia" by James Lovelock and Lynn Margulis; a single massive self-regulating organism engineered by the smallest organisms within it:

> That on which we depend, and which has so often been defined as the "given," the globally stable context of our histories and our calculations, is the product of a history of co-evolution, the first artisans and real, continuing authors of which were the innumerable populations of microorganisms which, for billions of years, have been the effective co-authors of her [Gaia's] ongoing existence.[29]

This extended line of scientific, philosophical, and political thought about mutualism that emerged out of bacteriology is not an ethical philosophy to apply to architecture, but an architectural philosophy from the beginning – a rethinking of the concept of interior, the materials of which it is made, and of its inhabitants.

16 Donna Haraway in *Donna Haraway: Story Telling for Earthly Survival*, 2017 film

1 Patrick Geddes, "Further Researches on Animals Containing Chlorophyll," *Nature* 25, no. 639 (January 26, 1882): 304. Darwin wrote to Geddes appreciating the paper, even if it challenged his emphasis on competition as the driving force of evolution.

2 Geddes had earlier demonstrated that some of the seemingly simplest organisms, like flat worms living at the water's edge, constituted a "vegetating animal" because they used the oxygen produced by the green chlorophyll permanently resident within them as within plants. Patrick Geddes, "Observations on the Physiology and Histology of *Convoluta Schultzii*," *Proceedings of the Royal Society of London* (January 1, 1879): 449–57. The crucial advance of the later research was to show the mutual advantage of such cohabitation.

3 Patrick Geddes, "Researches on Animals Containing Chlorophyll," *Nature* 25, no. 642 (February 16, 1882): 361–62.

4 The concept of "mutualists" in which two species benefit from living together (as opposed to exploitative parasitism or non-exploitative commensalism) had been introduced in Pierre-Joseph van Beneden, *Les commensaux et les parasites dans le règne animal* (Paris: Gemer Baillière, 1875). The term "symbiosis" is associated with Anton de Bary's 1878 lecture on "The Phenomenon of Symbiosis" that argued that the range of symbiotic cohabitations of dissimilar species exceeds the three described by van Beneden and proposed a simpler division between antagonistic competition and mutualistic collaboration to form a "joint household." Nathalie Oulhen, Barbara J. Schulz, and Tyler J. Carrier, "English Translation of Heinrich Anton de Bary's 1878 speech, '*Die Erscheinung der Symbiose*'," *Symbiosis* 69 (May 2, 2016): 131–39.

5 De Bary's lecture described a similar relationship between the mass of fungi that gathers around much smaller photosynthetic algae to form lichen, which benefits the cyanobacteria even if they could otherwise live without the fungi, while the fungi cannot survive without the bacteria. Oulhen, Schulz, and Carrier, "English Translation," 137.

6 See, for example, Geddes' summary of the research, including his own, on mutualistic symbiosis. Patrick Geddes, "Parasitism," in *Encyclopaedia Britannica*, eds. T. S. Baynes and William Robertson Smith, vol. 18 (Edinburgh: Charles Black, 1885), 268–69.

7 Patrick Geddes, "Environment," in *Chambers's Encyclopedia*, vol. 4 (London: William & Robert Chambers, 1901), 390.

8 Patrick Geddes and J. Arthur Thomson: *Life: Outline of General Biology*, vol. 2 (London: Williams & Norgate. 1931), 1255.

9 Geddes' first book on city planning, focusing on a small town in Scotland, rehearses the call for an evolutionary philosophy of "mutual aid" to replace the prevailing "crude Darwinism" of competition. Patrick Geddes, *City Development, a Study of Parks, Gardens, and Culture-Institutes; A Report to the Carnegie Dunfermline Trust* (Edinburgh: Geddes and Co., 1904), 76.

10 G. P. Fournier, K. R. Moore, L. T. Rangel, et al., "The Archean Origin of Oxygenic Photosynthesis and Extant Cyanobacterial Lineages," *Proceedings Royal Society B* 288, no. 1959, (September 29, 2021): 675.

11 Jacob A. Kegerreis, Sergio Ruiz-Bonilla, Vincent R. Eke, et al., "Immediate Origin of the Moon as a Post-impact Satellite," *The Astrophysical Journal Letters* 937, no. 2 (2022): L40.

12 Edmund R. R. Moody, Sandra Álvarez-Carretero, Tara A. Mahendrarajah, et. al., "The Nature of the Last Universal Common Ancestor and its Impact on the Early Earth System," *Nature, Ecology and Evolution* 8 (July 12, 2024): 1654–66.

13 Ron Milo, "What is the total number of protein molecules per cell volume? A call to rethink some published values," *Bioessays* 35, no. 12 (2013): 1050–5.

14 David Enard, Le Cai, Carina Gwennap, and Dmitri A. Petrov, "Viruses are a Dominant Driver of Protein Adaptation in Mammals," *eLife*, no. 12469 (May 17, 2016).

15 Viruses are an integral part of the history of life, are more numerous than other microbes, and have their own satellites, drifting packages of even smaller amounts of genetic code that never enter cells but replicate by using viruses that do. The evolutionary microbiologist Eduardo Rocha has recently called this "the Microbiome within the microbiome." Manuel Ares-Arroyo, Charles Coluzzi, Jorge A. Moura de Sousa, and Eduardo P. C. Rocha, "Hijackers, Hitchhikers, or Co-drivers? The Mysteries of Mobilizable Genetic Elements," *PLoS Biology* (August 29, 2024).

16 Arshan Nasir and Gustavo Caetano-Anollés, "A Phylogenomic Data-Driven Exploration of Viral Origins and Evolution," *Science Advances* 1, no. 8 (September 25, 2015).

17 The differences between bacteria and archea were only recognized in 1977.
18 If all the bacteria that are integrated into cells are counted, the number of bacteria in all environments increases dramatically. The total number of bacteria and amount of bacterial DNA in the human body, for example, would be one hundred times larger. Miroslav Oborník, "In the Beginning Was the Word: How Terminology Drives Our Understanding of Endosymbiotic Organelles," *Microbial Cell* 6, no. 2 (January 21, 2019): 134–41.
19 Schimper, whose teacher had initiated the concept of symbiosis, noted that the relationship between green chloroplastids and the colorless plant cells they occupied resembled symbiosis and that perhaps green plants had actually been made possible by the "union" of two different organisms. Andreas Schimper, "Über die Entwicklung der Chlorophyllkorner und Farbkörper," *Botanische Zeitung* 41 (February 16, 1883): 111. Mereschkowski drew on Schimper's research to argue that choroplastids were "foreign bodies, foreign organisms, that invaded the colorless plasm of the cell and entered into a symbiotic coexistence with it." Konstantin Mereschkowski, "Über Natur und Ursprung der Chromatophoren im Pflanzenreiche," *Biologisches Centralblatt* 25, no. 593–604 (1905): 596.
20 Ivan Wallin, *Symbionticism and the Origin of Species* (Baltimore, MD: Williams & Wilkins Company, 1927), 135. Wallin argued that the mutual adaption of bacteria and cell probably even includes the complete fusion of the two symbionts.
21 Lynn Margulis, *Symbiotic Planet: A New Look at Evolution* (New York: Basic Books, 1998), 38.
22 Patrick Geddes, "Variation and Selection," in *Encyclopaedia Britannica*, eds. T. S. Baynes and William Robertson Smith, vol. 24 (Edinburgh: A. & C. Black, 1888), 85.
23 Peter Kropotkin, "Mutual Aid Among Animals," *The Nineteenth Century Magazine* (September 1890): 342.
24 Richard Altmann, *Die Elementarorganismen und ihre Beziehungen zu den Zellen* (Leipzig: Veit & comp., 1890). Altmann noted that the highly organized patterns of granules within cells resemble bacteria in form, patterns, replication, and reaction to staining. He argued that these "bioblasts," as he called them (later named mitochondria), are elementary living beings in their own right. They were once free and but are now permanently absorbed into the larger collective cell of diverse elements they made possible, long ago losing those capacities that can be accomplished more efficiently by the collective. They are as dependent on the collective as the host is on them. Altmann describes this codependency as producing capacities beyond those of the collaborating individuals, just as the codependence of bacteria within colonies produces capacities beyond any individual.
25 Peter Kropotkin, "Recent Science," *The Nineteenth Century Magazine* (August 1893): 261. Italics in the original.
26 Lewis Mumford, "The Case Against 'Modern Architecture'," *Architectural Record* (April 1962): 161.
27 Lewis Mumford, *The Conduct of Life*, (New York: Harcourt Brace, 1951), 32, 91.
28 Donna Haraway, *The Companion Species Manifesto: Dogs, People, and Significant Otherness* (Chicago: Prickly Paradigm Press, 2003), 32.
29 Isabelle Stengers, *In Catastrophic Times: Resisting the Coming Barbarism* (London: Open Humanities Press, 2015), 44.

1 Antimicrobial products from supermarket, installation photograph, *We the Bacteria: Notes Toward Biotic Architecture* exhibition, 24th Milan Triennale International Exhibition *Inequalities*, 2025

The battle against microbes starts at home. Domestic space is ground-zero of a continuous war that has escalated ever since bacteria were proven to cause epidemic diseases in the late nineteenth century. Each home deploys a dizzying array of antimicrobial products, chemicals, technologies, and routines. There is a sense that bacteria would take over the house the moment we drop our guard, as if feeling at home requires the eviction of as many invisible roommates as possible. Yet this everyday battle is bound to fail. We share our home with countless microbes, and the very attempt to exclude them encourages more deadly strains to appear.

DOMESTIC ARSENAL

Cupboards under kitchen sinks, bathroom cabinets, and hallway closets are filled with chemicals and equipment to cleanse every surface of building and body. Each space, object, and orifice has its own array of products. Soaps, sprays, washes, pastes, gels, creams, and powders are applied to body and building and removed with sponges, brushes, pads, cloths, towels, tissues, wipes, and mops. **[1]** This antimicrobial arsenal is ever-increasing, and deployed in daily rhythms of specific repetitive movements – wipe, scrub, scrape, spray, suck, brush, wash, dry, dust, sweep, remove. The basic cleaning tools since the five-thousand-year-old invention of soap remain essential – broom, cloth, bucket – but are now aided by vacuum cleaners, fridges, dishwashers, and washing machines. **[2–3]** The microbial limits of the interior are further defended by water and air filters, door mats, pest repellants, and insect screens. All of these everyday technologies

2 California Shipbuilding Corporation employee Doris Jensen tying ribbons to brooms to be auctioned off for war bonds, 1944

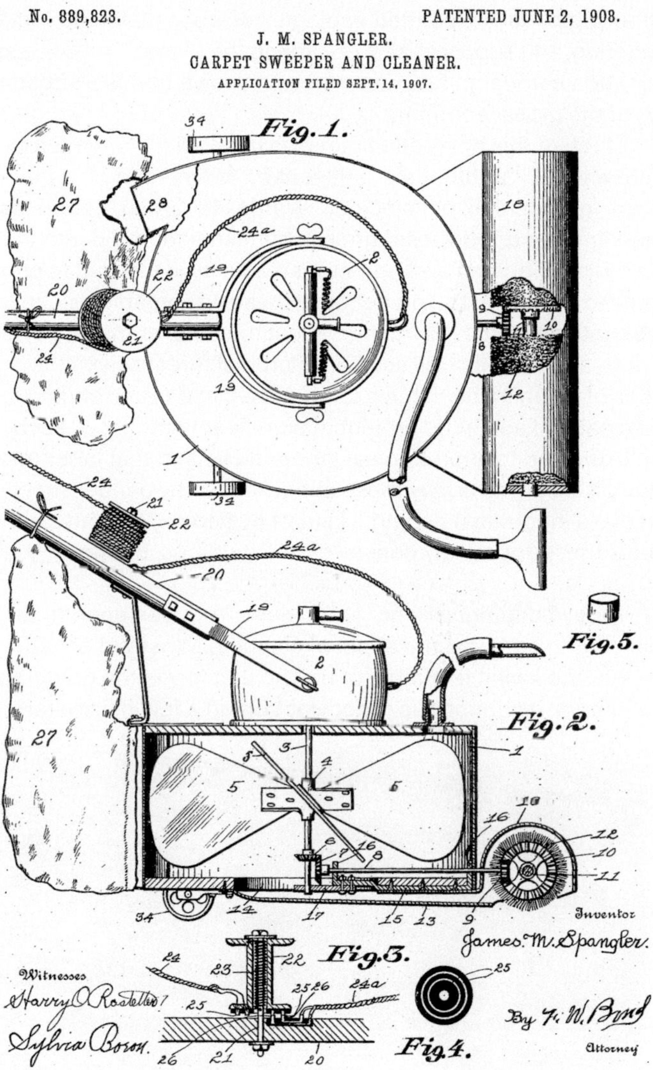

3 James Spangler, 1908 patent for
the first practical domestic vacuum cleaner

devoted to the exclusion and death of invisible enemies are supported by vast expanded ecologies of labor, materials, industry, marketing, and supply chains encircling the planet. The domestic sanitation campaign has become so massive that is a substantial part of the global economy.

Much of this domestic arsenal is labelled as "antimicrobial," "antibacterial," "antifungal," "antiseptic," "disinfecting," "sanitizing," "germicidal," or "biocidal." Words like "fresh," "spotless," "sparkling," and "odorless" are euphemisms for the death of microbes. All human and non-human activity is thought to contribute to the unwanted presence of these tiny organisms. Cleaning systematically removes the biological traces of humans, pets, insects, and rodents – all seen as microbial threats. Even the traces of cleaning itself have to be erased in a never-ending biochemical and aesthetic project. A significant amount of each day is devoted to antimicrobial labor and veiling that labor (most of which is carried out by those subordinated by gender, race, and class inequities) behind a kind of hygienic glow and synthetic smells that supposedly convey clean buildings, bodies, and minds.[1]

Today buildings are not just cleaned but designed to be cleaned and highlight the effect of cleaning. What is cleaned is in fact the invisible bubble of plastic that forms the contemporary interior, a continuous prophylactic skin a few millimeters

4 Micrograph cross-section of particleboard with polyurethane finish

thick that covers most surfaces. [4] This skin is hostile to microbes, prevents them from entering the material of the building itself, and facilitates their removal. Many of the most touched materials – in countertops, appliances, and flooring – are already plastic or laminated with plastic. Porous materials like plasterboard walls and ceilings are sealed with plastic paint, while polyurethane and acrylic seals the countless openings in wood, concrete, stone, and ceramics. [5] Even wool carpets, upholstery, and curtains are treated with stain guards that include plastic. Not to mention the fact that the cleaning tools for all these surfaces are likely made of plastic, applying chemicals from a plastic bucket that are stored in smaller plastic containers, perhaps using plastic gloves. To touch an interior is to touch a plastic skin with almost no gaps or cracks. This continuous film is smooth, and dry. Only kitchens and bathrooms offer the moisture microbes thrive in, and therefore attract the most vigorous and repeated cleaning with the most chemicals. The whole building supports this sanitary campaign. It tries to draw a line between human and microbes, as if defending humans from the organic world and their own animality. The spaces that humans wrap around themselves are a kind of "desert" or "wasteland" for microbes.[2]

Moreover, domestic space now cleans itself. Antimicrobial chemicals are impregnated into the materials forming interior space (paint, mortar, wall coverings, carpets, mats, handles,

5 SEM image of wood

countertops, faucets, light switches, bedding, shower curtains, bath mats) and objects within it (appliances, furniture, textiles, clothing, cutting boards, utensils, baby carriers, food storage containers, toys, keypads, pens). Their ubiquitous presence is accompanied by slogans like "germ-free," "odor fighting," "keeping foods fresher," and "stain inhibiting." These highly toxic chemicals are now found in all dust, soil, surface water, waste-water, and breastmilk worldwide. They are associated with numerous health disorders and actively contribute to the rise of antibiotic-resistant microbes, which are predicted to be the biggest global killer by 2050.[3]

Antimicrobial nanoparticles of metal (e.g. titanium, copper, silver, zinc, etc.) are increasingly embedded within building materials or coating them to resist bacteria, viruses, fungi, algae, and bio-deterioration caused by microbes. **[6]** They are in glass, concrete, metal, wood, stone, bricks, mortar, ceramics, plastic, gypsum, paint, tiles, pipes, furniture, carpets, upholstery, textiles, bedding, cookware, floors, countertops, water filters, and air filters. **[7]** These nanoparticles are now found in 97 percent of wastewater samples worldwide. They accumulate within most species, including humans, and are increasingly understood as a major health threat. The war on microbes is backfiring, creating bigger problems than it is solving.

6 Nanostructures in a titanium dioxide antibacterial coating on stainless steel are revealed under a scanning electron microscope. The coating kills bacteria under visible light

BUILDING MICROBIOMES

Despite all this hostility to microbes – prophylactic architecture, the relentless programs to sanitize it, and the antimicrobial materials it is made of – every home hosts dense communities of microbes on or in all surfaces, air, dust, furniture, fittings, plumbing, crevices, and even within the building materials themselves (not to mention clothes, cell phones, bags, and books). There is nothing without microbes. We are suspended within microbes just as they are suspended within us. These organisms are mobile, growing in colonies, surviving as biofilms of different species attached to all surfaces, or in spores that can easily be activated. Just add moisture to almost any building surface and wait a few days to see colonies of microorganisms on the surface and in the air come to life as dark patterns.

All interiors host microbial communities, including portable buildings in the form of cars, trains, and planes. Even the most sensitive spaces of hospitals that set the standard for the assault on microbes – operating theaters and intensive care rooms – are teaming with microbes. Cleaning only temporarily diminishes their population. Disinfected surfaces repopulate themselves within a few hours. The whole microbiome of a hospital room subjected to the most extreme cleaning restores itself within a few days. Many microbes survive even the harshest biocides by forming resilient biofilms or adapting themselves to not just

7 Cotton fabric covered with silver and copper nanoparticles that kill bacteria in six minutes of sunlight. Red color indicates presence of silver nanoparticles

resist the chemical attack but to feed on it. Extreme cleaning fosters extreme organisms that thrive under assault and dominate because they no longer have to compete with other microbes for resources.[4] The very hostility to organic life acts as a selection pressure to develop new organisms. Antimicrobial attitudes breed microbes. One study showed that homes in the United States have an average of seven thousand species of bacteria in their dust, along with two thousand species of fungus.[5] Another study showed that intensive care units typically have more than twelve thousand species of bacteria on the surfaces of each room.[6]

Less than a quarter of the microbial cells on building surfaces are living cells with the ability to recolonize humans. Most are dead, disintegrated, dying, or dormant. Yet dormant spores are easily reactivated within moist humans, and living ones are still vast in number, which use their dead companions as nutrients. Dead organisms are uncannily an active part of the domestic ecosystem.[7] Furthermore, the microbial communities are unrelated to social expectations and fears. After a week of use, pillowcases have seventeen thousand times more bacteria per square centimeter than toilet seats. What gives psychological comfort because it is supposedly clean often harbors more organisms than what produces anxiety.

The majority of these microbial housemates are human-associated – from skin, oral, anal, and uro-genital communities – with the rest coming from outdoor air, soil, and water along with pets, other animals, plants, and insects. They are deposited through direct and indirect contact, with each human shedding around thirty-seven million bacteria and as many viruses per hour, along with seven million fungi.[8] This cloud lingers in the air, in dust, and on surfaces. Recent occupants of a space can be forensically identified just by the microbial signature they leave behind in it.[9] A desktop reveals who has touched it. The air around a couch reveals who has been sitting there. These ghostly signatures are often related to the particular parts of the body making contact with different parts of a building – a door handle versus a toilet set, for example. The microbial communities of floors, walls, and ceilings are also different, with the floor having more microbes from the outside brought in on the soles of shoes.

Yet the overall microbial community of a space is spread without direct contact, via the air or in the dust that is constantly re-suspended by human movement. A quarter of the species of microbes on untouched surfaces are skin-associated.[10] Each specific microbial niche includes some microbes from all the other niches. To be in any one spot is to encounter the whole community. To occupy an interior is to share space with countless invisible companions that are only temporarily outside you and the other humans and non-humans in the space.

The microbiomes of humans and buildings are not just linked but co-evolve as one larger entity. The microbiome of a home is highly specific to its inhabitants. It is carried to a new space if they move, changes when someone leaves home for a few days, and can quickly be detected in a newly occupied home.[11] Humans living in the same house are likely to have more similar microbiomes since they live inside the microbes that live inside each other. Since many bacteria and fungi can survive for months on the surfaces of an interior – or years in the form of spores – the microbiome of a space is an evolving community largely defined by current inhabitants, but also by previous ones as well as short-term visitors. Each house is an archeology of microbes.

In a comparative study of seven ethnically diverse homes, only a third of all species detected were found in all homes, but those that were constituted around 95 percent of all microbes in them.[12] The real microbial signature of a space is therefore the exponentially smaller numbers of rarer species – with the unique species found only in one home being less than 0.6 percent of the total microbes in all homes. This mirrors human microbiomes. No two people have the same set of species, but a small number of species is shared by most humans and constitute the vast majority of their microbes. It is the wider range of less-shared species in much smaller numbers that hold the key to the health and resilience of humans.

Likewise with buildings. No two spaces have the same microbial footprint. The microbiome of buildings varies with activity, geography, seasons, temperature, dryness, time of day, proximity to soil, cleaning chemicals and regimes, light and carbon sources, ventilation, and plumbing – but, above all, the occupants. Each room in a building is different, and each niche within a room is different, offering a kind of forensic portrait of its inhabitants, their number, activities, gender, whether they have pets, etc. Neighborhoods and cities likewise have distinctive microbiomes determined largely by their occupants. In reverse, the microbiome of the occupants is affected by the spaces they share.

The immediate outside of a building has a very different microbiome than the inside, and the city has a very different microbiome to the countryside, which is different again from the deep forest. Architecture and urbanism cultivate particular microbiomes. A 2016 study called "Walls Talk: Microbial Biogeography of Homes Spanning Urbanization" compared the microbiome of the built environment of those living in the jungle with those living in rural villages, small cities, and large cities. It reveals a progressive narrowing of microbial diversity from a multiplicity of soil, plants, human, and other animal microbes toward only human-associated microbes.[13] It also shows an increasing microbial specialization between houses and between spaces within those houses. In the urbanized West, each building and room has a different microbiome. Heterogeneous mixture gives way to specialized communities. The researchers were able to predict what a space is used for based solely on the microbes found within it. Urbanization and modernization are marked by spaces that are increasingly detached from the microbes outside.

COLONIZING THE HUMAN

Buildings are a way to share microbes. In a sense, they form an expanded gut shared with others. They are part of the body and make bodies part of each other. People moving into a space soon pick up some of the microbiome of that space and start to contribute to it. Even the microbiome of a frequently cleaned hospital room resembles the microbiome of the previous patient, but starts to resemble that of a new patient after twenty-four hours.[14] The human microbiome cannot be thought of independently of the built spaces that are part of the organism's digestive system. Any simple line between body and building is dissolved. Each individual's thirty-two square meters of gut (along with seventy-five square meters of lung and two square meters of skin) is part of the building and vice versa, receiving microbes and conveying them to other spaces, other buildings. [8] Buildings make all inhabitants breathe each other in, absorbing the same microbially rich air. Buildings link all the lungs, skin, mouth, guts, and pores of an expanded more-than-human community. To occupy a room is to inhabit the bodies of the others in the room, including animals, plants, and insects, but also those who are no longer in the room, or outside, or connected to the same infrastructure of water or air. Architecture acts as a microbial reservoir and means of exchange. It seems to be made of clear lines but actually hosts communities in which the limits are never clear.

The built and social environment plays a huge role in the formation of the human microbiome, which is the basis of physical and mental health. Babies are born sterile and acquire their microbiome from their surroundings, starting with the mother who passes on a starter kit of microbes during vaginal birth – with vagina and anus close together to maximize microbial transfer. Yet the built environment immediately plays a huge role in

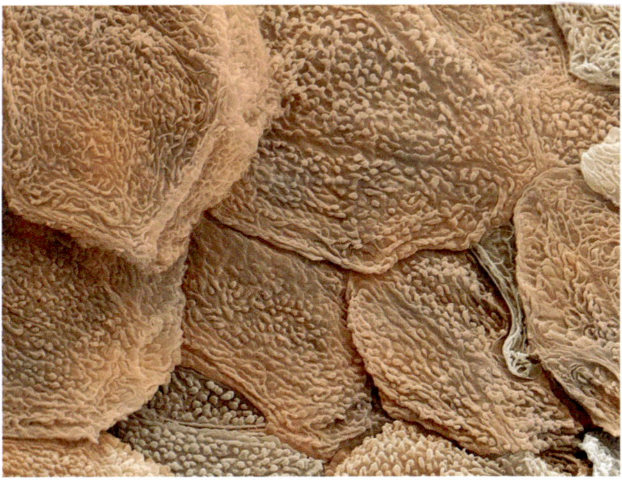

8 SEM image of human skin

the colonization of guts in early childhood, starting with hospital, home, and daycare spaces. Living in the same neighborhood or city produces some microbial overlap, but their unique microbiome is shaped more locally. A child's microbiome at first resembles that of its mother and other members of the household, but is quickly more similar to those it plays with in daycare, who share their microbes from different places and mingle with microbes from soil, plants, and other animals in playgrounds.[15] Each individual's unique microbiome is established by the age of three and keeps reconstituting from then on – with the most unique microbes of each individual being the most stable.[16]

The microbial ecologist Maria Gloria Dominguez-Bello has shown that babies delivered by caesarean section have microbes up to a year after their birth that were in the delivery room. These children tend to have worse health outcomes than those who had passed through the beneficial bacteria in the mother's vagina.[17] The microbes on the walls, surgical lamps, and ventilation systems change the sequence of gut colonization, and compromise the child's immune system and metabolism. **[9]** A microbially unfriendly room occupied just once for around

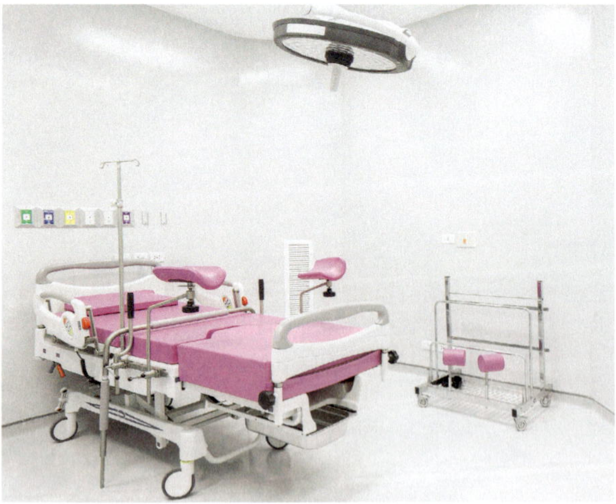

9 Medical bed in labor room

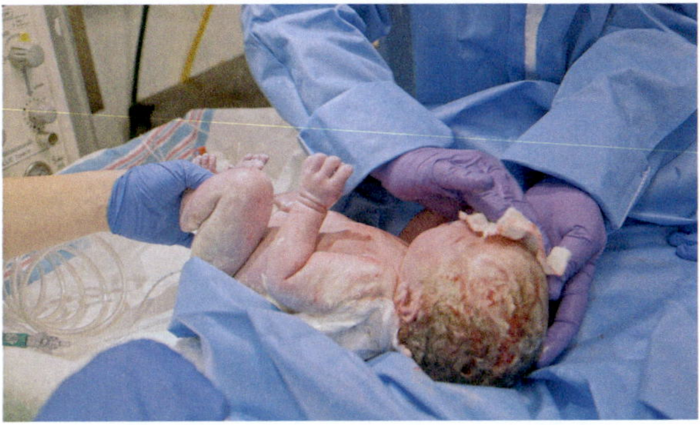

an hour can permanently shape a newborn's microbiome and life. Dominguez-Bello and her colleagues initiated the practice of "maternal-child microbial seeding" to counter this intrusion of the building by wiping the mother's vaginal fluid onto the newborn – reestablishing a typical pattern of colonization.[18] **[10]**

In another study, the gut of premature babies in intensive care neonatal units was shown to be colonized by gut-associated microbes from hospital room surfaces that the baby then releases back into the room in a self-reinforcing loop. The repeatedly sanitized room that nevertheless contains twelve thousand species of microbes acts as an external "reservoir" for the gut: "gut microbes are introduced from room sources, thrive in the gut, and are disseminated to the immediate environment, creating a cycle of room to infant colonization."[19] The gut and the room effectively become a single connected space. The gut is a pocket of the room but equally the room is an externalized gut shared with other humans – in this case, patients and medical staff. All the loops between individual microbiomes and spaces intersect, so that the microbes of neighboring babies, even in neighboring rooms, become intimately entangled.

Similar loops are set up with each successive space inhabited during the first years of childhood. No space is empty. Each is already defined by the microbes of previous or current occupants. Each both transforms and is transformed by new occupants. After

10 Maria Gloria Dominguez-Bello swabbing baby with its mother's microbes immediately after being born by cesarean section the child's unique microbial signature is established, it may broadcast this more than it receives others, but its micro-community continues to be affected by the spaces in which it finds itself. Or, to say it the other way around, each microbiological community is constantly suspended within other communities, sustaining itself within and outside the body through a kind of active curatorial work. Humans maintain their microbes outside them, and this reservoir of microbes in their spaces likely helps recolonize them after illness or antibiotic treatment.[20]

As with the microbial colonization of humans after birth, new buildings are colonized after construction. A newly constructed building has the same microbiome as its outside environment, but a distinctly different indoor microbiome gradually builds up when the interior is occupied.[21] It is human activity, not the building itself, that constructs the microbial environment. In other words, space is formed by the microbes that form its diverse inhabitants. Architecture is literally made of microbes.

1 Structural inequities are not just applied to the organization of cleaning. Ascending levels of social hierarchy are treated as ascending levels of cleanliness, understood as minimizing microbes.
2 Sean M. Gibbons, "The Built Environment is a Microbial Wasteland," *mSystems* 1, no. 2 (2016).
3 Mohsen Naghavi, Stein Emil Vollset, Kevin S. Ikuta, et. al., "Global Burden of Bacterial Antimicrobial Resistance 1990–2021: A Systematic Analysis with Forecasts to 2050," *The Lancet* 404, no. 10459 (2024): 1199–1226.
4 Martin Täubel, Emmanuelle Castagnoli, Tunga Salthammer, et. al., "The Impact of Cleaning on the Microbiomes of Indoor Surfaces," *Indoor Environments* 1, no. 3 (2024).
5 Albert Barberán, Robert R. Dunn, Brian J. Reich, et al., "The Ecology of Microscopic Life in Household Dust," *Proceedings of the Royal Society B* (September 1, 2015).
6 Brandon Brooks, Brian A. Firek, Christopher S. Miller, et al., "Microbes in the Neonatal Intensive Care Unit Resemble those Found in the Gut of Premature infants," *Microbiome* 2, no. 1 (January 28, 2014).
7 Rachel I. Adams, Seema Bhangar, Karen C. Dannemiller, et. al., "Ten Questions Concerning the Microbiomes of Buildings," *Building and Environment* 109 (2010): 225.
8 J. Qian, D. Hospodsky, N. Yamamoto, et al., "Size-Resolved Emission Rates of Airborne Bacteria and Fungi in an Occupied Classroom," *Indoor Air* 22 (2012): 339–51. Aaron J. Prussin II, Ellen B. Garcia, and Linsey C. Marr, "Total Concentrations of Virus and Bacteria in Indoor and Outdoor," *Environmental Science & Technology Letters* 2, no. 4 (2015): 84–88.
9 James F. Meadow, Adam E. Altrichter, Ashley C. Bateman, et. al., "Humans Differ in their Personal Microbial Cloud," *PeerJ* 3, no. 1258 (September 22, 2015).
10 John Chase, Jennifer Fouquier, Mahnaz Zare, et.al., "Geography and Location Are the Primary Drivers of Office Microbiome Composition," *mSystems* 1, no. 2 (April 19, 2016).
11 Simon Lax, Daniel P. Smith, Jarrad Hampton-Marcell, et al., "Longitudinal Analysis of Microbial Interaction Between Humans and the Indoor Environment," *Science* 345, no. 6200 (August 29, 2014): 1048–52.
12 Lax, Smith, Hampton-Marcell, et al., "Longitudinal Analysis."
13 Jean F. Ruiz-Calderon, Humberto Cavallin, Se Jin Song, et al., "Walls talk: Microbial Biogeography of Homes Spanning Urbanization," *Science Advances* 2, no. 2 (February 12, 2016).
14 Simon Lax, Naseer Sangwan, Daniel Smith, et al., "Bacterial Colonization and Succession in a Newly Opened Hospital," *Science Translational Medicine* 9, no. 341 (May 24, 2017).
15 Amnon Amir, Ortal Erez-Granat, Tzipi Braun, et al., "Gut Microbiome Development in Early Childhood is Affected by Day Care Attendance," *NPJ Biofilms and Microbiomes* 8, no. 1 (January 11, 2022).
16 Xin Zhou, Xiaotao Shen, Jethro S. Johnson, et. al., "Longitudinal Profiling of the Microbiome at Four Body Sites Reveals Core Stability and Individualized Dynamics During Health and Disease," *Cell Host & Microbe* 32, no. 4 (2024): 506–26.
17 Hakdong Shin, Zhiheng Pei, Keith A. Martinez II, et. al., "The First Microbial Environment of Infants Born by C-section: The Operating Room Microbes," *Microbiome* 3, no. 59 (2015).
18 Suchitra K. Hourigan, Maria Gloria Dominguez-Bello, and Noel T. Mueller, "Can maternal-child microbial seeding interventions improve the health of infants delivered by Cesarean section?," *Cell Host & Microbe* 30, no. 5 (2022): 607–11.
19 Brooks, Firek, Miller, et al., "Microbes in the Neonatal Intensive Care Unit."
20 Katharine Michelle Ng, Andrés Aranda-Díaz, Carolina Tropini, et al., "Recovery of the Gut Microbiota after Antibiotics Depends on Host Diet, Community Context, and Environmental Reservoirs," *Cell Host & Microbe* 26, no. 5 (2019): 650–65.
21 Gregory R. Young, Angela Sherry, and Darren L. Smith, "Built Environment Microbiomes Transition from Outdoor to Human-Associated Communities After Construction and Commissioning," *Science Reports* 13, no. 15854 (September 22, 2023).

1 Martin Oeggerli, SEM image of *Yersinia pestis*

5 BUILDING – NETWORK – EMPIRE

Humans started to separate themselves from the soil and most other species ten thousand years ago when they moved into permanently occupied buildings increasingly sealed off from the exterior world. They were accompanied inside by microbes that flourished and evolved, including pathogens that cause infectious disease. The expansion of buildings into settlements, cities, and interlinked empires magnified the capacities of both humans and the diseases that threaten them. Yet this threat paradoxically drives architecture. The built environment pulsates. Growth feeds microbes that feed collapse that feeds new growth in a continuous cycle. Multiple diseases coexist and interact to continuously shape the urbanization they repeatedly provoke, terrorize, collapse, and provoke again. Architecture shapes microbes and is shaped by them.

GOING INSIDE

The invention of freestanding rectangular buildings in southwest Asia around ten thousand years ago launched the so-called "Neolithic transition." Small dispersed nomadic bands of around fifty hunter-gathers foraging resources across 300–500 square kilometers gave way to larger communities in settled agrarian villages – domesticating themselves, other animals, and plants. This transition was non-linear and took several thousand years as it expanded across most of Eurasia. A polycentric mosaic of dispersed groups became increasingly linked by networks of exchange and migration.[1] The temporary hunter-gather base camp – typically consisting of semi-subterranean mud-lined oval spaces with mud-plaster floors and a wood-and-brush canopy overhead – was eventually displaced by a new type of permanently occupied right-angled building constructed on top of the ground with a fully enclosed interior, internal divisions, and different levels. Humans had begun to separate themselves from the soil and most other species, a separation that would ultimately transform their own biology and that of countless other species, both inside the new enclosures and outside.

2 10,800-year-old architecture in Kharaysin, Jordan, with newly invented right angles and polished white lime-plaster floor, unpainted in the space on the right and painted with red in the adjacent space on the left

The excavation of early Neolithic buildings from over ten thousand years ago on a hillside in Kharaysin, present-day Jordan, revealed lime plaster floors made of successive layers from rough to smooth until a final layer of finer material finished with a wash of the very finest lime plaster that was either left as unpainted white or painted on with powdered red pigment.[2] **[2]** These buildings immediately preceded the domestication of plants and animals. They are permanently occupied, but transitional since the community they housed still foraged for food across a large territory. They are also transitional in being half-way through a two-thousand-year evolution on the same site from small semi-sunken oval buildings cut into the sloping ground to larger freestanding square buildings sitting in rows on a human-made flat ground when farming began.[3] The successive archeological layers of the site offer a portrait of the early evolution of architecture.

Intermediate structures on the site are already orthogonal and internally subdivided with walls. Their plaster floor is unlike the soil outside and continues up the walls to form a sealed smooth prophylactic skin. **[3]** To enter the building is literally to enter another world, an insulated and isolated bubble of space

3 Reconstruction of a partially subterranean dwelling with a red-painted lime floor, dated to about 9800 years ago, discovered in Kharaysin, Jordan

formed by material that cannot be found outside and is suspended on a ground that is itself already a human construction – compacted earth terracing made on the top of the remains of previous buildings. Strictly speaking, architecture is not just a separation from the ground but the construction of an artificial ground, a ground that is already separate from the microbially rich soil.

This early use of lime plaster to define the interior space of buildings would become the general practice throughout southwest Asia, and survive in successive Egyptian, Phoenician, Hellenic, and Roman architectural systems. Lime plaster was cutting-edge technology. It is the first artificial material invented by humans and required the largest single investment of collective energy in early settled societies – magnified by the fact that buildings were regularly re-plastered. The right kind of limestone had to be gathered, often from a distance, along with a substantial amount of wood to cook it in extreme heat to turn it into quick lime, which was then mixed with water to produce a putty that can be smeared on surfaces and becomes hard. This material had a whiteness nowhere to be found in the environment. Like the newly invented right angles of buildings, it constituted a whole new environment, a new dryness and temperature within buildings, a new acoustic and visual space, even a new way of seeing, but also a new biological system. The lime plaster was itself antimicrobial because it is highly alkaline and resistant to the moisture that microbes multiply in. It maintained a new kind of line between inside and outside, between humans and other species, visible and invisible.

Such archeological sites offer forensic clues about change in human societies, but no assumption should be made about how the buildings were actually lived in: no association between building and social unit, no matter how tempting, or any familiar idea of domesticity.[4] Yet they were obviously central to daily life, and even crafted intersections between life and death. Human and non-human bodies were buried within the white surfaces. Some body parts, mostly skulls, were covered in white plaster and protruded from walls to occupy the interior as fellow inhabitants. The interior never simply sheltered humans. It sheltered the very idea of the human, which also means a specific set of companions, alive and dead, visible and invisible.

The Neolithic invention of a form of self-isolation that represented and accelerated a single species was also the invention of new forms of connection with other species. Early permanently occupied architecture was a genetic experiment, a separation from the majority of species, but also the curation of a specific community of humans, animals, and insects inside. The new interior – of the building, adjacent buildings, and the increasingly domesticated environment surrounding them – was a new architecture of trans-species community, a new microbial system.

CONNECTION THROUGH DISCONNECTION

Pathogens, the bacteria and viruses causing disease in humans, thrived in this new environment. They could easily move between bodies living so closely together (via direct contact, the air, surfaces, domestic animals, rodents, and insects), and between closely adjacent buildings, aided by the microbially rich human, animal, and food waste generated within and between the buildings. Disease took up residence, not just as an uninvited guest but as part of the ecosystem. The ever denser and more expansive networks interlinking settlements offered it the chance to become epidemic.

Dispersed nomadic hunter-gatherers did not offer such an ideal home to pathogens. They were never simply "in nature" but actively modified their surroundings in ways that must be understood as architectural, through structures for hunting and transformation of the soil over time when cycling between base camps.[5] This included oval brushwood huts associated with the first evidence of small-scale planting twenty-three thousand years ago in the Jordan Valley, and semi-subterranean circular limestone buildings with standardized wooden roof elements of the early Natufian culture in the same valley fifteen thousand years ago.[6] Monumental constructions, as in the almost five-meter-high rings of the Göbekli Tepe complex built almost twelve thousand years ago in present-day Türkiye, supported collective festivals. The use of stone and monumentality is paradoxically related to the need to return to these sites after being dispersed throughout much of the year.[7] But that dispersal, along with the lack of proximity to their own and other animals' waste for most of the year, limited the circulation of microbes. Human-associated pathogenic microbes required permanently occupied and interlinked buildings to achieve epidemic momentum.

With the continuous, year-round inhabitation of buildings, human health dramatically declined. Settled humans became shorter and lived shorter lives.[8] Ancient infectious bacterial diseases such as tuberculosis became epidemic. Some of the skeletons of the first permanent inhabitants of buildings are visibly distorted by the disease. **[4]** DNA analysis reveals that many other skeletons from this time also have the traces of *Mycobacterium tuberculosis*, the bacteria that killed around half of those that developed symptoms. **[5]** Humans started to reproduce more often to compensate for the losses. The dramatic increase in human population upon moving indoors was paradoxically a symptom of the dramatic increase in the mortality rate. Those that survived the tight circuit between growth and disease typically had resistance. Buildings remade the biology of the species that made them.

4 Collapse of spine initiated by tuberculosis infection in skeleton from early Neolithic site in central Germany

Settlement did not offer an increase in efficiency of resource extraction and utilization as is usually assumed. On the contrary, humans started to use an ever-greater amount of energy per person, and the eventual development of farming to support the larger populations created additional health problems caused by a less diverse diet.

As if in an effort to reduce the diseases provoked by buildings, hygiene was an integral part of the transition from nomadism to settlement. The fully plastered interior was divided between clean and dirty zones, and specific buildings associated with collective rituals – interlaced with burials and the communal processing and storage of plant material as food – received special attention to cleaning. Analysis of the floors and where they smoothly curve up into walls shows that they were regularly swept, washed, and periodically re-plastered. The separation from the surrounding world in such buildings was also accompanied by increasing separation from excretions, food waste, and combustion waste into designated places between buildings.[9]

This implied concept of health evolved as the line permanently occupied buildings drew around human life also threatened that life. Shelter brought new forms of exposure.

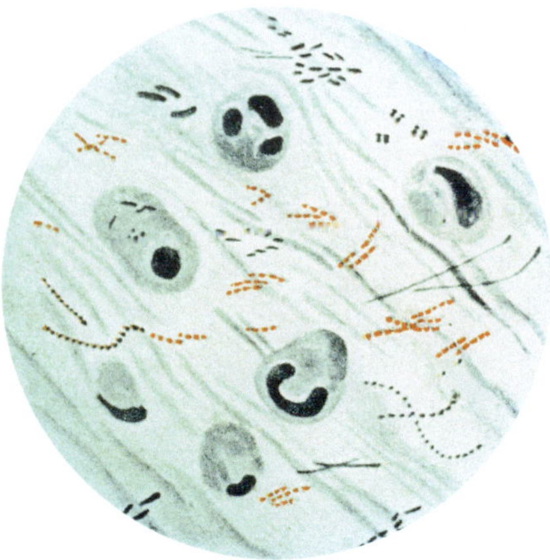

5 Photomicrograph of *Mycobacterium tuberculosis*, the organism that causes tuberculosis, in sputum, 1954

THE PULSE OF DISEASE

Humans, microbial pathogens, and architecture modified themselves in response to each other and have continued to co-evolve for millennia. Recent research suggests that the first permanently occupied buildings didn't just act as an ideal home for pathogens but were already a response to them.[10] Settlements were likely a way of managing the larger communities that were the paradoxical effect of producing more children to survive the emergence of a more virulent form of tuberculosis. But the dense settlements accelerated the disease, which provoked further increases in population density that provoked more disease, and so on. Epidemic disease has a pulsating effect. Which is to say that architecture has a pulsating effect.

These pulsations of disease are, as it were, the engine of urbanization, and vice versa. The majority of the inhabitants of plaster-lined buildings in the first proto-cities, such as the eight thousand-or-so residents of Çatalhöyük nine thousand years ago in present-day Türkiye, increasingly suffered from multiple infectious diseases as population density, workloads, and death rates grew until the settlement was completely abandoned.[11] **[6–7]**

6 Rendering of Çatalhöyük

Ever-larger, denser, interlinked settlements created not only the ideal conditions for contagious disease but also social hierarchies and systemic inequity. Over the thousand years that people lived in Çatalhöyük, houses increasingly had different sizes, amounts and diversities of resources, tools, decoration, storage, and burial practices.[12] The subdivision of interiors into specialized rooms paralleled the increasing stratification of the inhabitants. The built environment is inseparable from inequality, which is the single biggest driver of poor health. All microbial diseases that became active during early settlements (including hepatitis, syphilis, the plague, measles, smallpox, polio, and leprosy) disproportionally affected the disadvantaged. The poor were, as they are now, more vulnerable to illness, less able to treat it, and made even poorer by it in a deadly spiral. **[8]**

Any image of the seemingly inevitable expansion of humans across the planet in ever-larger populations, supported by technological advances in their ability to control the environment, has to give way to an image of repeated devastation by pathogens that shaped cultures, technologies, philosophies, genetics, and economies. Wars are ultimately microbial, with the outcome

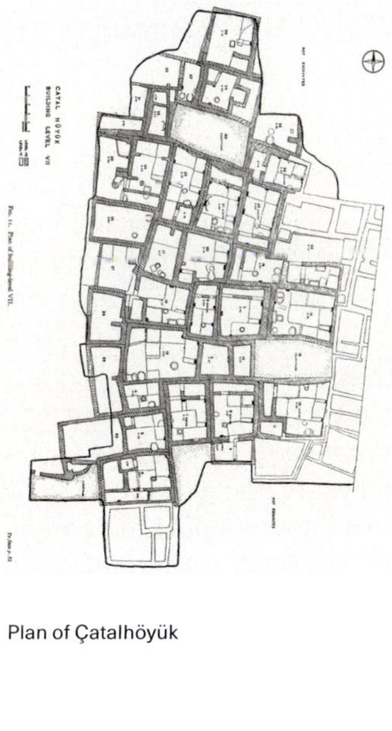

7 Plan of Çatalhöyük

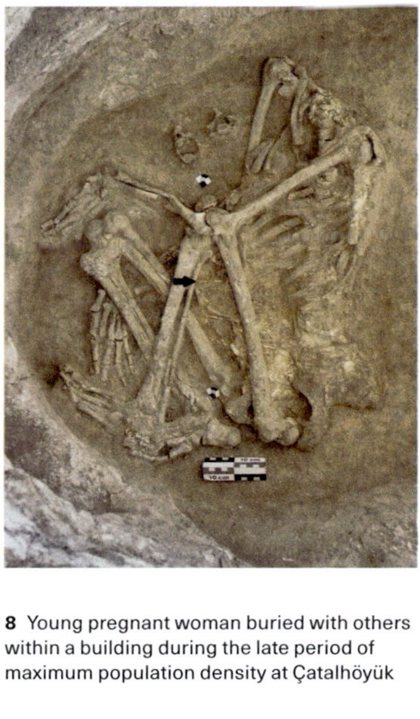

8 Young pregnant woman buried with others within a building during the late period of maximum population density at Çatalhöyük

of many battles determined by who can survive particular pathogens. In a sense, microbes are the real battlefield. Most transcontinental movements of humans can be explained in terms of one group with a high disease load eventually developing immunity and overcoming groups lacking that immunity.[13] Buildings, settlements, cities, and the networks between them incubate epidemics which occasionally devastate the population but also create immunity, which renders other populations susceptible. Resistance to tuberculosis, for example, is selected by cities that expose so many to it.[14] Paradoxically, the more people die from a disease, the more become resistant to it.

In this cycling between devastation and growth, each magnification of the built environment creates the condition for its collapse through infectious disease, which spurs further growth – even if that growth can take a long time to pass the levels at which the disease struck. The history of architecture is the history of dramatic pulsations as pathogenic microbes take shelter in built spaces alongside and within humans, domesticated animals, plants, and insects, repeatedly decimating their populations. As the built environment evolves in response to epidemics and pandemics, microbes evolve in a continuous dance, generating new diseases in humans and variations of ancient ones.

FROM AMOEBA TO CITY AND BACK

The microbes whose effect on humans is magnified by buildings are typically distributed across vast territories and stretches of time. Take the plague, caused by the bacteria *Yersinia pestis*, which is second only to tuberculosis in the number of humans it has killed in history. Humans have been entangled with it since moving indoors. The microorganism diverged from an intestinal bacterium around twenty thousand years ago, then started to diversify itself around six thousand years ago while repeatedly visiting human settlements. Every now and then over millennia, it took over vast parts of the built environment in pandemics until it ran out of fresh bodies to infect, only to periodically return via trade networks to find fresh bodies in newly recovered communities.

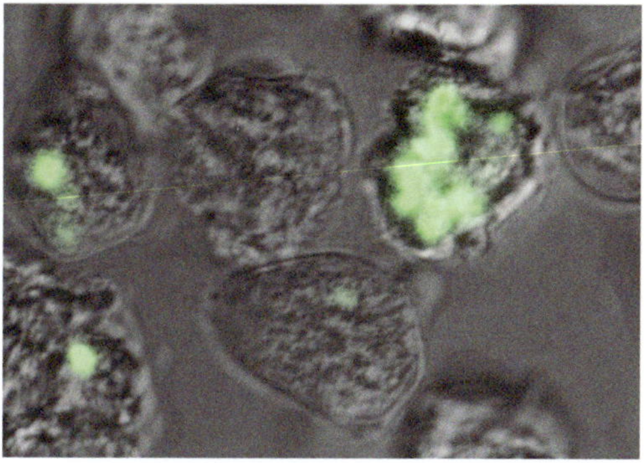

The bacteria's home base remains its ancient reservoir in Central Asia where it lives within amoeba in the soil and infects burrowing rodents that are immune to it, especially the marmots largely disconnected from human habitation in present-day Kyrgyzstan and Mongolia.[15] [9–10] When hunters made contact with the marmots, or when marmots were forced to look for food near humans, villages would be devastated by the plague. In 2011, archeologists unearthed a grid of semi-underground rectangular wood-and-mud houses in Hamin Mangha in Inner Mongolia that was occupied between 5600 and 5100 years ago with a hybrid way of life combining agriculture with hunting and foraging. Some of the houses had been hastily filled with a three-deep pile

9 Confocal fluorescence image of *Yersinia pestis* surviving and replicating within amoeba structures

10 *Marmota baibacina* (gray marmot), Altai Mountains, Kazakhstan

of up to ninety-seven bodies of all ages, and all the houses had been burned to the ground as the village was abandoned along with all the artifacts of everyday life, presumably in an attempt to escape the plague. [11]

The oldest confirmed traces of *Yersinia pestis* in human bodies are found in 5400-year-old burials of hunter gatherers in present-day Siberia at the beginning of the so-called "Neolithic decline," when the population collapsed by 90 percent across Eurasia, and at the decline's end in 4900-year-old burials of farming communities in present-day Sweden. [12] It is now thought to have caused pandemic waves that radiated out from mega-settlements in present-day Ukraine 6000 years ago.[16]

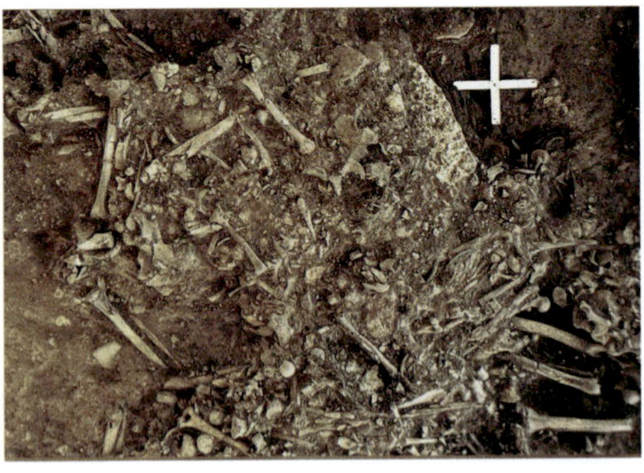

11 Burned-down pithouse filled with ninety-seven bodies in Hamin Mangha village, Mongolia

12 Skeleton of a woman who died of bubonic plague 4900 years ago, found among the remains of seventy-seven people in the Frälsegården village grave in western Sweden

These large oval-shaped settlements of clay-covered wooden-framed buildings housing around twenty thousand inhabitants may have attempted to resist contagious disease with an open organization that separated quarters, and separated the neighborhoods within them, to create social distancing. Groups of houses were periodically burned down to eradicate disease, as if having learned the lesson of densely packed Çatalhöyük.[17] **[13–14]** But even these low-density settlements, such as Nebelivka's almost fifteen hundred widely-spaced houses, had to be abandoned within two hundred years of their founding, as waves of the plague arrived and traveled out along the trade routes across Eurasia thousands of kilometers long. In the loop that both drives and disables the built environment, new networks and larger settlements hosted the bacteria that ultimately weakened them – forcing both bacteria and human to keep evolving.

Genetic trees of the different varieties of *Yersinia pestis* are related to the built environment. **[15]** One of the different strains of the microorganism spread over vast distances developed the ability to be transmitted between humans via fleas associated with rodents around four thousand years ago.[18] **[16–17]** This enabled it to move even more easily between buildings and settlements in the network. In other words, it had adapted itself to more efficiently move within the built environment it invariably weakened.

The intensity of interconnection magnifies the possibility of collapse. The dramatic rebuilding over two thousand years of the Bronze Age after the collapse of the Neolithic once again fed an even bigger collapse. Waves of epidemic disease played a role in the twelfth-century-BCE rapid dissolution of so many interconnected civilizations and empires across Eurasia and North Africa with large urbanization, monumental architecture, advanced technology, and dense trade networks. As with all the rise and fall of previous circuits, multiple diseases had coexisted and interacted to continuously shape the urbanization they provoked, terrorized, and periodically collapsed.

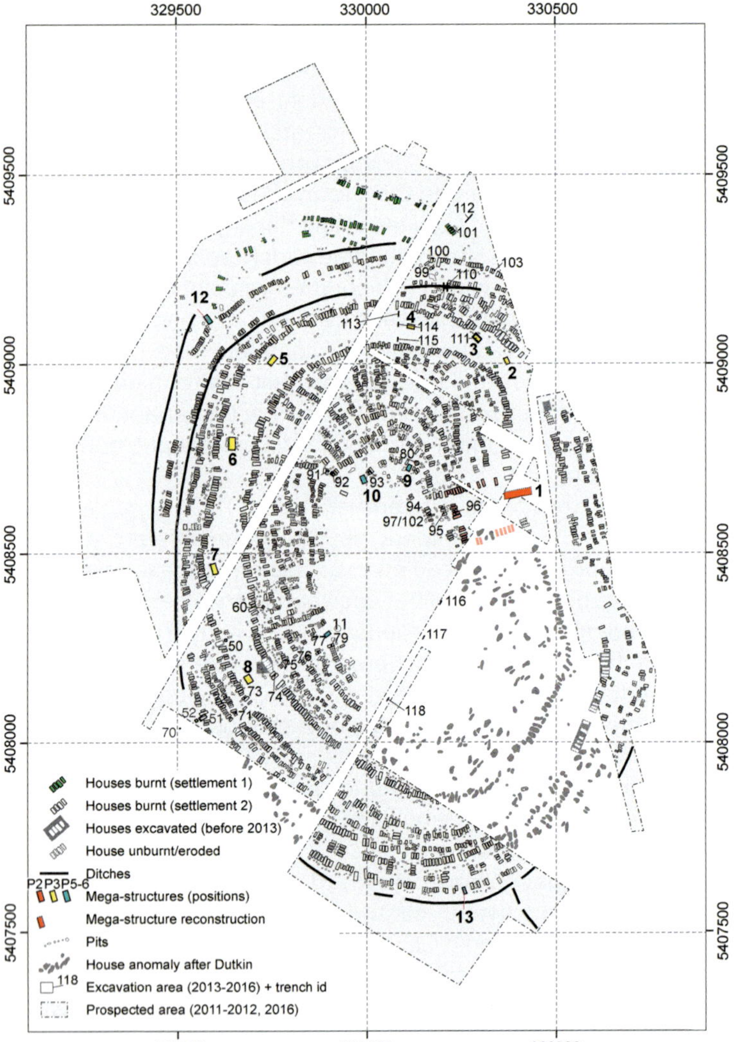

13 Plan of the city of Maidanetske in present-day Ukraine, showing quarters (each with its own assembly house) and burned houses

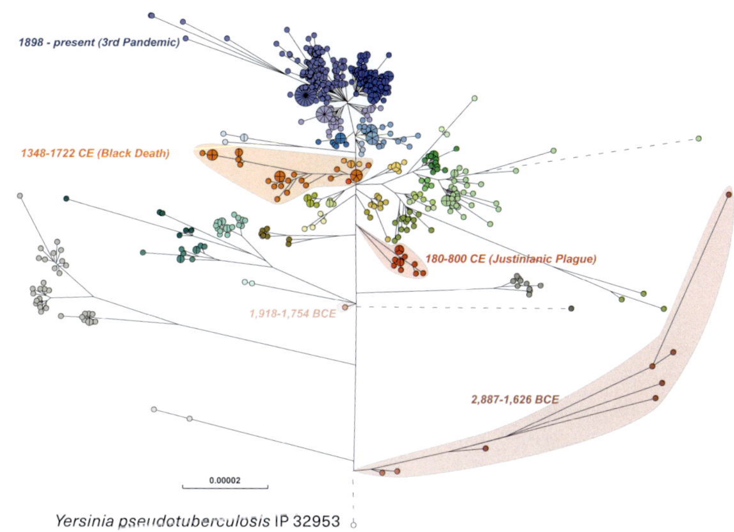

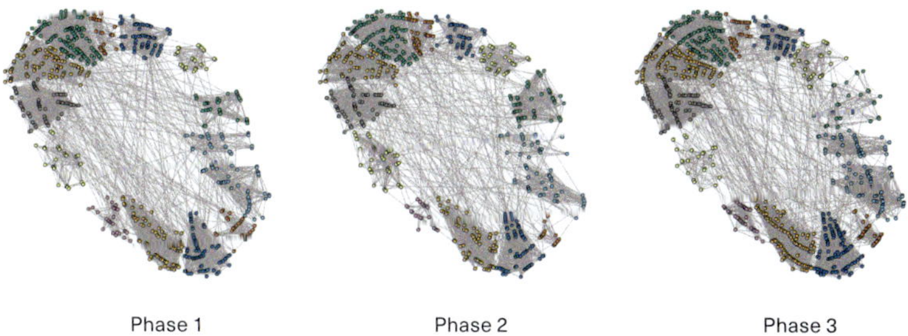

14 Genetic tree of *Yersinia pestis* from 2887 BCE to the present

15 Model of spread of infections in Nebelivka with dots representing households colored by quarter. Different rates of the endemic infection and resistance depend on degree of contact between quarters

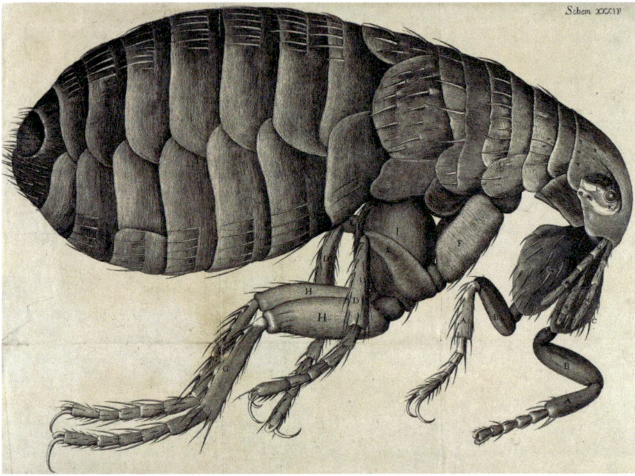

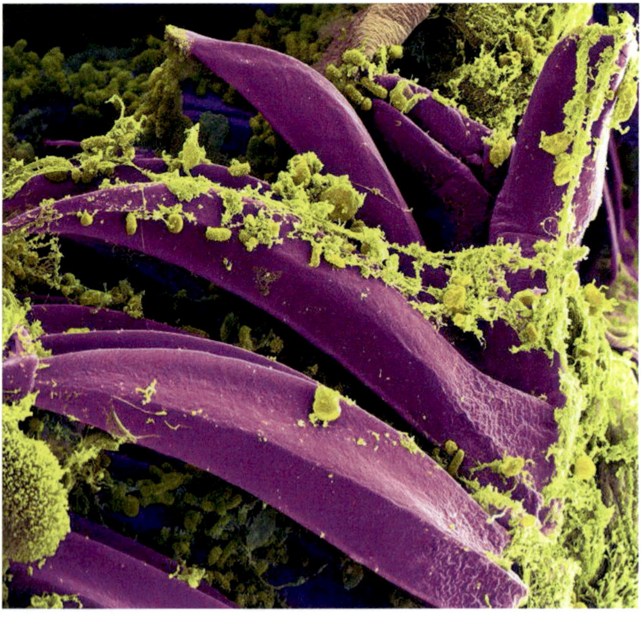

16 Robert Hooke's 1665 illustration of a flea from *Micrographia* – one of the first scientific works to employ microscopy

17 Scanning electron micrograph of *Yersinia pestis* accumulating in the foregut of a flea before being regurgitated into a bite wound

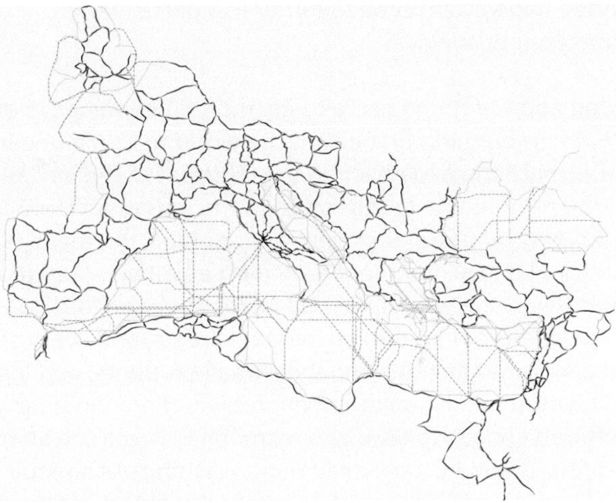

PLAGUES OF EMPIRE

The emergence of empires magnified the capacities of microbes. The trans-continental networks that allowed imperial powers to extract resources from vast territories enabled pathogens to quickly travel across the same territory. The unprecedented net of the Roman Empire, and corresponding rapid growth of population and density, especially in Rome itself, efficiently distributed microbial diseases such as a new strain of tuberculosis across Europe, the Middle East, Africa, India, China, and southeast Asia.[19] **[18]** Rome was the overcrowded unsanitary epicenter of disease, despite its celebrated sewer system and the fresh water provided by its aqueducts. Pathogens would arrive from distant parts of the empire, multiply rapidly in the city, and then move back out through the entire network. As the historian Kyle Harper puts it:

> The Roman Empire threw open "all the gates of the inhabited world." ... The drama of disease history lies in the incessant collision of pathogen evolution and human connectivity. In the Roman Empire,

18 The Roman Empire as a network of land, sea, coastal, and river links those two forces came together in a particularly consequential way.[20]

The population of Rome had already tripled between 175 and 28 BCE, becoming the first city in the world to reach one million people without the expansion of the footprint of the city itself. For all the remarkable architecture of the aqueducts, public baths, toilets, and the sewer systems – notably the massive underground Cloaca Maxima that channeled all city waste out to the Tiber River – most people lived in dense unsanitary conditions, with human excrement thrown into the streets, and every space shared with other animals and their waste, rodents, and insects. **[19–21]** It was an ideal habitat for microbial urban companions that were offered spaces to flourish and mobility via all the animals and insects, aided by the lack of hand washing. As a result, there were high levels of infant mortality and lower life expectancy for those that survived childhood.[21] The web of transportation links on land and water interconnecting a vast territory inhabited by a quarter of the world's population – which was in turn connected to much of the rest of the world population by even wider global

19 Giovanni Battista Piranesi, Cloaca Maxima, from *Vedute di Roma*, ca. 1770

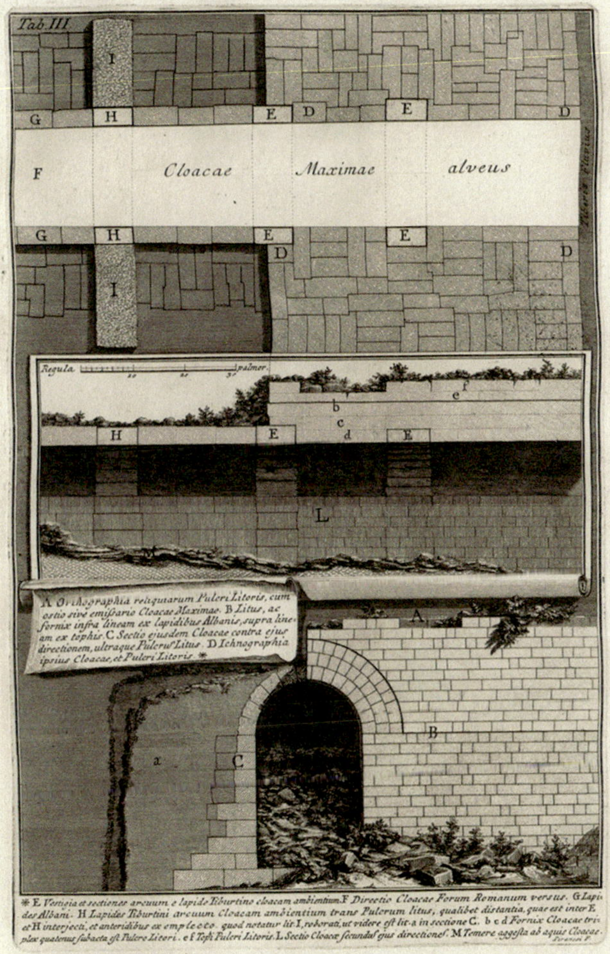

20 Giovanni Battista Piranesi, plan, section, and elevation of the Cloaca Maxima, ca. 1761

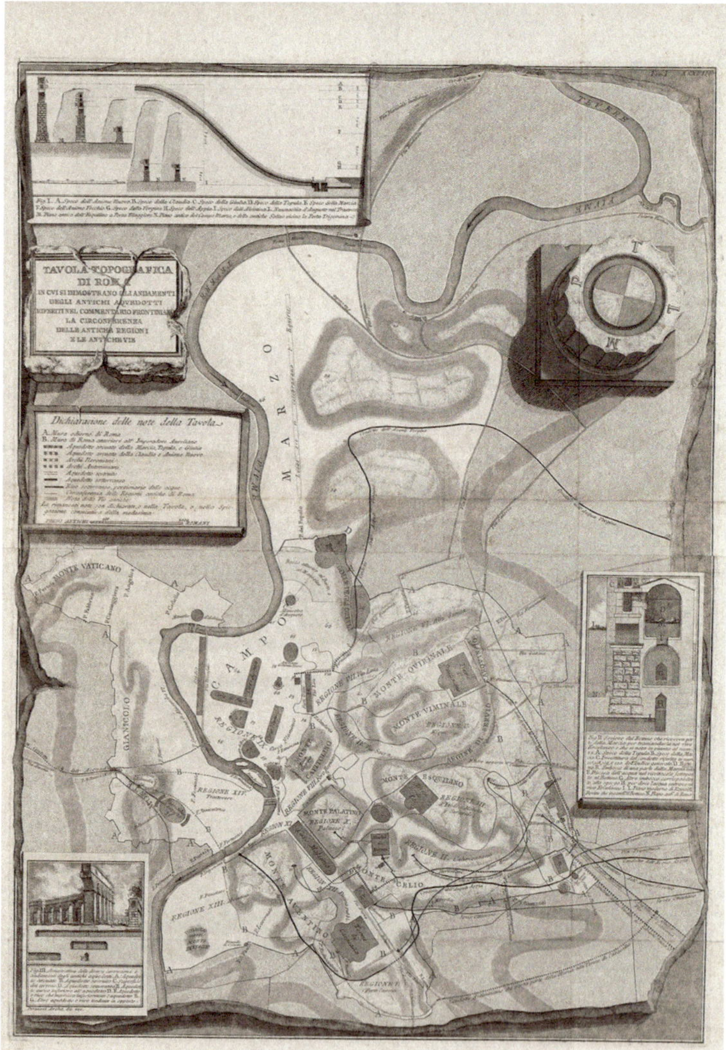

21 Giovanni Battista Piranesi, *Tavola topografica di Roma*, 1756, showing the aqueduct system circuits of exchange – meant that a microbe at any distant point could quickly arrive at the dense microbial incubator at the heart of the web, and from there go back out to other distant points. A map of the Roman Empire, and of the form of urban life it established, is a map of infections.

Vitruvius wrote his ten scrolls of architecture that initiated the tradition of Western architectural theory at the very moment that Caesar Augustus established a unified empire and Rome had reached its highest density and levels of epidemic disease. The treatise argued that architects need to have a "working knowledge" of medicine and always aim at "healthful" dwelling, identifying tuberculosis as one of the illnesses that architecture can not only cure but prevent. Design can rebuild the balance of those "whose strength has been sapped by disease" and make the healthy less likely to get sick.[22] Every aspect of buildings – location, orientation, air, light, water supply, drainage, materials, and finishes – has to be designed with the prevention of disease and recovery from disease in mind.

Vitruvius didn't just try to formalize a classical aesthetic tradition based in Greek precedent but integrated ancient Greek medical theories into architectural theory, particularly the idea that health is environmental: an internal balance of four elements associated with earth, air, fire, and water. As experts in constructing the environment, architects had to play a crucial role in maintaining that balance by guiding the quality of air, light, and water. Vitruvius writes about avoiding "pestilent" places with unhealthy air and water in favor of those with fresh air with the right humidity and unpolluted water – reinforced by hygiene of body, building, and streets, and the healthiest orientation of rooms. Architecture must be placed in the healthiest environment and modify that environment to make it even healthier since disease constantly lurks as a threat to be preemptively countered.

The Antonine Plague, likely a smallpox pandemic that had originated in Africa and worked its way across Arabia, arrived in Rome in 166 CE, devastating the city and its empire at their peak, destroying labor, food supply, and trade. **[22]** A contemporary pharmacological text described the plague: "like a kind of wild beast, does not just kill a few, but spreads over entire cities and destroys them horribly."[23] Urbanization itself was the victim.

Over the next six years, the disease killed around a fifth of the population of the empire and is credited with its demise, cemented by a second devastating wave reaching Rome in 191 CE.

Likewise, the massive Justinian bubonic plague started in 521 CE, just as the empire had reestablished itself around the Mediterranean and is thought to have led to its disintegration. Its network had enabled a particular strain of the *Yersinia pestis* bacteria to steadily work its way around North Africa, Europe, and the Near East for eight years, killing half of the world's population at the time. **[23]** Once again, the built environment was undone by a pathogen well adapted to it. Four strains had traveled across Asia via the nomadic Hun Empire for the previous century in a series of smaller epidemics marked by mass burials before the density and interconnectedness of the revived empire exponentially increased their effect. The plague would keep returning to the empire's weakened network in smaller waves for another two hundred years, as the recovery of urbanization kept providing sufficient fresh bodies.[24]

Pathogens never fully leave the built environment that hosts them and is threatened by them. In a deeper sense, the marmot

22 Jules Gabriel Levasseur, *The Angel of Death Striking a Door During the Plague of Rome*, 1894, engraving after a painting by Jules-Élie Delaunay communities, and even the amoeba home of the microbe, have to be understood as part of the ecology of the human-built environment they seem so disconnected from and remain so today, with the bubonic plague still a killer in many parts of the world. Rooms, buildings, cities, networks, empires, and the even wider interconnections between empires are permanently haunted by pathogens that keep returning but never in exactly the same form, reigniting crises that force rebuilding. Microbial disease is the paradoxical engine of the built environment it so deeply threatens.

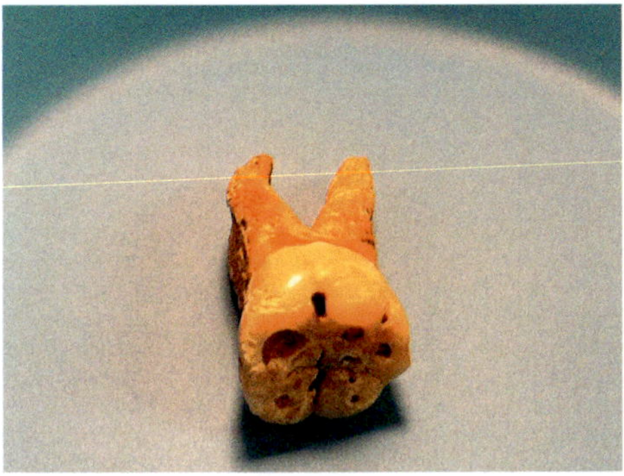

23 Tooth containing *Yersinia pestis* of Justinian plague victim found in burial ground in farmland outside Munich

1 Juan José Ibáñez, Jesus González-Urquijo, Luis Cesar Teira-Mayolini, and Talía Lazuén, "The Emergence of the Neolithic in the Near East: A Protracted and Multi-Regional Model," *Quaternary International*, no. 470 (2018): 226–52.
2 Juan José Ibáñez, Juan Muñiz, Eneko Iriarte, et al., "Los primeros agricultores y ganaderos. Excavaciones en el yacimiento del Neolítico Precerámico A y B de Kharaysin (Zarqa, Jordania). Campañas de 2015 y 2016," in *Informes y Trabajos* 17, *Excavaciones en el Exterior* (Madrid: Ministerio de Cultura y Deporte, 2019), 103–23.
3 Juan José Ibáñez, Juan Muñiz, Luis Teira, et al., "Architecture in Kharaysin from the late PPNA to the middle PPNB," *Archeological Research in Asia* 41, no. 100584 (2025).
4 Bill Finlayson, Steven J. Mithen, Mohammad Najjar, et al., "Architecture, Sedentism, and Social Complexity at Pre-Pottery Neolithic A WF16, Southern Jordan," *The Journal of the Council for British Research in the Levant* 47, no. 2 (2015): 8183–88.
5 Brian Andrews and Danielle Macdonald, eds., *More Than Shelter From the Storm: Hunter-Gatherer Houses and the Built Environment* (Gainsville: University Press of Florida, 2022).
6 Over time, these buildings were often abandoned, only to act as the site and source of materials for new buildings in a dense archeology of buildings, buried bodies, and tools. Fanny Bocquentin, Elisa Caron-Laviolette, Niels Fourchet, et al., "Hunter-gatherer-builders: 70 years of research at the Natufian hamlet of Eynan-Mallaha (upper Jordan Valley, Israel)," *Archaeological Research in Asia* 42, no. 100618 (2025).
7 Rémi Hadad, "Re-Territorializing the Neolithic: Architecture and Rhythms in Early Sedentary Societies of the Near East," *Comparative Studies in Society and History* 66, no. 3 (2024): 557–83.
8 Clark Spencer Larsen, "The Agricultural Revolution as Environmental Catastrophe: Implications for Health and Lifestyle in the Holocene," *Quaternary International*, 150 (2006): 12–20.
9 Flip Havlíček and Martin Kuča, "Waste Management at the End of the Stone Age," *Journal of Landscape Ecology* 10, no. 1 (2017).
10 Tuberculosis is an ancient disease. The bacteria traveled with humans out of Africa and survived without devastating its host because the disease was latent within an infected body for more than a generation before becoming active. This enabled it to be passed to other hunter-gatherer groups, when contact occurred, and to eventually infect younger, more susceptible bodies, without wiping out whole communities. But as the human population grew tenfold when expanding across Eurasia forty thousand years ago, new strains of the bacteria appeared, one of which became active soon after infection and had the ability to decimate a whole hunter-gatherer group in the course of a generation. This forced humans to modify their behavior to survive. Hunter-gatherer women developed increased resistance to the disease and started to have children more frequently – annually rather than every four years – by weaning earlier. As a result, the population grew another tenfold, despite the increased death rate. Pere-Joan Cardona, Martí Català, and Clara Prats, "Origin of Tuberculosis in the Paleolithic Predicts Unprecedented Population Growth and Female Resistance," *Scientific Reports* 10, no. 42 (2020).
11 Clark Spencer Larsen, Christopher J. Knüsel, Scott D. Haddow, et al., "Bioarchaeology of Neolithic Çatalhöyük Reveals Fundamental Transitions in Health, Mobility, and Lifestyle in Early Farmers," *PNAS* 116, no. 26 (June 17, 2019): 12615–23.
12 Katherine I. Wright, "Domestication and Inequality? Households, Corporate Groups and Food Processing Tools at Neolithic Çatalhöyük," *Journal of Anthropological Archeology*, 33 (2014): 1–33. The relationship between the Neolithic transition and systemic inequality is widely debated by scholars with an increasing resistance to any one-to-one association between permanent settlements and inequality, yet the evidence of the initiation and parallel growth of inequity is not disputed. As Kathryn Twiss et al. put it in a recent analysis of Çatalhöyük buildings, already "some were more equal than others." Katheryn C. Twiss, Amy Bogaard, Scott Haddow, et. al., "'But Some Were More Equal than Others': Exploring Inequality at Neolithic Çatalhöyük," *PLoS One* 19, no. 9 (September 6, 2024).
13 Jonathan Kennedy, *Pathogenesis: A History of the World in Eight Plagues* (New York: Crown, 2023).
14 Ian Barnes, Anna Duda, Oliver G. Pybus, and Mark G. Thomas, "Ancient Urbanization Predicts Genetic Resistance to Tuberculosis," *Journal for the Study of Evolution* 65, no. 3 (2010): 842–48.
15 David W. Markman, Michael F. Antolin, Richard A. Bowen, et al., "Yersinia pestis

Survival and Replication in Potential Ameba Reservoir," *Emerging Infectious Diseases* 24, no. 2 (2018): 294–302.
16 Nicolás Rascovan, Karl-Göran Sjögren, Kristian Kristiansen, et al., "Emergence and Spread of Basal Lineages of Yersinia Pestis during the Neolithic Decline," *Cell* 176, no. 1–2 (2019): 295–305.
17 R. Alexander Bentley, Simon Carrignon, Bisserka Gaydarska, et al., "Modelling Cultural Responses to Disease Spread in Neolithic Trypillia Mega-settlements," *Journal of the Royal Society* 21, no. 219 (October, 2024).
18 Aida Andrades Valtueña, Gunnar U. Neumann, Maria A. Spyrou, et al., "Stone Age *Yersinia Pestis* Genomes Shed Light on the Early Evolution, Diversity, and Ecology of Plague," *PNAS* 119, no. 17 (April 26, 2022).
19 Mary B. O'Neill, Abigail Shockey, Alex Zarley, et al., "Lineage Specific histories of *Mycobacterium Tuberculosis* Dispersal in Africa and Eurasia," *Molecular Ecology*, 28 (April 23, 2019): 3241–56.
20 Kyle Harper, *The Fate of Rome: Climate, Disease, and The End of an Empire* (Princeton, NJ: Princeton University Press, 2017), 97–98.
21 Jared J. Eddy, "The Ancient City of Rome, its Empire, and the Spread of Tuberculosis in Europe," *Tuberculosis* 95, (2015): 523–28.
22 Vitruvius Pollio, *Vitruvius: Ten Books on Architecture*, eds. Ingrid D. Rowland and Thomas Noble Howe, trans. Ingrid D. Rowland (New York: Cambridge University Press, 1999), 29.
23 Robert Leigh, *On Theriac to Piso, Attributed to Galen: A Critical Edition with Translation and Commentary* (Leiden: Brill, 2016), 149.
24 Monica H. Green, "The Four Black Deaths," *The American Historical Review* 125, no. 5 (December 2020): 1601–31.

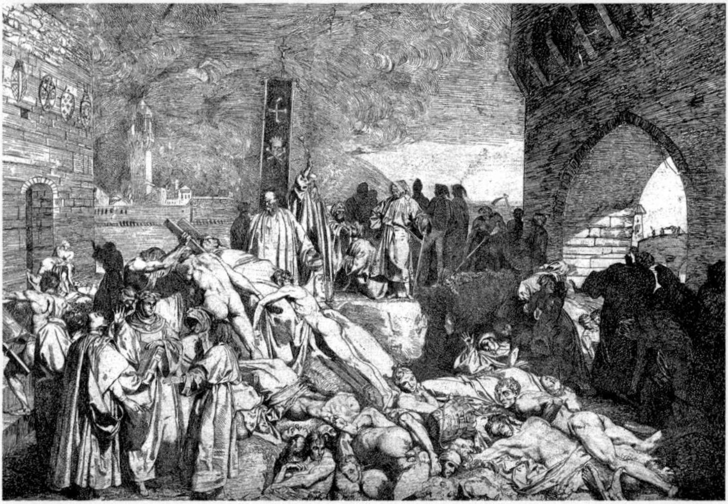

1 Plague in Florence of 1348 as described in Boccaccio's *Il Decamerone*, featuring Boccaccio holding a book in the foreground. Etching by Luigi Sabatelli the elder, 1801

6 PLAGUE ARCHITECTURE

The biggest single pandemic in human history, retroactively called the Black Death, killed more than half of the population of Asia, Europe, the Middle East, and North Africa between 1346 and 1353, permanently transforming societies, economies, and political orders. It was caused by the *Yersinia pestis* bacteria, which used the international trade and pilgrimage routes on land and water to steadily work its way through most human bodies across the most densely populated – but still largely rural – quarter of the planet in just eight years. The plague kept returning to devastate communities every decade or so afterwards for four hundred years. In a kind of immune response, cities gradually adapted themselves to the bacteria with new kinds of buildings and social protocols that left permanent traces in the urban fabric.

DEADLY WAVES

Villages and cities heard of the plague long before it arrived, yet death came too fast for them to respond. People died more quickly than could be buried. Streets filled with bodies. Farms went fallow. Labor collapsed, along with most social norms. It felt everywhere like the end of the world – especially in the larger cities, which suffered the greatest proportion of deaths. Urbanization itself was under attack. **[1–2]**

The higher the degree of urbanization – connectivity within and between human settlements – the higher the death rate.[1] **[3]** Constantinople (present day Istanbul), the capital of the Byzantine Empire and the largest city in Europe and the Middle East at the time, was deserted in 1347, reeking of the smell of unburied corpses and the burning down of the infected's houses. A year later, local chroniclers said Cairo, almost as large, was like "an abandoned desert."[2] Major economic hubs like Siena "appeared uninhabited."[3] Giovanni Boccaccio's *Il Decamerone* – a book of short stories told to each other by a group of ten people sheltering from the plague in a villa outside Florence, as Boccaccio himself had done – describes how most people in the city had confined

2 Piérart dou Tielt, Burial of plague victims in Tournai, miniature, ca. 1353

themselves to their houses and died there while the rich ran away to the countryside, assuming "the whole of the population would be exterminated and that the city's last hour had come."[4] The built environment itself had seemingly been defeated by a stealthy invader.

The devastation was understood as divine punishment from a Christian perspective and divine mercy from an Islamic perspective. The leading medical authority in both worlds was Ibn Sina (Avicenna), whose eleventh-century encyclopedic *al-Qānūn fī al-ṭibb* (*Canon of Medicine*) elaborated Galen's ancient Greek theory explaining disease as an effect of corrupted air. The source of bad air can be either celestial, through certain alignments of planets, or terrestrial, through putrefaction. There is no disease in the bad air itself, but breathing it can provoke disease in vulnerable bodies by unbalancing them. A cloud of corrupt air can arrive on wind from afar, or from a local swamp, or from rotting bodies and excrement. It lurks in a plague-stricken city, within buildings, and around the sick. To share a house with a sick person is to risk getting sick, not through contact with them but by breathing the bad air they exude that lingers in their clothing and bedding.

Hundreds of so-called "plague treatises" warned people not to enter the houses of the sick and called for either increased ventilation when the air outside was healthy or sealing the

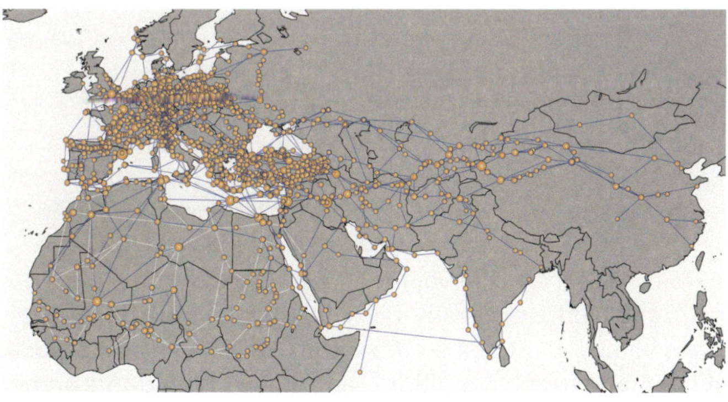

3 Networks connecting European and Asian cities via pilgrimage and commercial routes during the fourteenth century. The degree of connectivity of each node correlates with the number of plague deaths

windows with carpets when it was not and burning aromatic fires within them. Excrement was to be removed from houses and streets, and the ditches and canals used as sewers cleared. Echoing Avicenna, treatises especially recommended maintaining a well-balanced body and mind, which is less easily provoked into illness. Being alarmed about the plague was thought to increase susceptibility to it. The readers of plague treatises were the political, religious, and economic elites who could imagine escape and impose urban cleansing on others. Plague historian Ann Carmichael notes that some cities, like Florence, did try to preemptively forbid entrance of the sick and those from certain plague-stricken cities, clear putrid matter from streets, and remove the sick when the plague arrived.[5] But in most cities these protocols were adopted only after the disease had already come and gone.

The unseen microorganism eventually ran out of victims. The medical doctrine that some people were more susceptible than others was not wrong. Those that survived likely did so because of a genetic variation in their immune system that became a genetic legacy of their descendants.[6] The bacteria had effectively modified the human species. Since it took more than eight years to complete its devastation, cities had by then become vulnerable again by partially rebuilding their social structure, populations, and the networks between them. The microorganism was therefore able to return each decade or so to find fresh bodies. In a sense, full recovery from the plague was marked by new waves of attack – each supported by some return of the economy, social order, and population.

It took two centuries for population levels to return to pre-pandemic levels of 1345, which required a dramatically new growth rate to overcome the periodic collapses of each new wave. As with diseases fostered by the very first permanent Neolithic settlements, devastation paradoxically spurred faster growth, and a different economy. The plague had unexpected positive effects. It increased the value of labor. Surviving workers could demand better conditions, and wages for farmers and artisans increased. Serfdom was no longer sustainable and life expectancy grew. *Yersinia pestis* was ultimately an active agent of social, urban, and economic restructuring.

The plague's transformative arrival in Europe in the fourteenth century was preceded by a long transcontinental journey of urban devastation that has been overlooked from a Eurocentric perspective but documented by Arabic chroniclers and recent genetic analysis.[7] The bacteria initially migrated from its ancient reservoir in the mountains of present-day Kyrgyzstan during the thirteenth century as a series of epidemics associated with the Mongol invasions across China, Iraq, and Syria. It reached the Black Sea and the port of Kaffa in 1346 – from which trading ships promptly carried it to Genoa, and from there across Europe. The waves of plague returned to the region around a decade apart for a century, then more frequently and locally for another three centuries, with around thirty major epidemics – with the one in the 1570s almost as big as the first – and countless smaller ones before fading in Western Europe in the early eighteenth century and later in Eastern Europe, North Africa, and the Middle East.

The disease finally went away, only for an industrialized global economy to emerge that created another set of opportunities for the microorganism to genetically rebuild itself and reoccupy cities and networks. This so-called third pandemic started in the late nineteenth century in China and became the most global of all, spreading to all inhabited continents. This pandemic continues today with thousands of people still being infected around the world every year. Urban life has always taken place in the shadow of the plague.

TRANS-SCALAR DEFENSE

The first substantial and sustained immune response from cities came after the biggest devastation of all in the mid-fourteenth century. A new architectural and urban system emerged that was effectively designed by the disease it tried to resist. In this sense, pathogens were at once inhabitant, saboteur, and architect of buildings and cities. Medical tracts on the plague increasingly became architectural treatises – even offering more comprehensive prescriptions of buildings, cities, and their maintenance than those offered by architects.

With the arrival of the second deadly wave after the Black Death in Milan, Bernabò Visconti, the lord of the city-state, disregarded medical orthodoxy to recognize that the plague was not simply a product of bad air but a living entity spread though contact between people, their clothing, goods, and the spaces they occupied. His plague regulations of early 1374, "to preserve our subjects from contagious illness," expelled the sick outside the city to either die or recover in huts or the woods, and those in contact with anyone who died to be quarantined for ten days before returning to society.[8] Travel into Milanese land from plague-infested places was also blocked. This combination of separating the sick and suspected from the healthy, restriction of entry, and appropriation for destruction of all "movable and immovable" goods of the sick and those from infected places, would become the norm. Gian Galeazzo Visconti expanded the strategy after deposing Bernabò in 1385, refusing to let pilgrims come close to any settlements and using the Adda River as a natural *cordon sanitaire*. In September 1399, sites were chosen within the city to which the sick could be removed. A month later, when the plague struck again, two plague hospitals (*mansions ad receptandum infirmos*) were opened and soon moved into buildings outside the city walls. Doctors visited suspected cases in houses, sending the sick to the new hospitals and anyone who had been near the infected to makeshift camps out of town, marking the boarded-up house as *domus infecta*.

A trans-scalar system of defense was established that treated house, city, and city-state as a set of ever-expanding prophylactic rings. [4] Each ring was policed to prevent the disease from entering and to move it further outwards. A new type of building and urban structure emerged to either exclude or house the disease. Plague hospitals outside the limits of the city – typically, appropriated monastery buildings that were already designed as a form of isolation from society – were completely sealed, regularly cleaned, buildings in which the ill were segregated from their clothes, possessions, and society – and to some extent each other – until the majority died. These buildings were usually "whitewashed" (using the Neolithic invention of heating limestone to produce powdery quicklime that is mixed with water and applied thickly as a plaster or thinly as a coat) to produce and

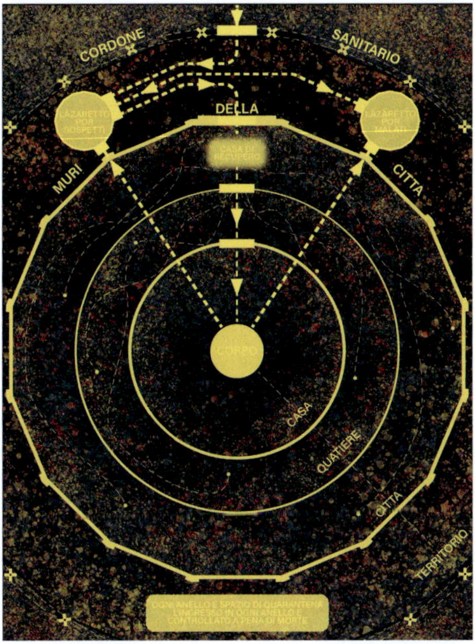

preserve cleanliness. The association of whitewash and health was so ancient and strong that no doctor or political authority calling for whitewash in the face of disease had to explain why. The antibacterial property of whitewash would not be identified until the end of the nineteenth century but its effect on smell, the main association with disease, was always evident.

Anyone who had been in the house of the sick, or who had contact with the household, would be treated as a suspected case and sent outside the city limits to another isolated building, a temporary shack or another appropriated monastery, only to go to the other building if they sickened. In reverse, those in the building for the sick who survived would move to the space of the suspected, and from there back to the city after sufficient time had passed. But the original houses of the sick could not be entered until everything inside was burned, the space fumigated

4 Diagram of prophylactic plague defense system

and aired for ten days, and the walls and ceilings scraped and whitewashed. This cleansing was carried out by those who had been infected but survived, as were burials. The whole city would be cleaned and whitewashed when an epidemic had passed.

The heart of this system was the understanding that clothing, furniture, rooms, buildings, neighborhoods, cities, and regions were nested spaces that could be infected and needed treatment like any other patient. The trans-scalar system of defense presupposed a model of contagion. The buildings isolating the sick outside city limits could have been rationalized with the miasma theory – as places to sequester the bad air coming off sick and dead bodies – but symptomatically were not. The system mobilized the strategy used for leprosy since ancient times, a bacterial disease that had always been understood to be contagious, with protocols to isolate its victims in special buildings outside the city – run by an order named after Saint Lazarus, the patron saint of lepers.

City-states across Italy and elsewhere took over Saint Lazarus' buildings and monasteries to establish isolated plague hospitals – later called "lazarettos" – for the infected and suspected. **[5]** They also instituted policed rings of *cordon sanitaires* further out again in land and water to isolate cities and regions, blocking anyone coming from an infected place with quarantine rules to delay entry for the others, isolating them and their possessions, and destroying suspect goods. **[6]** Sometimes, whole neighborhoods would be seen as infected and isolated from the rest of the city. All these buildings, neighborhoods, cities, and even whole territories, were treated as sealed enclosures – either sealing the disease in or out.

As the waves of disease kept coming, a specialized plague architecture evolved, as surveyed in the late eighteenth century by the British prison reformer John Howard, who wanted to design the best possible lazarettos for England in the belief that the long absent plague would inevitably return there. In 1774 he persuaded the British government to mandate the sweeping, ventilation, and annual scraping and whitewashing of all prison cells to prevent typhus, another bacterial infection. He checked himself into lazarettos throughout Europe to research what would become his illustrated survey of lazarettos, hospitals, and

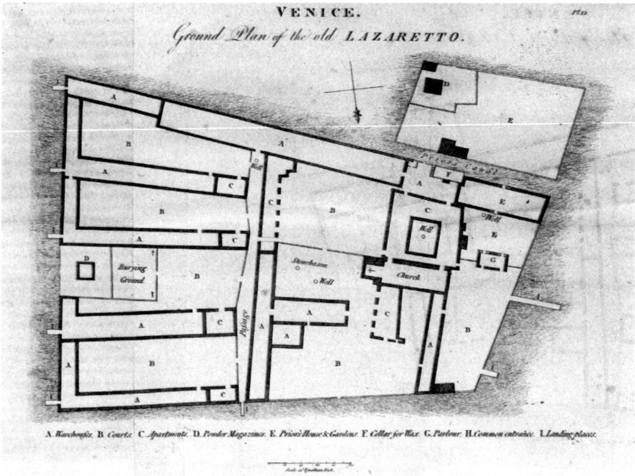

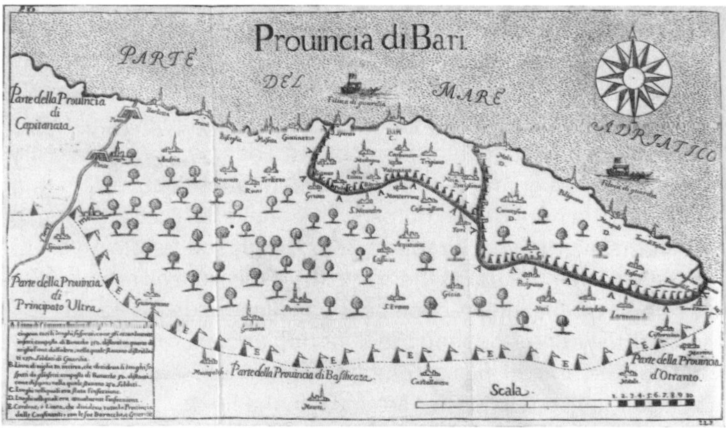

5 Lazaretto Vecchio, Venice, from John Howard, *An Account of the Principal Lazarettos in Europe*, London, 1791

6 Military-enforced *cordon sanitaires* isolating Bari and its province during the plague of 1690–1692 prisons of 1789. Strangely, lazarettos resembled in plan the ideal cities of the Renaissance and were technically the most modern buildings. The places where so much suffering and death took place were disconnected from an imperfect world. Their perfected geometries systematically segregated different kinds of humans and goods, and water was typically used to produce the effect of an island and operate the most advanced sanitation systems.[9] **[7–8]** After an outbreak of the plague in Milan in 1484–1485 that killed fifty thousand people – one third of its inhabitants – Leonardo da Vinci sketched a compact vertical ideal city with wide streets, fresh air vents in buildings, and separate canals for sanitation and transportation to prevent the spread of disease. All buildings were effectively floating in a cleansing system.

The permanent lazaretto of Milan was an island on land. Designed by Lazarro Palazzi in 1468 and finished in 1488, it was a vast square building outside the city walls, as big as the city castle and likewise surrounded by a moat as a new kind of military defense against an unwanted invader. **[9–10]** The square with four-hundred-meter-long sides was formed by a single story of 288 tall whitewashed rooms for 8–10 people with their own cooking-heating fireplace and an integral built-in latrine depositing human waste directly into the moat. **[11]** There was a single entry across the moat guarded by an observation room above it. The portico in front of the rooms, which sheltered the sick when the rooms overflowed, wrapped a vast enclosed field with a simple wooden chapel at the center – visible from all rooms – that presided over the intersection between life and death – as if the spiritual center pushed the suffering and excrement to the outside. The chapel was a completely open structure without walls so the ill could gather around it in the field.

Similar modernization occurred within cities. The Ca' Granda Hospital in Milan, for example, was built in parallel with the city's lazaretto after another devastating plague epidemic killed thirty thousand people in the city. It was designed by Antonio di Pietro Averlino (Filarete) in 1456 and admitted its first patients in 1472. The geometry of bisected squares maximized ventilation and light, and featured almost continuous windows, a special canal for fresh water supply, integral washbasins and toilets between each pair of beds, an innovative system of internal

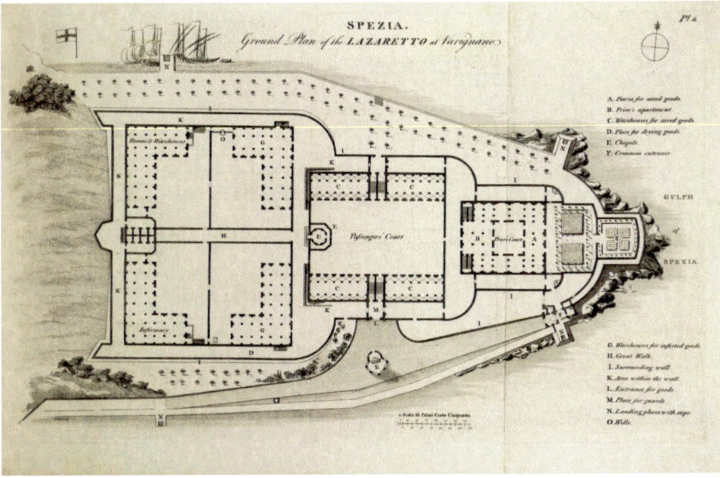

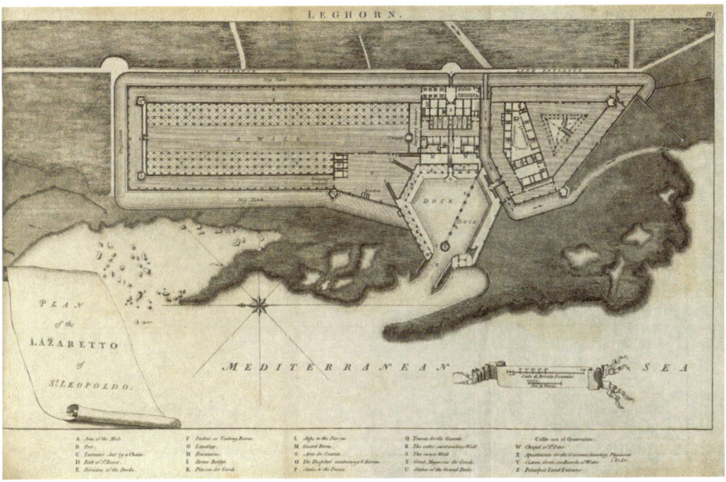

7 Lazaretto in Spezia, from John Howard, *An Account of the Principal Lazarettos in Europe*, London, 1791

8 Lazaretto in Leghorn, from John Howard, *An Account of the Principal Lazarettos in Europe*, London, 1791

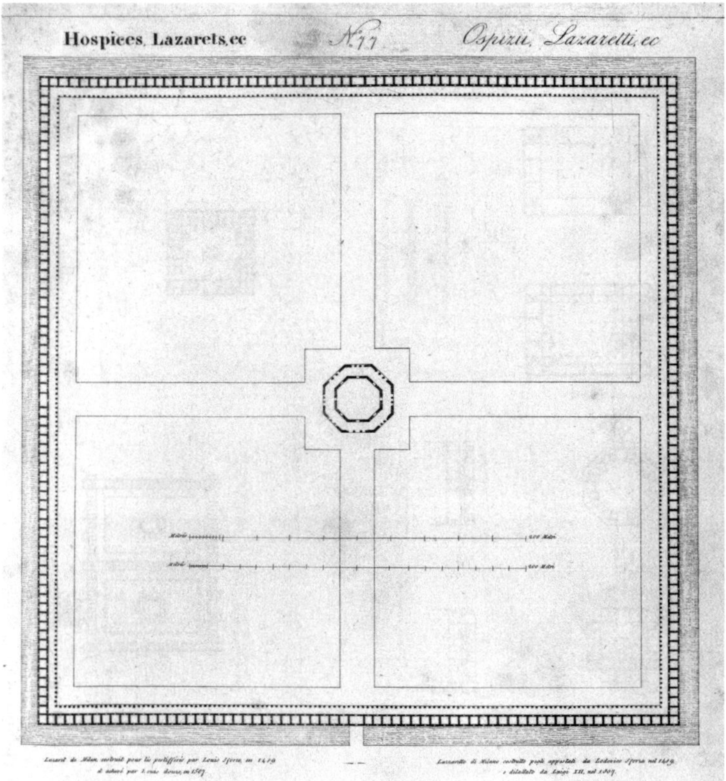

9 Jean-Nicolas-Louis Durand, 1833 illustration of Lazaretto of Milan, completed 1488

10 View of Milan showing lazaretto outside city walls, engraving from Georg Braun and Frans Hogenberg, *Civitates orbis terrarium*, 1572

11 Attributed to Luca Beltrami, room with fireplace and latrine in the lazaretto of Milan, watercolor, 1899 plumbing, tubes venting sewer air above the building, and twice-daily cleaning and airing of the floors.[10] **[12]** The building also acted as the center of a new network of fourteen smaller hospitals. It became the model throughout Europe for a new type of central hospital using the latest sanitary design and orchestrating a network of more specialized hospitals, such as that in Lisbon in 1492 and Valencia in 1512.[11] Emergency conditions provoked a restructuring of building typologies and urban infrastructure. Cities carried the permanent imprint of disease, just as they carried the permanent imprint of war.

Ca' Granda was a major urban statement of the new idea that hospitals treat diseases, and treat each disease differently – with sections of the building devoted to different illnesses. Only those that were poor and had a chance of recovery from illness or starvation were admitted. Care for the poor and plague control had become overlapping missions since the end of the fourteenth century.[12] Lazarettos outside the city and hospitals inside were the anchors of an urban system based on a new philosophy of health: that to care for the poor was to care for the necessary labor force to rebuild the economy and the city. The

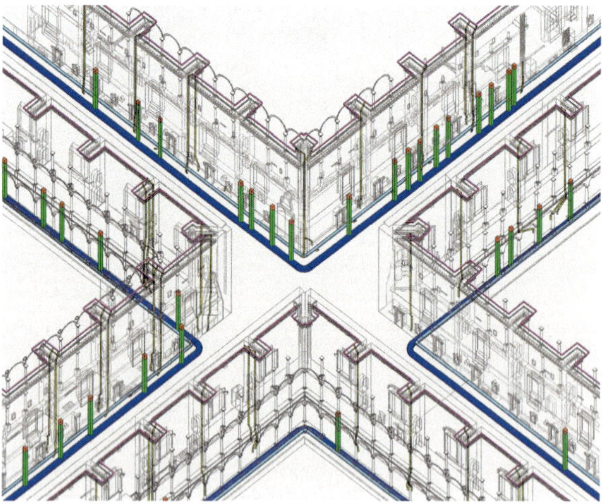

12 Computer model of the sanitation system – canals, latrines, and ventilation tubes – embedded into the Ca' Granda hospital wards by Filarete

devastation of entire populations incubated a new investment in the care of the vulnerable, the ill, and children.

Florence's population, for example, went from ninety to thirty-seven thousand as a result of the Black Death. The architecturally celebrated Ospedale degli Innocenti (Hospital of the Innocents), designed by Filippo Brunelleschi in 1419 and inaugurated in 1445, was not so much a hospital as an institution to care for orphaned and abandoned children, which were not accepted in the Santa Maria Nuova hospital.[13] The building was commissioned by the Silk Weavers Guild of Florence, of which Brunelleschi was a member, in response to the extraordinary decline of the population. Like Ca' Granda, it had a major symbolic urban presence – placed on axis with the dome of the cathedral – and role in reimagining the city.

AMNESIA

European cities became permanently marked by spaces to manage disease, yet plague protocols would typically be forgotten between epidemics. Miasma theory maintained its dominance even after the Verona physician Girolamo Fracastoro's much discussed *De Contagione et Contagiosis Morbis* of 1546 elaborated the first fully fledged theory that each disease was the result of specific tiny invisible organisms – living "seeds of contagion" carried on "formites" like linen, clothing, and objects – that could multiply rapidly and quickly "invade" any space or body.[14] Only in emergencies would protocols based on principles of contagion be belatedly reestablished and gradually strengthened. Giovanni Filippo Ingrassia's eight-hundred-page treatise of 1576 chronicling his recent successful medical defense of Palermo against the plague, which repeatedly cited Fracastoro, is as much an architectural treatise as a medical one, detailing every aspect of the built environment – complete with drawings of plague buildings – and the protocols to preserve its occupants.[15] **[13–14]**

Even Ingrassia's original diagnosis turned on architecture. He describes his original doubt that the Palermo outbreak was contagious until he learned that all the people who sat on carpets spread out in a house in Messina were quickly infected, dying,

13 Giovanni Filippo Ingrassia, illustration of new lazaretto outside Palermo's city walls, showing operations, isolation, and sanitation protocols, 1576

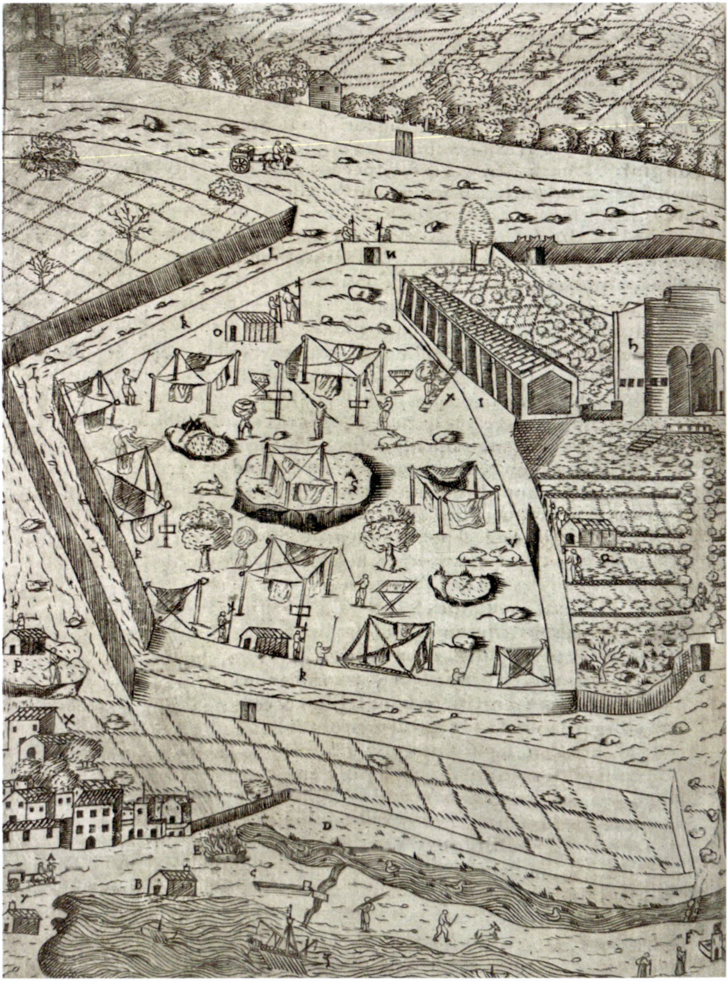

14 Giovanni Filippo Ingrassia, illustration of an isolated facility for ventilating and disinfecting clothing from city households, located outside Palermo's walls, 1576

or dead. The carpet had been unloaded from a galley that had previously discharged two infected people in Palermo. Mobile domestic objects can, Ingrassia recognized, "infect from afar," conveying disease between distant houses. Every element of the domestic interior becomes suspect. The Messina outbreak was reportedly stopped by closing the house and isolating everyone who had touched the carpets.

Miasma and contagion paradigms share the sanitary war on excrement and all forms of putrefaction in houses and streets, but defense against contagion calls for much stricter regimes of isolation and disinfection. In addition to cleaning the city, Ingrassia instituted a complex system of separating healthy, sick, suspected, and convalescing into nine new plague hospitals set up in existing buildings – starting with an existing leprosarium. Those who recovered spend twenty-one days in a convalescent hospital before going to another one within the city for twenty-one more days "for the last purification," and from there rejoin the city – likely into one of hundreds of minimal houses built out of rubble and planks, since their infected houses had been sealed. Anything in a house touched by the infected had been destroyed and the clothing of the others in the house had been systematically disinfected and aired in a garden of a duke's house outside the city walls. Ingrassia analyzed every element of the built fabric and the movements of people and goods within it in terms of either isolating or conveying invisible "pestilential seeds" – what would three hundred years later be known as pathogenic microbes. Every protocol is described in exacting detail, from how to move the sick or dead through the streets to how to enter a house to purify it without coming into contact with its surfaces or contents, and what treatment to give to everything inside.

Quinto Tiberio Angelerio, who was practicing medicine in Messina at the time, introduced even more prophylactic layers to his system for defending Sardinia during the eight-month epidemic of 1582–1583. The strategy was so successful that it became a model in subsequent centuries, and was formalized as fifty-seven plague instructions in his 1584 booklet – including everyone carrying a six-foot-long stick to maintain that distance between each other.[16] A triple *cordon sanitaire* was set up around the city, streets were cleaned, and the entire city disinfected house by house, whitewashing the darkest and least ventilated. Windows of unsuspected houses had to be kept open and all surfaces washed with vinegar, and inhabitants were not allowed to go outside. All fittings and furniture of infected houses were burned and clothes, textiles, and objects were sterilized using new method of dry heat in ovens after being washed – to kill what Angelerio called the *malefica semina*, "bad seeds."

A final prophylactic layer was added to the ever-more-elaborate plague system in the form of sealed outfits. Ingrassia had recommended that the women disinfecting and fumigating clothes should wear "well-smoothed waxed cloth" to avoid picking up the seeds of disease on their own clothing and passing them on to the uninfected. During the plagues of the 1630s, doctors wore long cloaks of waxed fabric with hoods and built-in eyeglasses.[17] And during the 1656 Plague of Rome that killed about 20 percent of the city, the sealed outfit included an extended beak packed with aromatic herbs at the tip to keep distance from patients. **[15–16]** Doctors descended from carriages also covered in waxed fabric and entered the houses of the poor wearing a portable architecture.

15 Physician in plague costume, engraving after Jean-Jacques Manget, *Traité de la peste*, 1721

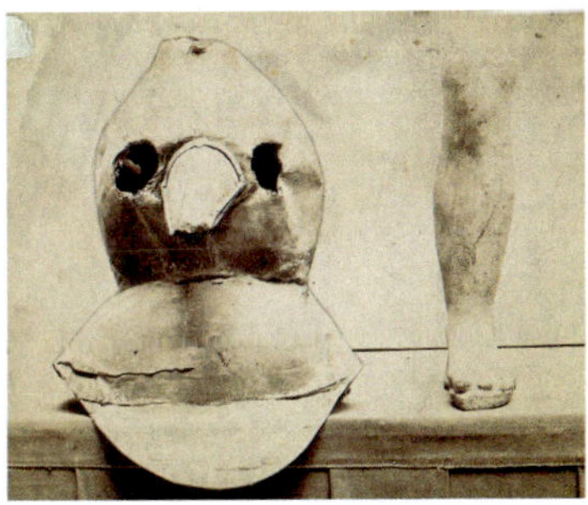

16 Plague mask and leg model from a Venetian lazaretto, nineteenth-century photograph

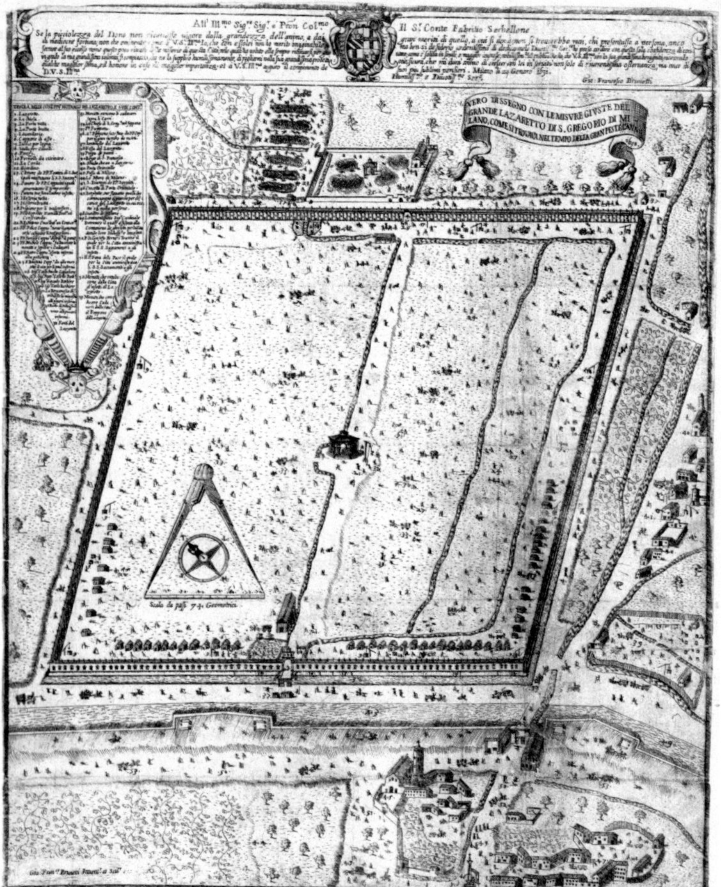

17 Giovanni Francesco Brunetti, Lazzaretto of Milan during the 1630 plague, etching, January 29, 1631; Brunetti survived the plague in the lazaretto

Ingrassia and Angelerio spoke of the need to provide care for the poor. Yet inasmuch as most of the rich left the cities for the more isolated countryside, and with different isolation rules for those who stayed, the main burden remained on the poor – who were, according to Fracastoro's theory, more likely to infect others. The new city structured by disease control therefore also sustained the inequity of the majority. Plague defense was ultimately defense of structural injustice.

The plague defense system was all too easily overwhelmed if any part of it was neglected, as in the 1630 plague of Milan, the last and biggest to hit the very city that had inaugurated the system. Plaque regulations were relaxed during a time of famine, and the poor from the countryside wandering the city streets without sustenance were eventually moved into the lazaretto for shelter and care, only to be joined by the sick as the plague returned. Its vast central field filled with rows of huts as around fifteen thousand people overflowed the rooms. Giovanni Francesco Brunetti, who survived the disease in the lazaretto, portrayed the scene in a January 1631 etching in intimate detail, including the position of his own room near the main entrance,

18 Details from Brunetti etching showing church, hangings, social distancing, bodies on the ground and piled on wagons, and burials

carts bringing “the infected” from the city, guard posts around the perimeter of the building, rods that people carried to warn that they were sick, the distance maintained between them, the wells, cooking, temporary huts, priests, confessions, disciplinary hangings, bodies loaded onto carts, and continuous burials. **[17–18]** The city too was awash with cruelty, panic, suffering, and the stench of death. **[19]** Regulations were eventually reestablished but too late to have an effect. Almost a half of the city died. The built environment was once again undone by its invisible guest.

19 Attributed to Orazio Colombo, Torture and execution of alleged plague carriers in Milan, 1630, etching, 1839

1 The proportion of epidemic deaths in a city, understood as a node in a network, is directly correlated with the number of other nodes it is directly connected to, and whether those nodes are directly connected to each other. José M. Gómez and Miguel Verdú, "Network Theory May Explain the Vulnerability of Medieval Human Settlements to the Black Death Pandemic," *Scientific Reports* 7, no. 43467 (2017).
2 Ahmad Al-Maqrizi, "A History of the Ayyubids and Mamluks," in John Aberth, *The Black Death: The Great Mortality of 1348-1350: A Brief History with Documents* (New York: Bedford, 2017), 69.
3 Agnolo di Tura, "Sienese Chronicle," in Aberth, *The Black Death*, 82.
4 Giovanni Boccaccio, *Decameron*, trans. G. H. McWilliam (London: Penguin Books, 2003), 8.
5 Ann Carmichael, "Plague Legislation in the Italian Renaissance," *Bulletin of the History of Medicine* 57, no. 4 (Winter 1983): 508–25.
6 Jennifer Klunk, Tauras P. Vilgalys, Christian E. Demeure, et al., "Evolution of Immune Genes is Associated with the Black Death," *Nature* 611, no. 7935 (November 2022): 312–9.
7 Nahyan Fancy and Monica H. Green. "Plague and the Fall of Baghdad (1258)," *Medical History* 65, no. 2 (2021): 157–77.
8 "Plague regulations of Bernabo Visconti, Lord of Milan," in *The Black Death*, ed. and trans. Rosemary Horrox (Manchester: Manchester University Press, 1994), 203.
9 Howard scathingly describes all the imperfections of the lazarettos, particularly the lack of sanitation and regular whitewashing. John Howard, *An Account of the Principal Lazarettos in Europe: with various papers relative to the plague : together with further observations on some foreign prisons and hospitals, and additional remarks on the present state of those in Great Britain and Ireland* (London: William Eyres, 1789).
10 Daniel Savoy, "Cleansing the Soul: Filarete and the Sewers of the Ospedale Maggiore in Milan," *Renaissance Quarterly* 77, no. 3 (2024): 735–88.
11 The Lisbon hospital explicitly followed Filarete's organization and had an integrated system of toilets directly feeding a new sewage system. Danielle Abdon, "Epidemics and the Royal Control of Public Health in Lisbon, Portugal, 1480–95," in *Epidemic Urbanism: How Contagious Diseases Have Shaped Global Cities*, eds. Mohammad Gharipour and Caitlin DeClerq (Bristol: Intellect Ltd, 2021), 162–70.
12 Ann Carmichael, "Contagion Theory and Contagion Practice in Fifteenth-Century Milan," *Renaissance Quarterly* 44, no. 2 (Summer 1991): 217.
13 Britta Hentschel, "Ospedale degli Innocenti: The Loggia and the Creation of the Public Sphere," *Treatment* (e-flux Architecture, January 2025). Diana Bullen Presciutti, *Visual Cultures of Foundling Care in Renaissance Italy* (Abingdon: Ashgate, 2015).
14 Girolamo Fracastoro, *De Contagione et Contagiosis Morbis* (Venice: Heirs of Lucantonio Giunta, 1546). Frascatoro's preventive measures were limited to social distancing; regular cleaning of the body, clothes, and linen; and burning the furniture of the infected.
15 Giovanni Filippo Ingrassia, *Informatione del pestifero, et contagioso morbo il quale affligge et haue afflitto questa citta di Palermo, & molte altre città, e terre di questo Regno di Sicilia, nell'anno 1575 et 1576* (Palermo: Giovan Mattheo Mayda, 1576).
16 Raffaella Bianucci, Ole Jørgen Benedictow, Gino Fornaciari, and Valentina Giuffra, "Quinto Tiberio Angelerio and New Measures for Controlling Plague in 16th-Century Alghero, Sardinia," *Emerging Infectious Diseases* 19, no. 9 (September 2013): 1478–83.
17 Francesco Pona, *Il gran contagio di Verona nel milleseicento, e trenta. Descritto da Francesco Pona* (Verona: Bartolomio Merlo, 1631), 30.

1 William Heath, *Monster Soup*, satirical etching on Thames water pollution, 1828

7 SANITARY REFORM

The history of cities is the history of disease. The pandemics of the nineteenth century brought us the infrastructure we still have today: clean water and sewage systems, urban parks, etc. They also revolutionized the design of buildings, interiors, and furniture. Overcrowded industrializing cities were hit by waves of infectious microbial diseases – smallpox, typhus, typhoid fever, yellow fever, scarlet fever, cholera, and tuberculosis. An alliance of doctors and social reformers campaigned to turn the emergency protocols used in previous centuries to combat epidemics into permanent regulations, policing lifestyles and redesigning every scale from toilet to territory. Buildings and cities were modernized as these reforms rapidly spread around the world. Death rates dramatically declined and the concept of public health was normalized as a right and responsibility.

SICK WATER

In a cartoon of 1828 by William Heath titled *Monster Soup commonly called Thames Water*, a middle-class woman drops her teacup in horror upon looking through a microscope at a sample of the polluted river running through the city and its citizens via neighborhood pumps. **[1]** The Thames was a prime source of diseases such as cholera and typhoid fever, even if scientists kept rejecting the idea. The dominant medical idea remained the miasma theory that blamed disease on foul air. Nevertheless, the illustration depicts the "microcosm" of London's water as a fearful world of tiny malevolent creatures of different sizes and shapes, with text quoting the evocation of hell in John Milton's *Paradise Lost*. The Thames was both the open sewer of the city and its water supply, and therefore the source of infection – a fact suspected at a popular level long before the medical establishment accepted it.

These monsters were not just imagined by the cartoonist. The microscope-maker Philip Carpenter had opened a popular corner store called "Microcosm" on Regent Street in London in 1826. It featured a continuous show in which a solar microscope projected three-foot-wide circular images of microscopic life onto the wall of a darkened room, including one of "a single drop of water, filled with innumerable living creatures."[1] **[2]** An 1827 visitor reported on the "shocking" sight of the "infernal world" produced by adding a little animal or vegetable matter to water:

> What it shows is really enough to drive a man of lively imagination mad. Nothing can be more horrible, – no more frightful devilish figures could possibly be invented, – than the hideous disgusting water animalculae (invisible to the naked eye, or even to glasses of inferior power) which we daily swallow. They look like damned souls darting about their filthy pool with the rapidity of lightning, while every motion and gesture seemed to bespeak deadly hate, horrid torture, warfare and death.[2]

Scientific images of these diverse microorganisms living in their "billions" in stagnant water were soon published in popular magazines, including the smallest bacteria that constantly

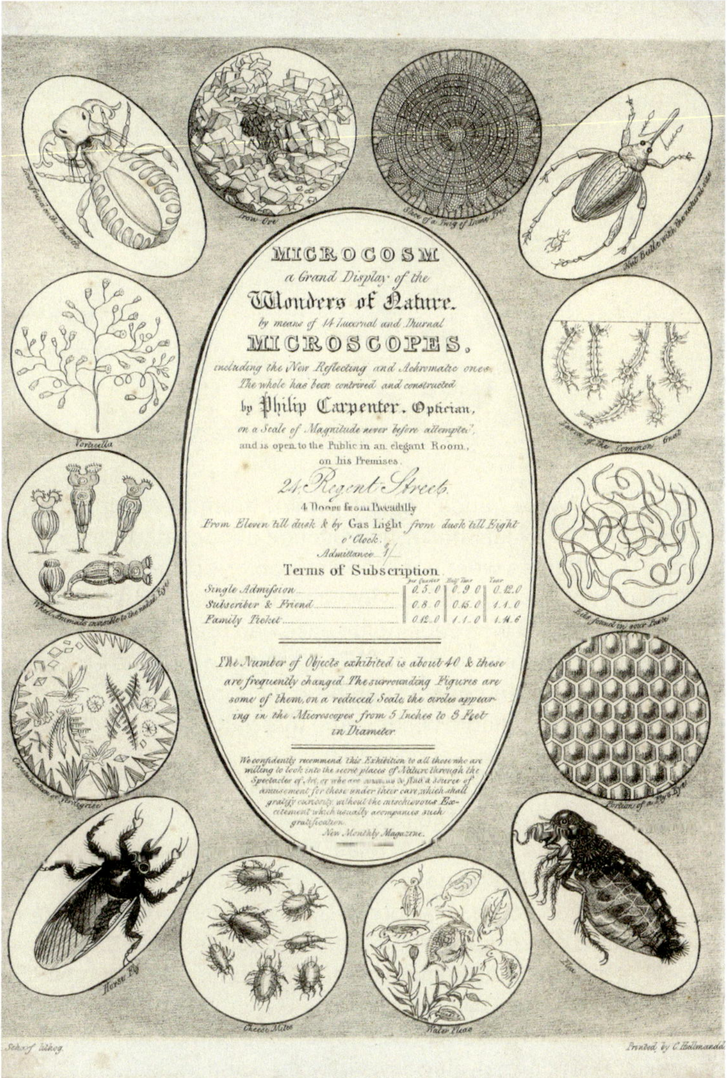

2 Advertisement for Philip Carpenter's Microcosm solar microscope exhibition, 1826

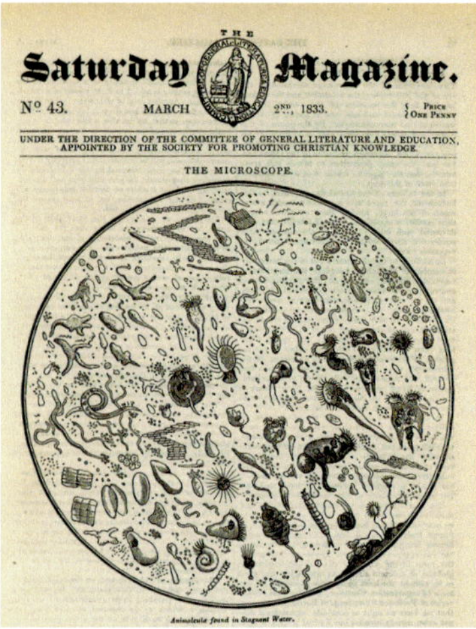

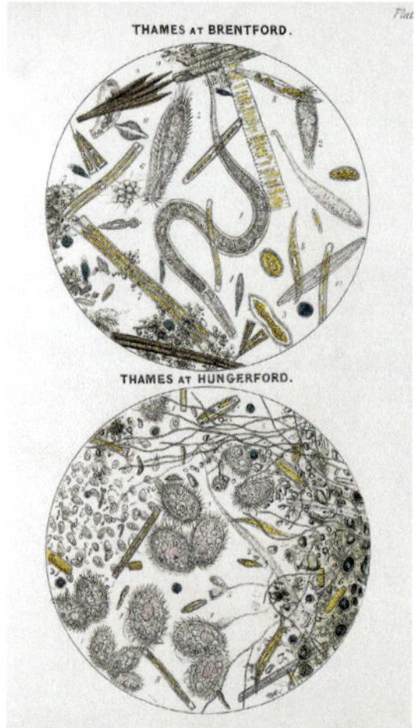

wriggle – and were hence named "vibrio" (from the Latin for "vibrate") in 1773.[3] **[3]** Similar microscope images of organisms living in the Thames were published by doctor Arthur Hassall in 1850 as part of the ongoing call for water reform.[4] **[4]** The suspicion that polluted water was causing disease had been growing for decades until Dr. John Snow in 1854 finally demonstrated that the cholera rapidly spreading through his own Soho neighborhood was coming from a single water pump that had been contaminated by the excrement of someone with the disease.[5]

Earlier cholera maps showed the disease as a kind of menacing cloud hovering over the poorer neighborhoods of the city, as if conveying the very idea of miasma. **[5]** Snow produced a new kind of map showing disease as a kind of urban citizen, with each death at an address recorded by a black bar, and the biggest stacks of bars clustered around the pump. **[6]** He wanted to prove that the disease infecting human intestines was a contagious "poison" transmitted by contact with the excrement of the ill.[6] He asked Hassall to examine water from the pump, the river, and houses of the infected, along with diarrhea and intestinal samples from recently deceased patients. Hassall found "myriads" of a

3 Microbial life found in stagnant water, including vibrio bacteria

4 Microbial life in Thames river water, from Arthur Hill Hassall, *A Microscopic Examination of the Water Supplied to the Inhabitants of London ...*, 1850

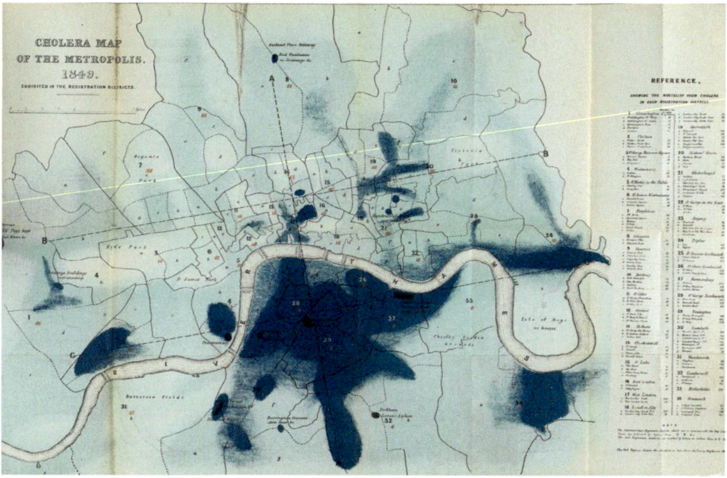

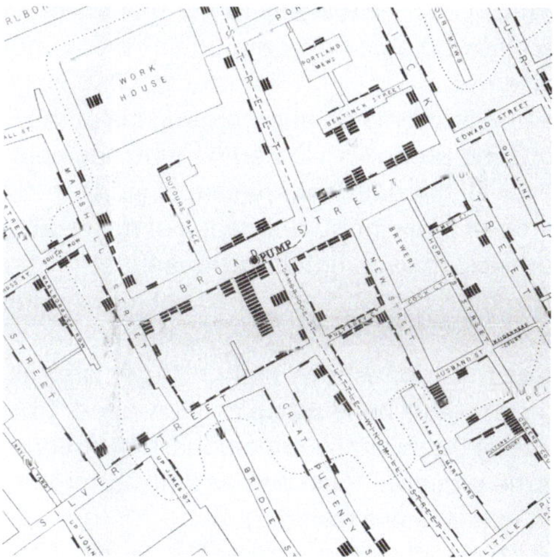

5 Cholera map of London in 1849, showing cloud of deaths in relation to overcrowding, prisons, workhouses, asylums, pollution, and defective sewers

6 Detail of John Snow's map of 1854 cholera outbreak in Soho, from John Snow's *Report to the St. James Vestry, London*, 1855

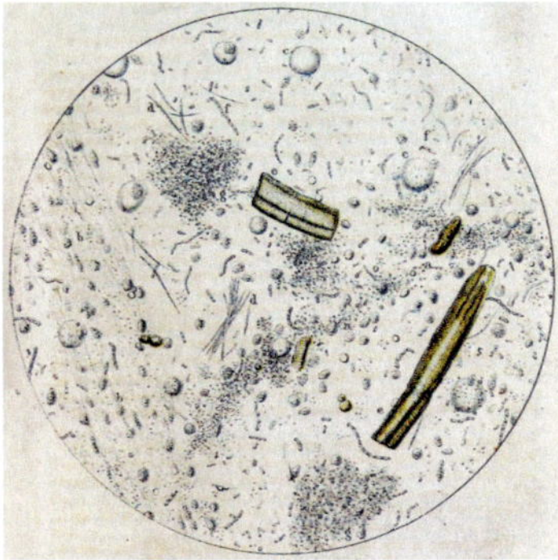

particular species of *vibrione* in "every drop" of the human samples that he did not see in healthy patients, and published images of them in his report submitted to the Royal Commission investigating the epidemic.[7] **[7]** Yet he presented them as an important symptom of the disease rather than its primary cause, and the scientific and political communities were unpersuaded by Snow's research.[8]

The leading authority on microorganisms at the time, Christian Gottfried Ehrenberg in Berlin – who had coined the word "bacterium" for all the different species of vibrio in 1828, and was the source of many popular images of microorganisms in tainted water – explicitly rejected the idea that they produce disease during both the 1831 and 1848 cholera epidemics across Europe.[9] He treated microbes as complex creatures with the same status as the supposedly "higher" organisms like humans that depend on them – building up an illustrated "atlas" of the diverse life of these vital companions, from traces in ancient fossils up to the present.[10] **[8]** It was as if he admired microbial life too much to see it as a threat.

The idea that each disease might be provoked by a specific tiny living organism – including the microbes first seen through a microscope, drawn, and named "animalcules" by the Delft draper and microscope maker Antonie van Leewenhoek in 1683 – had periodically been raised in the eighteenth century – notably in

7 Doctor Arthur Hill Hassall's microscope analysis showing vibrio bacteria in the diarrhea of a cholera patient

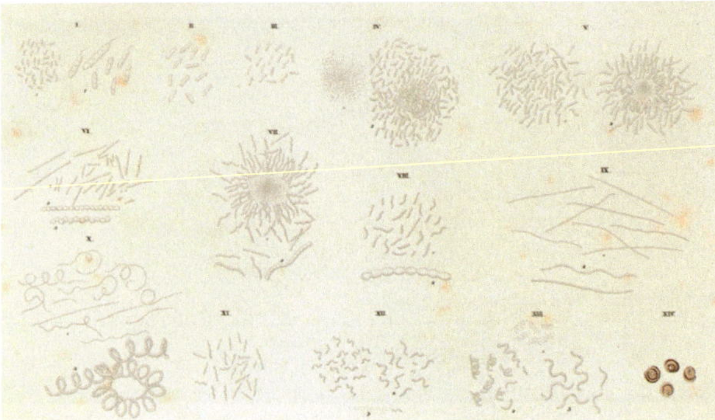

1757 by the Swedish biologist and doctor Carl Linneaus, the founder of the modern system for classifying all living organisms. But it was repeatedly dismissed until the little-known Italian microbiologist Agostino Bassi published his 1835 demonstration that microscopic living fungi cause disease in silkworms, and in 1844 reactivated what would eventually be known as the germ theory of disease by arguing that many diseases of plants and animals, especially humans, are likewise caused by "living parasites."[11]

A few months after Hassall saw and disregarded them, the anatomist and expert in microscopes Fillipo Pacini saw "millions" of the same bacteria in the intestines of the dead during a major cholera outbreak in Florence in August 1854.[12] He identified the microorganism as the living cause of the disease, calling it *Vibrio cholerae*, with his original hand-inscribed slides now preserved in the Florence anatomy museum. **[9]** Pacini immediately published his research and circulated it to scientists around Europe – expanding it later in longer, published studies – yet was overlooked by the scientific community.[13] When almost thirty years later, Robert Koch discovered the same microorganism in Calcutta in 1883, the Cholera Commission of the Imperial Health Office in Berlin recognized it and also Pacini's previous discovery. The little creature was finally acknowledged as a new kind of migrant urban citizen that had forced buildings and cities to be redesigned long before its deadly agency was recognized.

8 Microorganisms, including some later classified as bacteria *(Bacterium, Vibrio, Spirochaeta*, and *Spirillum)* from Christian Gottfried Ehrenberg's *Atlas von vier und sechzig Kupfertafeln zu Christian Gottfried Ehrenberg über Infusionsthierchen*, 1838

THE GREAT STINK

The so-called Great Stink of London during the hot summer of 1858 completely overwhelmed the largest city in the world. Between 1800 and 1850, the city's population had exploded from one to two-and-a-half million, which caused traditional waste management systems to collapse. A contemporary satirical illustration in *Punch* magazine shows Death rowing along the Thames thick with putrefying waste. **[10]** *The Builder*, the most widely read professional architectural magazine at the time, surveyed the riverbank at the heart of the city from the almost completed new Houses of Parliament to London Bridge, reporting that it was formed by a band of excrement one hundred feet wide on average and up to six feet deep. The illustration is a cross-section showing the "poisonous accumulation" exposed every low tide near a sewer outflow, with a smell "enough to strike down strong men."[14] **[11]** The stench made Parliament unoccupiable and forced British politicians to finally approve the construction of a massive sewage system for London. Every building and street was transformed by vast new infrastructural networks of pipes installed over sixteen years by the engineer Joseph Bazalgette. **[12–13]** One network guided fresh water from upstream into each interior of the city. The other guided all waste downstream beyond city limits.

9 Filippo Pacini, *Vibrio cholerae*, microscope slide, 1854

10 *The Silent Highwayman*, Death rows on the Thames during the Great Stink, from *Punch Magazine*, London, July 10, 1858

11 Illustration of "poisonous accumulation" of excrement on Thames riverbank, from *The Builder*, July 3, 1858

12 Joseph Bazalgette (top right) at the northern outfall sewer being built below London's Abbey Mills pumping station, 1860

13 Construction of a London sewage tunnel, 1859

This multi-scalar architecture of excrement stretched from toilets and washable fixtures at furniture scale to plumbing networks within and between buildings, to new kinds of buildings in which humans tended to new kinds of machinery and chemical reactions. [14–15] The biggest pipes were laid under the new embankment that formed a whole new architecture of the river – giving the city a new façade and set of civic spaces. [16–17] Such a monumental embankment diverting sewage away from the river and bringing fresh water to the city had already been envisaged by the painter and inventor John Martin in the 1830s, and was much discussed at the time during the first debates about the poor health of the city. [18] When the scheme was finally realized, it was accompanied by codes for light, air, water, and hygiene that sculpted urban form and largely persist until today. Every scale of the city was visibly redesigned by invisible and yet-to-be-acknowledged bacteria.

The massive demolition of medieval Paris and its reconstruction between 1853 and 1870 was likewise rationalized in terms of infectious diseases. Georges-Eugène Haussmann was commissioned by Napoleon III to be the Prefect of Police and normalized the police powers used to cleanse infected houses during the devastating cholera epidemics in 1832 and 1849 to dramatically transform the built environment – demolishing entire medieval neighborhoods and constructing wide avenues,

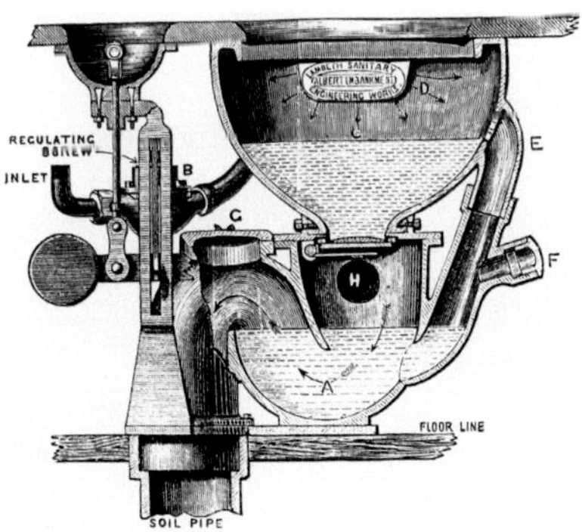

14 Doulton Valve Closet, 1881

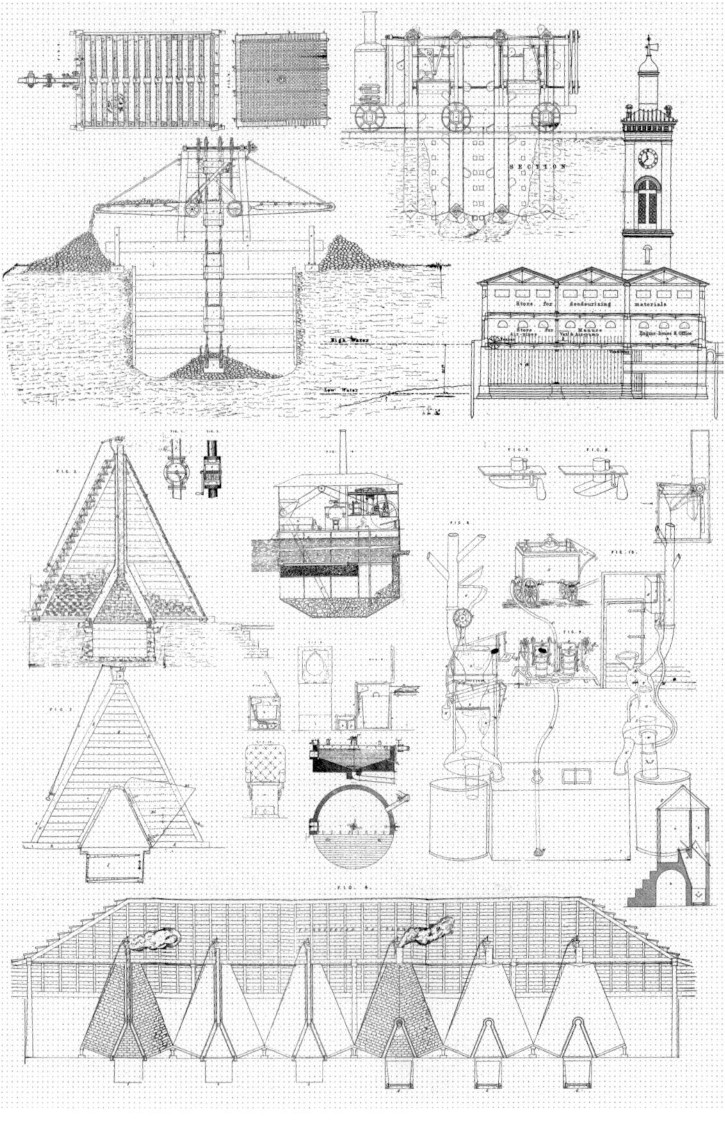

15 Sewage and manure patents from specifications by Rogers, Gibson, Wicksteed, Legras, and others, 1854–1860

16 Construction of the Thames Embankment, 1869

17 Section of the Thames Embankment showing low-level sewer and railway works, 1867

sewage systems, fresh water, ventilation, sunlight, and parks. **[19–20]** The strategy was to treat Paris as if it was in a permanent state of emergency – using health as a proxy for control. The population of Paris had doubled in the first half of the century to become the third largest city in the world after London and Beijing, and doctors had been portraying the overcrowded city as sick since the 1820s, referring to it as the "home of infection" and compiling statistics directly associating sickness and mortality with poverty. Haussmann radicalized and militarized interventions that had been called for decades earlier by sanitary reformers, such as doctors Alexandre Parent-Duchâtelet and Louis-René Villermé.

Parent-Duchâtelet was an early advocate for "public hygiene," presenting an excremental portrait of Paris in 1822.[15] His lengthy study of its sewer system argued that the city itself, "formerly only an infected marsh," was made possible by this overlooked underground "monument" that resists epidemics by removing the "corrupted" water that causes infection. The enemy was not excrement itself but its "infected emanations" that sicken whole neighborhoods.[16] Sewers make places "inhabitable." The very

18 John Martin, Plan for preventing the pollution of the water of the Thames and preserving the sewage for agricultural purposes, London, 1834

19 Demolition of Butte des Moulins for the avenue de l'Opéra, Paris, 1870

20 Water supply system of Paris, engraving from *La Nature*, France, 1886 act of habitation is an effect of controlling excrement. His goal was to mobilize change – proposing a series of new sewers and connections between existing ones, with every house required to be connected to the system with a cast-iron pipe. The book was ultimately about urban design and was intended to be accompanied by a similar, obsessive study on streets.

Parent-Duchâtelet soon joined forces with Louis-René Villermé and founded the first professional journal of public health in 1829. *Annales d'hygiène publique et de médecine légale* framed a set of protocols for producing and policing houses, streets, neighborhoods, and cities. The work became urgently relevant with the first cholera epidemic in 1832. All the coffins moving through the city traumatized the public, doctors, artists, and authorities alike. Dramatic newspaper headlines like "Cholera Morbus is Within our Walls" conveyed the sense that the nomadic illness had arrived from London to take up residence.[17] Emergency police powers were invoked to quarantine and cleanse those houses and streets affected, but it took decades for the first law against unsanitary dwellings in 1850 to grant the right to investigate and condemn suspect buildings. Haussmann took advantage of this law to completely transform the city.[18] For the Prefect of Police, the whole city was a suspect.

Distant colonies, such as British India, were treated the same way as the spaces of the poor in metropolitan cities. They were seen as the ultimate source of urban diseases such as cholera and forcibly "cleaned" with the same strict regimes of isolation, quarantining, and whitewashing that had been developed in Italy centuries before. In Karachi, during the bubonic plague outbreak of 1897, for example, entire neighborhoods were sealed off by a *cordon sanitaire*; sanitary brigades conducted invasive house-to-house inspections, whitewashing walls and destroying homes deemed unclean. **[21–22]** The sick and those suspected of illness were removed to segregation camps on the edge of the city. Urban planning concentrated on "cleaning" so-called "native" neighborhoods and segregating them from those of colonists, along with the revision of water and sewage networks, wider streets, etc.

21 Demolished plague-infected house on Gow Sitani Street, Karachi, 1897

22 Gulamsha Mahomedan segregation camp during bubonic plague outbreak, Karachi, 1897

The sanitary reform movement – launched in the imperial capitals of England and France and spreading rapidly through the rest of Europe, the United States, and beyond – identified buildings and the infrastructural systems supporting them as the agents of disease, and therefore the only way to resist it was with design. The movement transformed rooms, buildings, streets, and cities by making centuries-old emergency measures permanent. Cities were reshaped by what they tried to prevent.

SICK BUILDINGS

The attempt to normalize emergency protocols in England started in the late eighteenth century. Doctor John Haygarth, a close associate of John Howard, the surveyor of lazarettos, carried out the first systematic contact tracing, going building to building to monitor the epidemic movement of smallpox in the city of Chester in 1777–1778.[19] He blamed urban organization and revived a version of Italian plague regulations; quarantining all citizens at home, establishing a "pest house" for the infected; and systematically purifying rooms, furniture, and clothing.[20] Haygarth's so-called "rules of prevention" became influential within a circle of doctors in the north of England and was adopted by John Ferriar in Manchester at the epicenter of industrialization in 1796 in the face of repeated typhus fever outbreaks. Ferriar made detailed accounts of the unhealthy dirtiness, lack of light, fresh air, and waste disposal of the buildings inhabited by the laboring poor, seeing them as both the main victims of disease and the cause of its spread. The infected were isolated in "fever wards" that were airy and repeatedly cleaned, along with the patients and anything they touched including bedding, clothing, furniture, and utensils.[21] Walls and ceilings were regularly hot whitewashed, as were the homes of the infected, and a supply of whitewash was given to the inhabitants to regularly maintain their newly cleansed spaces. Workers were asked to pay continuous attention to the cleanliness of their bodies and buildings. Windows were added to the darkest houses and streets were cleaned of the waste of humans and other animals.

Ferriar's idea was to insert health-inducing spaces into the unhealthy city. Their whiteness countered the perceived darkness of dirt, soot, excrement, polluted water, vermin, the dirty skin of workers, and poverty itself. The ultimate ambition was to improve the air and light in all houses to prevent illness in the first place. Ferriar had started obliging all his patients, regardless of their state of health, to whitewash their houses in the face of the 1789–1790 typhus epidemic, blaming it, like Haygarth, on the "filthy," unventilated and overcrowded lodging houses of the rapidly growing city that acted as the "nursery" of disease.[22] The built environment itself was the real patient to be treated.

Similar protocols of isolating the ill in new healthy spaces while modifying, cleansing, and whitewashing existing spaces were repeatedly made in cities throughout England during nineteenth-century epidemics – especially during the national crisis of the 1830 cholera epidemic and its even more deadly return in the 1840s. **[23–24]** Reformers increasingly insisted that the unhealthy buildings and urban infrastructure that fostered disease should be preemptively transformed. **[25]** The lawyer and social reformer Edwin Chadwick became the first national leader of the sanitary reform movement, embracing the construction of a new built environment yet never accepting the concept of contagion. His massive 1842 national survey of the living conditions of the poor in the British Isles confirmed the association between the built environment and disease and launched the campaign for new "public health" laws governing cities, mandating the whitewashing of existing houses of the poor and supporting the construction of new types of "healthy houses" with improved air, water, light, ventilation, drainage, and cleanliness. The prescription for a healthy house became the same as for a healthy hospital – reinforced by fresh water and sewage systems.

Florence Nightingale, who had been a nurse treating cholera patients from John Snow's neighborhood before heading to the war in Crimea – where she would become famous for cleansing the Scutari hospital, which was killing more soldiers than the battlefields – took over the at-once architectural and medical leadership of the sanitary reform movement from Chadwick after her return in August of 1856. She quickly became an expert

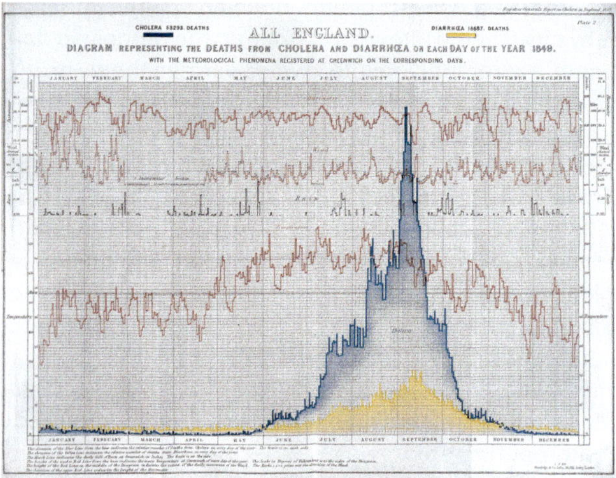

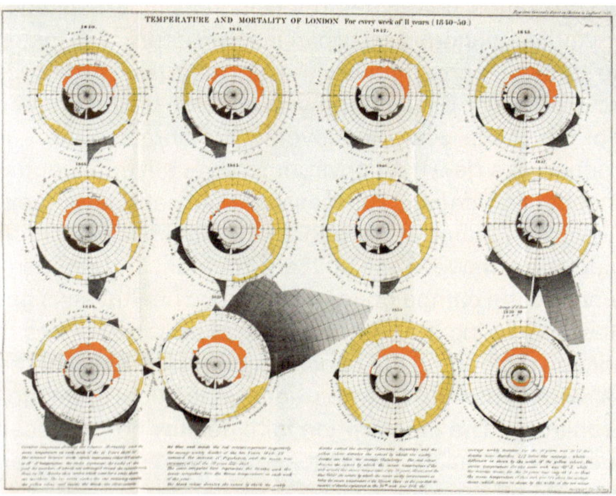

23 Daily cholera and diarrhea deaths in 1849, with meteorological data, from William Farr, *Report on the Mortality of Cholera in England*, 1852

24 Temperature and mortality in London, 1840–1850, chart from William Farr, *Report on the Mortality of Cholera in England*, 1852

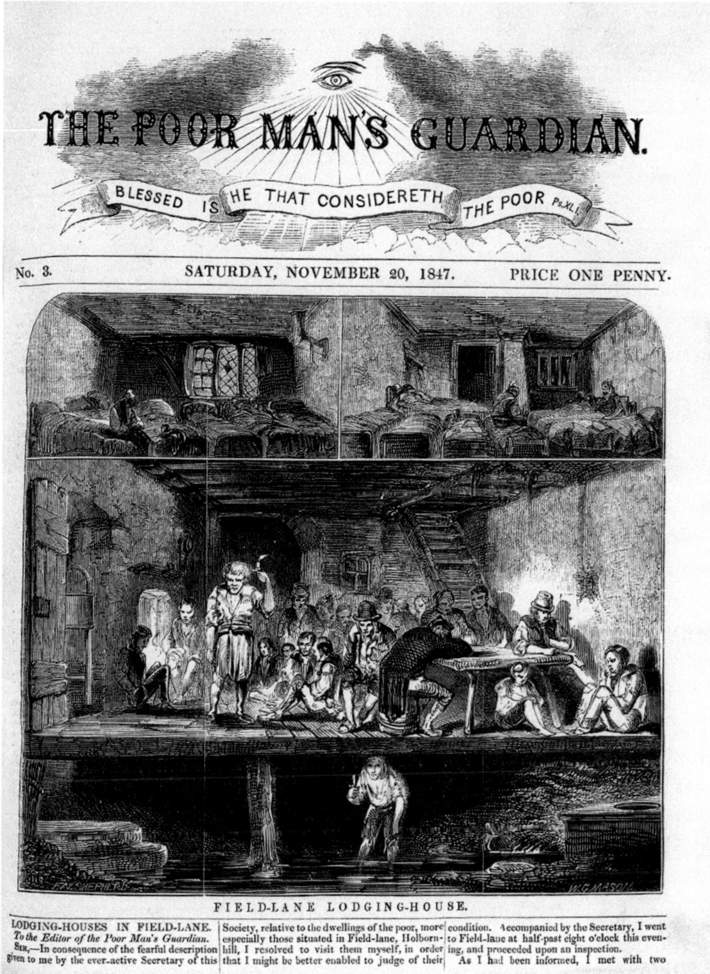

THE POOR MAN'S GUARDIAN.

BLESSED IS HE THAT CONSIDERETH THE POOR Ps. XLI.

No. 3. SATURDAY, NOVEMBER 20, 1847. PRICE ONE PENNY.

FIELD-LANE LODGING-HOUSE.

LODGING-HOUSES IN FIELD-LANE.

To the Editor of the Poor Man's Guardian.

Sir,—In consequence of the fearful description given to me by the ever-active Secretary of this Society, relative to the dwellings of the poor, more especially those situated in Field-lane, Holborn-hill, I resolved to visit them myself, in order that I might be better enabled to judge of their condition. Accompanied by the Secretary, I went to Field-lane at half-past eight o'clock this evening, and proceeded upon an inspection.

As I had been informed, I met with two

25 Illustration exposing unsanitary living conditions in Field Lane, London, from *The Poor Man's Guardian*, November 20, 1847

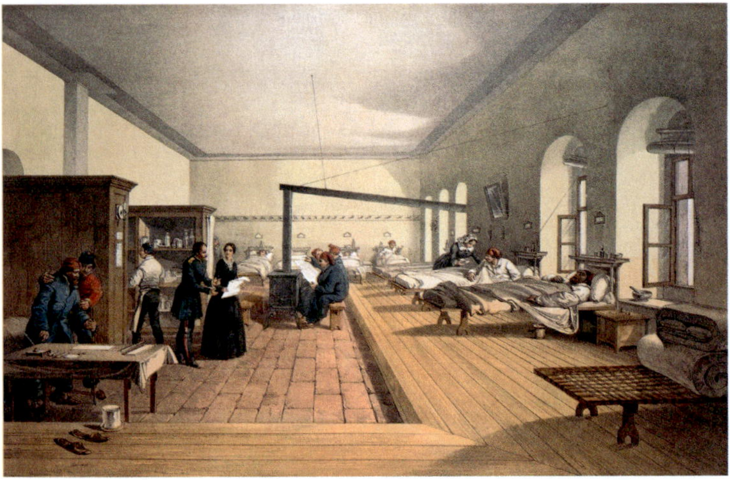

in building reform. [26] Her *Notes on Hospitals* of 1859 called for fresh water, continuous cleaning and dusting, ventilation, large windows, smooth floors without gaps and white walls (polished to be sealed, reveal dirt, and increase light levels), simple plans with few corners or moldings that could harbor dust, minimal utilitarian furniture, and no extraneous fabrics or decoration.[23] Her most famous book, *Notes on Nursing* of the same year, applied the same architectural prescription to "preserving the health of houses."[24] Each domestic space was treated both as a sick patient to be cured and as a medical facility for the sick. Taking care of buildings enabled buildings to take care of their inhabitants.

Nightingale, like Chadwick, didn't accept that epidemic disease was contagious, advocating instead the miasmatic theory. Her focus was the excremental "organic matter" attaching itself to every surface of the built environment, fouling the air and thereby provoking sickness in those breathing it. Nightingale's prescription was to develop systems whereby anything coming out of the human body passes through the building to the countryside via disposal systems that don't leave a trace on the

26 Edmund Walker, *Florence Nightingale at Scutari Hospital during the Crimean War*, lithograph (after William Simpson), 1856

building or city – starting with bandages, clothing, bedding, furniture, and the surfaces of rooms. The idea was to relentlessly clean the buildings and bodies, flood the space between them with health-inducing fresh air and light, and keep that space under constant surveillance. The blankness of a smooth wall surface from which all human traces have been removed allows the human to restore itself physically, but also mentally. Nightingale wrote extensively on the need to reduce noise and visual complexity to calm the nerves of patients so that the body could cure itself.

Nightingale argued that the role of the architect–nurse–doctor is not so much to provide hospitality to people as to construct an inhospitality to disease. The traditional house or hospital that cocoons humans in layers of their own excrement acts as a genuine "pest-house" in the sense of a home for disease. Yet in the miasma view, the building is not itself infected. Disease was not a thing moving in the world but an internal human response to its own toxic excretions. The healthy house is a machine for getting rid of excrement. Architecture was reimagined as a purification system, and the first thing to be removed, as in the opening chapter of *Notes on Hospitals*, is the "absurd" concept of contagious germs.

1 The dramatic effect was already described in 1815: "The solar microscope will magnify a single drop of the brightest water into a standing pool of many yards in diameter, wherein may be distinctly seen numerous tribes of animals, amusing themselves as larger animals are known to do in the ocean; some pursuing their prey with animated velocity, while others, having subdued it by superior force, are seen voraciously employed consuming the spoil. Thus is a wonderful microcosm displayed within the space of a fluid drop!" *The Critical Review; Or Annuals of Literature,* 1 (March, 1815): 269. Earlier encyclopedias describe the solar microscope projection of hundreds of vibrio in water that would be otherwise considered pure.

2 Letter of August 2, 1827, in Hermanvon Puckler-Müskau, *Tour in England, Ireland, and France, in the years 1826, 1827, 1828 & 1829 in a series of letters* (Philadelphia, PA: Carey, Lea, and Blahard, 1832), 172.

3 "The Microscope," *The Saturday Review* (March 2, 1833). The images were based on drawings published in Berlin by Christian Gottfried Ehrenberg in 1830.

4 Arthur Hassall, *A Microscopic Examination of the Water Supplied to the Inhabitants of London and the Suburban Districts* (London: Samuel Highley, 1850). As with the earlier images in *The Saturday Review*, they don't show an actual view through a microscope but place drawings of examples of a diversity of species seen through a microscope within a circle to convey the sense of such a view.

5 John Snow, "Doctor Snow's Report," in *Report on the Cholera Outbreak in the Parish of St. James, Westminster, during the Autumn of 1854 / Presented to the Vestry by the Cholera Inquiry Committee, July 1855* (London: J. Churchill, 1855), 97–120. Reverend Henry Whitehead, Snow's eventual partner in the interviews with neighbors, finally identified the first local case before the main outbreak, an infant whose diapers were washed in water that was emptied into what turned out to be an old leaking brick-lined cesspool only three feet from the well of the pump.

6 Five years earlier, Snow had already argued that cholera passes between people via their excrement, and therefore can be communicated by drinking water taken from rivers or wells contaminated by sewers, house drains, or leaking cesspools. John Snow, *On the Mode of Communicating Cholera* (London: John Churchill, 1849).

7 Arthur Hassall, "Report on the Microscopical Examination of the Blood and Excretions of Cholera Patients," in *Appendix to Report of the Committee for Scientific Inquiries in Relation to the Cholera-Epidemic of 1854* (London: George E. Eyre and William Spottiswoode, 1855), 289–93.

8 Hassall begins his report on the water samples by saying that the presence of microorganisms is the sign of impurity, rejecting the perception that the healthy human and what it consumes "teems with invisible and parasitical forms of life." Arthur Hassall, "Report on the Microscopical Examination of Different Waters (Principally Those Used in the Metropolis) During the Cholera Epidemic of 1845," in *Appendix to Report of the Committee for Scientific Inquiries*, 219.

9 Christian Gottfried Ehrenberg, *Ein Wort zur Zeit: Erfahrungen über die Pest im Orient und über verständige Vorkehrungen bei Pest-Ansteckung zur Nutzanwendung bei der Cholera* (Berlin: Mittler, 1831).

10 Christian Gottfried Ehrenberg, *Die Infusionsthierchen als vollkommene Organismen. Ein Blick in das tiefere organische Leben der Natur* (Leipzig: Voss, 1838). Ehrenberg even studied the active microbial life in Berlin construction sites, suggesting that it threatened to destabilize buildings. Mathias Grote, "Microbes Before Microbiology: Christian Gottfried Ehrenberg and Berlin's Infusoria," *Endeavour* 46, no. 100815 (2022).

11 Agostino Bassi, *Sui contagi in generale e specialiamente su quelli che affligono l'umana specie* (Lodi: Wilmat & Figli, 1844). Bassi argues that measles, syphilis, and the plague are caused by microrganisms.

12 Filippo Pacini, *Osservazioni microscopiche e deduzioni patalogiche sul cholera Asiatico* (Florence: Tipografia di Federigo Bencini, 1854).

13 Gian Piero Carboni, "The enigma of Pacini's *Vibrio cholerae* discovery," *Journal of Medical Microbiology* 70, no. 11 (2021). It was not until 1965 that Pacini was fully credited and the bacteria named *Vibrio cholerae Pacini.*

14 "The Condition of the Thames," *The Builder* 16, no. 854 (July 3, 1858): 449–50, 454.

15 Alexandre Jean Baptiste Parent-Duchâtelet, *Essai sur les cloaques ou égouts de la ville de Paris envisagés sous le rapport de l'hygiène* (Paris: Crevot, 1822). Parent-Duchâtelet presented a history of the "immense" changes made to the shape and infrastructure of ever-growing Paris since the fourteenth century in the ultimately unsuccessful attempt to control the human waste that provokes disease – including changing the level of the streets, the path of the Seine,

and the distribution of neighborhoods. He had prepared what he thought was the first complete map of the entire network of almost thirty-six kilometers of closed and open sewers. It was apparently too big and intricate to publish, but the book systematically documents the construction, flow, temperature, smell, discharge, method of cleaning, and policing of each part of it.

16 Parent-Duchâtelet was unsure that drinking polluted water produced disease but noted that many ancient and more recent figures believe that it did, including the surgeon Jacques-Rene Tenon's book on new hospital designs for Paris that called for the hospital for contagious disease be positioned downstream so that its waste water would not be consumed, *Mémoire sur les hôpitaux de Paris* (Paris: Pierres, 1788).

17 Villermé quickly assembled the statistics to show that infections and deaths impacted the laboring and itinerant poor the most and were "directly related to the poor conditions of their dwellings." The degree to which homes were confined, damp, dark, dirty, and unventilated spaces in narrow, dark, unairy, and unclean streets was "directly proportional" with the amount of disease. Louis-René Villermé, "Note sur les ravages du choléra morbus dans les maisons garnies de Paris depuis le 29 mars jusqu'au 1er août 1832," *Annales d'hygiène publique et de médecine légale,* 9 (1834): 385–409.

18 Kathryn J. Kudlck, "Learning from cholera: medical and social responses to the first great Paris epidemic in 1832," *Microbes and Infection* 1, no. 12 (1999): 1051–7.

19 John Haygarth, *An Inquiry How to Prevent the Small-pox. And Proceedings of a Society for Promoting Genneral Inoculation at Stated Periods, and Preventing the Natural Small-pox, in Chester* (London: J. Johnson, 1784), 86.

20 Even before adopting the model of contagion to explain the dispersal of small pox, Haygarth's architectural analysis of the health of Chester in 1774 that blamed the noxious air around the bodies and buildings of the poor concluded that a new specialized clean and well-ventilated building with fresh linens and separate apartments could be used to isolate fever patients. John Haygarth, "Observations on the Population and Diseases of Chester, in the Year 1774," *Philosophical Transactions* (January 1, 1778): 140.

21 John Ferriar, "Of the Prevention of Fevers in Great Towns," in *Medical Histories and Reflections* (London: Cadell & Davies, 1810), 213–47.

22 "In all offensive houses, I obliged the inhabitants to white-wash the whole," John Ferriar, "Epidemic Fever of 1789 and 1790," in *Medical Histories and Reflections*, 158.

23 Florence Nightingale, *Notes on Hospitals* (London: Longman, 1859), 15.

24 Florence Nightingale, *Notes on Nursing: What it is and What it is Not* (London: Harrison, 1859), 20.

1 Flasks used by Louis Pasteur for catching airborne microbes during his studies to refute the theory of spontaneous generation, 1860

8 THE BACTERIAL TURN

The idea that microbes are the agents of disease eventually infected the sanitary reformers who were trying to resist it. In fact, the reformers accelerated the idea before science caught up. Even Florence Nightingale, the fervent opponent of the idea of contagion, started calling for the disinfection of germs in the 1880s. By the time the germ theory of disease became dogma at the end of the century, architects and doctors had already shaped a modern architecture that supported it.

DUST

The main amphitheater of the Sorbonne was packed with the scientific and cultural elite on the evening of April 7, 1864 for a "*Soirée scientifique*." Louis Pasteur took to the lectern and echoed the late eighteenth-century form of popular entertainment by projecting live microscope images of the "highly agitated little cells, which rush back and forth" in a drop of water to which a little hay had been added.[1] But then he dramatically announced that the air of the theater was also full of such microorganisms. They were "passengers" in the dust steadily falling down onto the audience, their clothes, and every surface of the interior. Pasteur projected a microscope image of that dust, pointing to the "microscopic beings" in it, and therefore in every breath. The crowded audience was suddenly insignificant in relation to all the other occupants of the space, and vulnerable to them.

Pasteur's 1860 experiments, sampling dust with specially designed glass flasks containing highly filtered air and a sterile broth, had revealed that countless microorganisms are suspended within the air of any room – but much less in the air of the courtyards outside, even less in the countryside, and very few in "uninhabited regions" high in the Alps. **[1]** Symptomatically, the density went up in the alpine inn where Pasteur slept for one night – brought there, he thought, from all over the world by travelers like himself. Habitation in buildings and cities seemingly concentrated microbes. In the words of the lecturer, "the further one travels from inhabited regions, the fewer germs there are in the air ... Conversely, the further one ventures into inhabited regions, the greater the number."[2] These experiments became the basis for others to demonstrate that specific microbes cause disease.

Architectural spaces started to be visualized as microbial spaces. Pasteur's argument, and the germ theory of disease it supported, soon made its way into professional architectural journals. *The Builder* in London – whose editor, the architect George Godwin, had played a major role in pushing for sanitary reform since the 1840s – reported on the experiments of Pasteur in 1867, and a year later on follow-up work by Jules Lemaire, showing that the number of microbes in the air of a room is affected by the number of inhabitants. The Irish physicist John

Tyndall's 1870 paper "On Haze and Dust" became another key reference for architects in linking space and disease. It argued that all rooms in London – but especially the crowded rooms of the poor – were filled with microbes within the dust that might cause disease when absorbed by humans.[3] Tyndall eventually called the threat "bacterial clouds." He argued that microbes are not evenly distributed in interiors but float around in particular clusters as do clouds in the sky.[4] The question was how buildings could resist these formations rather than cultivate them. **[2]**

The longstanding sanitary campaign against dust because it was excrement fouling the air started to be rebranded as a campaign against the microbes living within it. Every element of the sanitary reform formula was reframed in terms of microbes. Personal and building hygiene protocols for cleaning bodies, buildings, toilets, and sewage systems were implemented to remove microbes. Whitewashing was necessary because lime is antimicrobial; ventilation because it reduces the density of microbes; fresh water because it is free of pathogens; and sunlight because it kills bacteria, as first demonstrated in 1877.[5] Foul smell, the very calling card of miasma, was now understood as

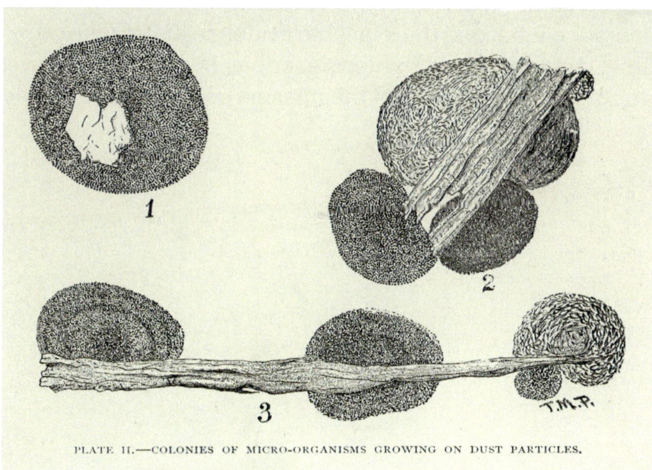

2 Colonies of microbes growing on dust particles, understood to cause disease, from T. Mitchell Prudden, *Dust and Its Dangers*, 1890

the smell of microbes at work, decomposing matter. Far from a threat to sanitary reformers dedicated to a healthier environment, microbiology was an accelerant to their project.

The germ paradigm didn't immediately take over in the scientific community. When Pasteur and Koch demonstrated that specific bacteria caused specific diseases, they were not believed by many scientists. The miasma theory still had strong advocates. During the extended debate, a hybrid of germ theory and miasma theory developed in medical, popular, and political discourse. This diplomatic compromise was possible because the respective architectural prescriptions were so similar. When John Snow had unsuccessfully argued that contagion occurs through a "poison communicated" through unclean water, that contagious element was in the very excrement targeted by his opponents. He also blamed the same suspects: crowding, lack of light, and poor hygiene of body and building. When bacteria finally entered the discourse as the likely active agents of disease, the microrganisms consolidated rather than disrupted the long-standing campaign to reform buildings and cities.

As Bruno Latour argued, sanitary reformers had actually propelled bacteria theory in the 1870s, not just absorbing it but accelerating it beyond the available evidence at the time.[6] In reverse, historian David Barnes describes how Pasteur actively contributed to the survival of the miasma paradigm as a member

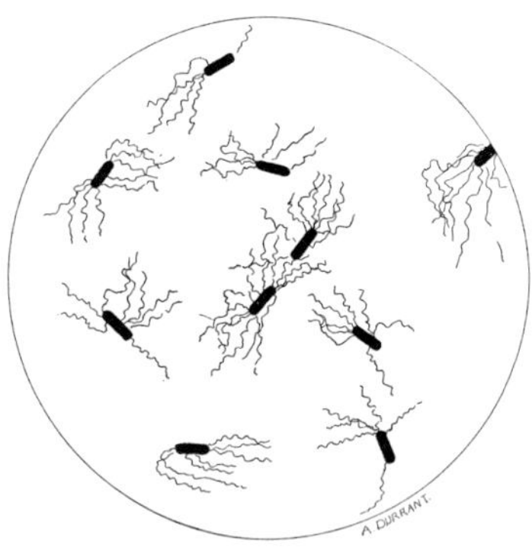

3 Bacilli of typhoid fever from Charles Singer, *A Short History of Medicine*, 1928

of the commission formed to analyze the Great Stink in Paris of 1880. A mixture of the contagion and miasma paradigms was useful to both doctrines. Outbreaks of typhoid fever, for example, were still blamed on miasma by doctors who paradoxically had already accepted the discovery of the bacteria that caused it by German pathologist Karl Eberth in 1880. **[3]** This elastic "sanitary-bacteriological synthesis," as Barnes puts it, meant that "the germ theory of disease changed everything and nothing at all."[7] Sanitary reform and bacteriology both gained momentum, with ambiguous symptoms. In the face of a crisis, people often held two theoretically incompatible ideas in their minds and deployed both strategically.

BUILDINGS UNDER THE MICROSCOPE

During this period of tactical compromise, the built environment was subjected to ever closer scrutiny for bacteria and fungi – from the air inside, below, and outside buildings, to the surfaces, crevices, cavities, plumbing, and building materials themselves. Buildings were the subject of laboratory study. Architecture became something to be seen through a microscope. Architectural magazines such as *The Builder* that had long reported for and against the germ theory of disease in relationship to the plague, cholera, typhoid fever, and tuberculosis increasingly adopted germ theory without debate and assigned a key role to architectural design. An unsigned 1880 article on "Health and the House-Builder," likely by the editor George Godwin, argued that architecture is an "intimate" part of the new "prophylactic" or preventive philosophy in medicine that isolates humans from the "living germs" that cause disease.[8] It asserted that cholera and tuberculosis are produced by specific germs a few years before Koch was credited with identifying them – a symptom of sanitary reformers pushing ahead of the science, as if willing some bacteria to be pathogens in order to preemptively counter them with design.[9]

There was a growing acknowledgment that microbes are everywhere in the built environment – in the air, surfaces, furniture, dust, materials, and plumbing of both "healthy" and "unhealthy" spaces. Detailed investigations were carried out by chemists, physiologists, and biologists across Europe into the density of microbes in the air and dust of buildings; comparisons of microbes in houses, schools, and hospitals; the effect on microbes of disinfecting building materials and interiors; and the microbes inside wallpaper, walls, plumbing, and materials like brick and timber. As the doctor Emile Vallin, one of the leading hygienists in Paris committed to germ theory, put it in 1883: "Show me your house and I will tell you what diseases threaten you."[10]

In an ever-denser exchange, international conferences, scientific publications, and professional magazines explored the relationships between microbes and buildings. University departments specialized in research on hygienic building, and microbes became part of architectural education in required classes on sanitary design.

The Leipzig-based biologist Rudolf Emmerich published extensive technical research on the diseases "whose breeding grounds are to be found in the home" in 1882.[11] He focused on the filler material traditionally put in the space between the ceiling and floor above for sound and thermal insulation in buildings throughout Germany and neighboring countries. He argued that this hidden matter, which was so close to domestic life, was ideal for breeding microbes. It was usually made out of fermenting organic matter from rubbish dumps, including the rubble of older potentially "sickly buildings," and thereby brought infectious bacteria and fungi into new buildings. The older buildings would have been cleansed and whitewashed after every illness and epidemic, but never the space between the floors where the "pathogenic germs" remained. Importing the materials of old buildings meant "domestic epidemics" could occur in even the apparently cleanest new buildings. The very act of cleaning buildings with water, Emmerich argued, paradoxically added further microbes as they seep through the inevitable cracks between floorboards. He remarkably speculated that it is hard to think of a better method of transferring the germs of epidemic disease "from century to century."[12]

Emmerich combined miasmatic and bacteriological arguments.[13] He obsessed about the excrement in the dumps where the filler was taken from, the fact that workers used it as a toilet during construction, and the excrement washed into it daily. In his view, the inside of building floors was more polluted than any soil near cesspools below or around buildings. Lifting floorboards exuded the "disgusting" smell of putrefaction. The space between floors had the ideal warmth, moisture, and nutrients to act as a "greenhouse" for microbes. Emmerich even suggested that the tuberculosis bacilli that Koch had only just identified a few months earlier could live within that environment as happily as within the human body. The goal of his research was to calculate how much nutrient the architectural filler provided to the microorganisms that spread infectious disease. In a newly constructed building in Leipzig, Emmerich calculated that the organic matter within the floors was equivalent to burying three thousand human corpses there. *Frankfurter Zeitung* could not resist this provocation and summarized the research into these "special breeding grounds for bacteria," inaccessible to traditional forms of cleaning, on its front page under the menacing title "A Source of Disease in our Homes."[14]

Techniques were developed to disinfect the material during construction, including a specialized oven with an internal zig zag intestine patented in 1883 by the Viennese architect Adolf Kessler for a kind of pasteurization of architecture.[15] **[4–5]** Eventually, the use of such material was banned, and it was removed from existing schools and hospitals. But an array of ovens, spray systems, and fumigation systems emerged to target microbes in every building element, furnishing, and space. **[6–8]**

Yet architectural and engineering discourse didn't simply demonize all microbes. It often pointed out the beneficial role played by many of them, particularly in sewage treatment and water filtration systems where "the great bulk of them are our greatest friends" since "bacteria remove bacteria."[16] The crucial role of microbes in sustaining the nitrogen cycle, and thereby so many lifecycles including the human, was first demonstrated in 1877 by the French agricultural chemists Jean-Jacques Schloesing and Achille Müntz. It became increasingly common to refer to bacteria as both friend and enemy. As the prominent sanitary reformer Dr. François de Chaumont wrote in an 1886 issue of *The Builder*:

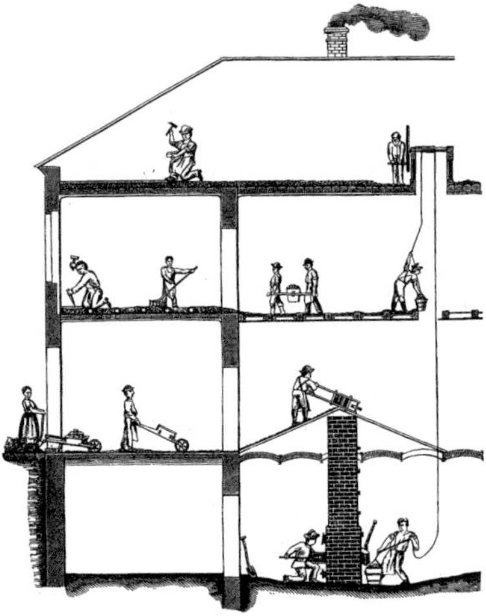

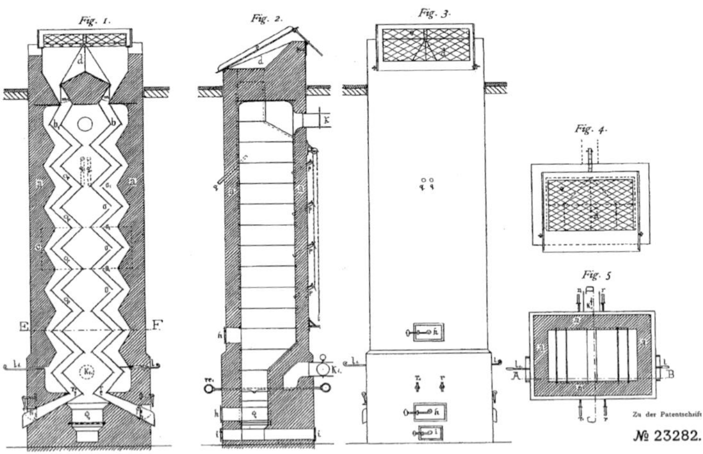

4 Adolf Kessler, oven for on-site disinfection of building materials, as illustrated in *Theorie und System der Deckenfüllmaterialien-Desinfection*, 1893

5 Adolf Kessler, 1883 patent drawing of on-site oven for disinfection of building rubble and filling material

6–7 Superheated steam apparatus for disinfecting walls and disinfection oven for furnishings presented at the Urban Hygiene Exhibition in Paris, from *La Nature*, 1886

8 Autoclave system of the chemist Auguste Trillat fumigating a house with formaldehyde vapor to "destroy all pathogenic germs," from *La Nature*, 1897

> We must thus look upon this bacterial or microbial underworld not as an utter enemy, but as a mighty agency for good or evil, as the case may be; we see that we could not exist without it, nor can we in some cases continue to exist in company with all of it. Our cue would seem to be to help the friendly microbes, and to fight those that are our foes.[17]

Our Secret Friends and Foes, a popular 1893 book by chemist and bacteriologist Percy Faraday Frankland, divided microorganisms into "useful" and "malignant."[18] **[9–10]** This double identity had already been implied in Pasteur's theatrical lecture of 1864. Having menaced the audience by saying that the dust they were breathing "sometimes" carries human sickness and death "in the form of typhus, cholera, yellow fever" – even though none of this had been confirmed yet – he said that to deprive water of the germs in dust is to deprive it of life itself:

> I have deprived it, and continue to deprive it, of the one thing it is not given to man to produce; I have deprived it of the germs floating in the air, I have deprived it of life itself, for life is the germ, and the germ is life.[19]

Pasteur shows a philosophical and empathetic tenderness to both water that needs microbes to have life, and microbes that

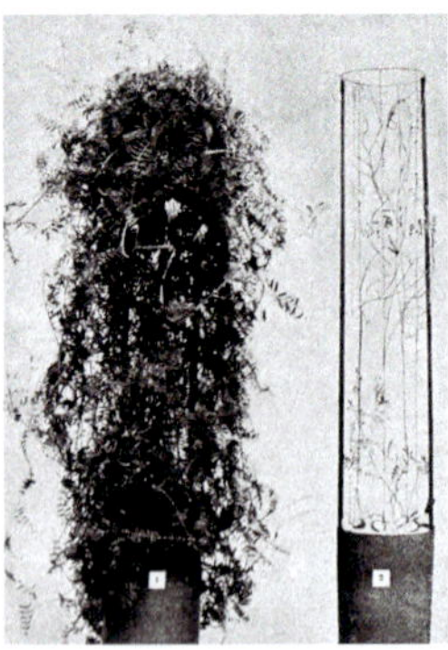

9 Image of plant with and without inoculation of nodule bacteria to illustrate bacterial friends, from Percy Faraday Frankland, *Our Secret Friends and Foes*, 1893

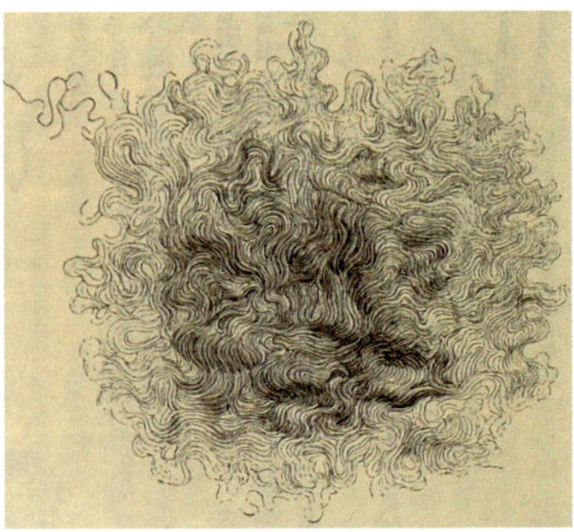

10 1886 image of anthrax colony by Carl Flügge, used to illustrate bacterial foes, from Percy Faraday Frankland, *Our Secret Friends and Foes*, 1893

need water to come to life. He had just developed a way to control microbes, cultivating some of them rather than others, using heat to kill the microbes that spoil wine and beer that had been fermented by other microbes, a technique then famously applied to milk. The work of pasteurization, as with all Pasteur's subsequent research, was to selectively edit microbial communities.

Architecture was on the frontlines of the battle with bacteria from the moment Pasteur and Koch demonstrated the link between specific bacteria and diseases like anthrax, tuberculosis, and cholera, and launched a kind of media campaign against these newly visible enemies. Koch exhibited the first photographs of pathogens in model laboratories within major health exhibitions in Berlin in 1882–1883 and London the following year. **[11–14]** The public could stare at deadly living bacteria through a series of microscopes. At a time in which tuberculosis was killing one in four people globally, and in big cities like Paris one in three, visitors could visualize the pathogen that was likely living within them. The exhibitions promoted a new set of protocols for the design of houses and cities.

The sanitary reform movement that had already dramatically transformed cities and buildings with sunlight, ventilation, plumbing, and hygiene started to be targeted on bacteria, and architecture became the first line of defense against the previously invisible enemy. Household manuals immediately framed their advice to women as the need "to destroy the germs of disease."[20] Disinfectants that had been developed for hospital operating theaters were rebranded to cleanse domestic spaces, and specialized equipment was developed to disinfect buildings, furniture, bedding.

Our Homes and How to Make them Healthy, a 1883 book prepared by group of sixteen doctors and architects for the International Health Exhibition in London – where Koch's pathogenic microbes were on show – seamlessly combined the architectural protocols formulated in terms of miasma with the new bacterial paradigm. One of the authors, the engineer Douglas Galton, who had worked closely with Florence Nightingale on the sanitary reform of hospitals, referred to the research of Koch and Pasteur. He accepted that the proposition that bacteria cause disease becomes "more probable day by day," but skeptically asked why

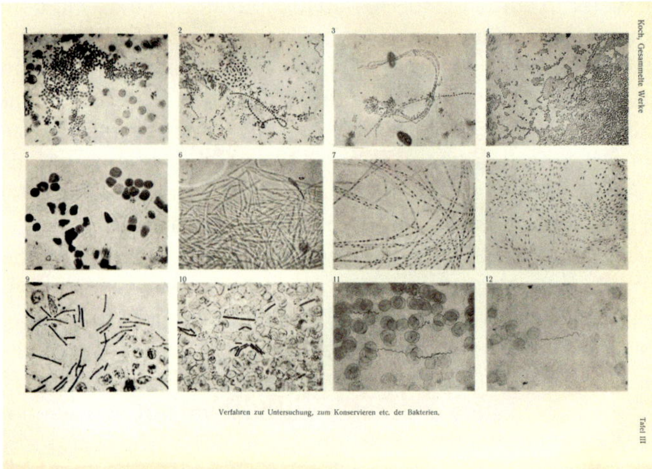

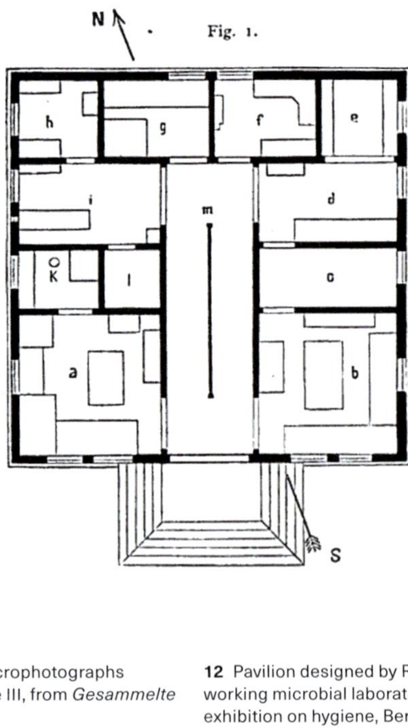

11 Robert Koch, first microphotographs of pathogens, 1877, Plate III, from *Gesammelte Werke*, 1912

12 Pavilion designed by Robert Koch for working microbial laboratorates at the German exhibition on hygiene, Berlin, 1882–1883

13 Cover of the official catalog of the German exhibition on hygiene, Berlin, 1882–1883

14 Cover of the official catalog of the International Health Exhibition, London, 1884

everyone exposed to the germs filling the air doesn't get sick.[21] The answer: it is the architecture that is sick. The Health Exhibition included a housing building divided in half between a sanitary and unsanitary design to make the point.

Over nine hundred pages long, the book systematically identifies each unhealthy architectural element: site, foundations, roof, floors, walls, windows, layout, corners, plumbing, joints, finishes, plaster, paint, wallpapers, carpets, curtains, blinds, ornament, moldings, cornices, mortar, absorbent surfaces, etc. The primary enemy remains the accumulation of the dust, dirt, and filth that harbors disease. Anything that attracts such build-up has to be removed in favor of smooth washable surfaces, regularly "cleansed" with whitewash. Decomposing traces of the human – microbially rich excrement from the gut, lungs, and the pores of the skin – are in the air and the water, steadily absorbed by the building or accumulating in its linings, ornament, unnecessary complexities, crevices, cavities, and coverings. In a self-conscious echo of Nightingale's formula but tinged with the looming threat of microbes, the house can only shelter the human by being cleansed of these unwanted human traces. The healthy house needs to be detached from the human in order to protect the human. This cleansing is mental, moral, and modern. The simplification of surfaces reduces stress on nerves, producing "healthy" decoration through an aesthetic sanitation of the visual field that rebuilds the morality of the occupant.

The very call to remove anything useless from architecture is treated as a form of sanitation, cleaning the eye, organization patterns, mechanical operations, and the mind. Sanitary reform was aesthetic reform, the production of a new visual order, and this order now signaled the control of invisible life.

AESTHETIC REFORM

In series of seven articles for *The Architect* in 1876, the British architect Edward William Godwin (who was about to be the architect of the houses of Oscar Wilde and James McNeill Whistler) described the recent design of his own London house in terms of an array of sanitary strategies: bare walls, light and airy rooms, ceilings with the same plaster as used in hospitals, whitewashed walls, no fabrics or molding to catch impurities, furniture reduced to the minimum and raised off the floor for ease of daily cleaning, removable seats on chairs to clean dust from crevices, minimum joints, no wallpaper, and small easy-to-clean carpets. The overall aesthetic effect was "simplicity," "economy," "freshness," and "cleanliness."[22] **[15]** The "White House" Godwin designed for Whistler in 1878 polemically took the unornamented sanitary aesthetic to the exterior with its façade of white bricks in shocking contrast to the buildings around it.[23] **[16]** Other British architects like Charles Voysey, Mackay Hugh Baillie-Scott, Margaret McDonald, and Charles Rennie Mackintosh would likewise develop a sanitary aesthetic based around smooth white surfaces.

Popular magazines relentlessly insisted on white as the basis of cleanliness in domestic management (on walls, countertops, towels, sheets, tablecloths, aprons, etc.). An 1899 article on "Household Art and the Microbe" by the feminist writer and home economics pioneer Helen Campbell in the magazine *House Beautiful* argued that "the microbe" has been the most active

15 Edwin Godwin, sanitary interior, from *The Building News*, November 17, 1876

16 Edwin Godwin, "White House" for James McNeill Whistler, 1877–1878 promoter of advanced interior design: "without him the best forms of interior finishing would still be but the dream of the too-progressive architect."[24]

In France, the Touring-Club de France led the way in cultivating an antimicrobial aesthetic on behalf of its membership of seventy-five thousand cyclists. One of the founders of the club was doctor E. P. Léon-Petit – an authority on the "hygienic treatment" of tuberculosis – who insisted that hotel rooms were hotspots for contagion, where members would inevitably pick up microbes deposited by previous unknown guests. He worked with the architect Gustave Rives on the design of a "*chambre hygienique*" to be installed in hotels. Their prototype "white room" – which contained sleeping, toilette, and toilet spaces – was displayed at world fairs, automobile shows, and congresses on tuberculosis, starting with 1900 Exposition Universelle in Paris – strategically placed just inside the entrance of the Palais de l'hygiène, next to the display of all known pathogenic microbes in the Salon Pasteur. [17] Seen by over a million visitors, it self-consciously looked "like a hospital room" with its complete medicinal arsenal against "terrible bacilli": Ripolin paint on all surfaces and furniture; no gaps, fabrics, cornice, or moldings; curved transitions between floors, walls, and ceiling; minimalist bent-wood and metal furniture; and large windows.[25] The club distributed a thirty-six-page manual on how to produce a hygienic

17 Second model "*chambre hygienique*," designed by Gustave Rives for the Touring-Club de France, exhibited at the 1902 Salon de l'Automobile Club de France, Grand Palais, Paris

interior complete with furniture, fittings, plumbing, water filtration, and regular disinfection. It reads like a manifesto for modern architecture – insisting on sunlight, air, ventilation, simplicity, and smooth washable whiteness without any gaps, protrusions, or ornament.[26]

The campaign was highly successful, with hotels applying the formula in rooms across France to earn the club's seal of approval. Yet the international jury of the Exposition Universelle already said the formula should be applied to all rooms of all houses, and republished most of the manual in its report.[27] The idea was immediately picked up by newspapers along with medical, family health, engineering, art, architecture, and popular magazines.[28] *L'art décoratif* argued that this "healthy, fresh, and happy" ensemble composed "without artistic pretension" was paradoxically a service to art in moving the sense of beauty from complex layers of ornament toward simplicity as a new form of decoration in its own right – an argument that would be much later associated with Adolf Loos and Le Corbusier.[29]

The hygienic imperative also had an immediate impact on architects in Vienna, where the public was already sensitized to bacterial life in houses. As put in "Bacterial Breeding Grounds in the Home," an 1892 article in the popular magazine *Wiener Illustrierte Zeitung*, the search for these "eerie, invisible guests" needs to start at home: "But where do they find these refuges from which they can repeatedly threaten humans? First of all, we must answer that they are found in human dwellings and their surroundings themselves."[30] A microscope image of the bacteria found in a crack in floorboards was offered to the public as a "weak image" of the much greater diversity of microorganisms it breeds. **[18]** Sealing and continuously cleaning the interior became a form of warfare.

Houses started to look like sanitized laboratories. The architect Leopold Bauer organized his design of Villa Kurz in his hometown of Järgendorf in 1902 on "the hygiene principle." The photograph of the kitchen shows it radiating polemical cleanliness. **[19]** In the same year, Otto Wagner, Bauer's teacher, complained in his *Moderne Architektur* about Vienna's "cultures of bacteria" (*Bakterienkulturen*).[31] The first edition of the book in 1896 already insisted that modern humans demand "maximum

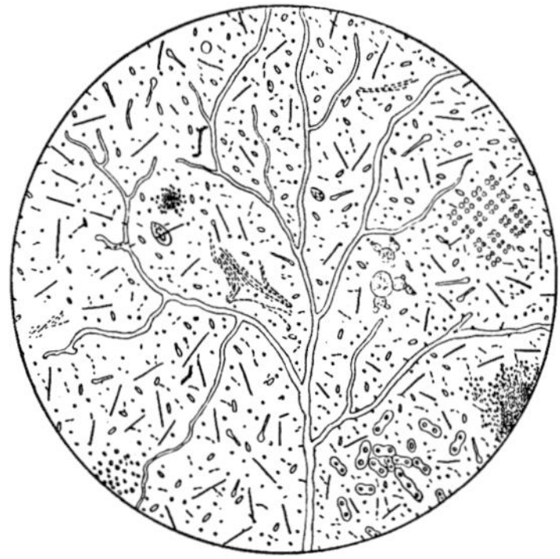

cleanliness" and all works without it have the "germ of death" (*Todeskeim*) within them.[32] Wagner called on architects to develop new art forms out of the latest hygiene techniques. He channeled sanitary reform mantras, saying that artistic effect is "inseparable from cleanliness," advocating for smooth white surfaces, systemic cleaning, fresh air, and sunlight. He argued that the design of a hotel room shouldn't be different from that of a hospital room. **[20]** Yet in a twist of fate, he still died of a bacterial infection in his own clean house before modern antibiotics were discovered.

Bauer's 1899 book on his own "modern" work equated utility and simplicity with cleanliness, physical exercise, and modern clothing. The "simple, clear, prismatic basic forms" with "large white wall surfaces" of vernacular houses on the island of Capri, Italy, were the model – along with English designs and attitudes to hygiene. In contrast, the excessively ornamental woodwork of the Austrian interior attracted dust and dirt that needed to be "repelled" by smooth, shiny, easy-to-clean surfaces in a continuous "war on dust" to be fought in the streets, exteriors, and interiors of buildings.[33] His two classmates at the German State Technical School in Brno ten years earlier, Josef Hoffmann and Adolf Loos, disagreed with each other about almost everything except the importance of the English hygienic model. Loos celebrated the leadership of English sanitary design in his 1898 newspaper article "Plumbers," arguing that that the

18 Illustration of bacteria between floorboards from "Bacterial Breeding Grounds in the Home," *Wiener Illustrierte Zeitung*, 1892

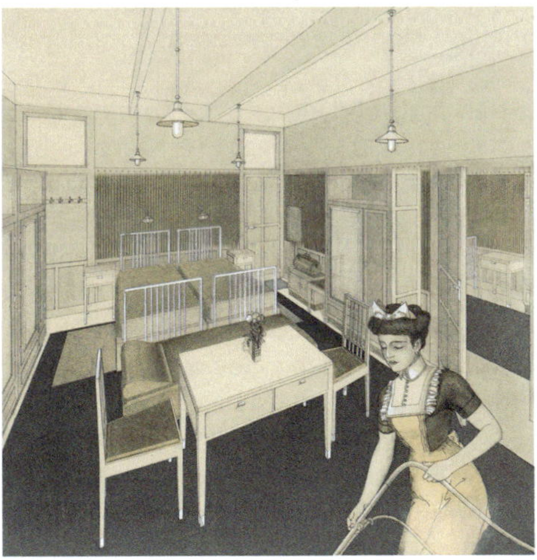

19 Leopold Bauer, hygienic kitchen of Villa Kurz, Jägerndorf, 1902

20 Otto Wagner, hygienic hotel room at Karlsplatz, Vienna, 1913

Austrian state should have a vested interest in cleanliness since only a people that use water as much as the English can hope to compete with them economically:

> The plumber is the pioneer of cleanliness. He is the state's chief craftsman, the quartermaster of culture, that is of today's prevailing culture. Every English washbasin with its spigot and drain is a marvel of progress.[34]

Likewise, a 1902 book by the German architect and critic Hermann Muthesius acknowledges the English fusion of sanitary and aesthetic motives, cleanliness and the look of cleanliness.[35] His 1904 book *Das englische Haus* concludes that "health" is what makes the English house a model, marked as much by its simplification of decoration as by its hygienic surfaces, materials, details, dimensions, light, ventilation, furnishings, sanitary fittings, and "veritable networks" of pipes.[36] The book predicts that hygiene will continue to transform architecture until the concepts of health and beauty "become identical." Muthesius would later argue that nothing is more important in a house than killing all the bacteria that breed within it by sealing all surfaces and using sunlight, ventilation, rigorous cleaning, and predominantly white surfaces.[37]

The Austrian critic and editor of *Dekorative Kunst*, Joseph August Lux, wrote in his 1905 survey of the Vienna-based architects he had published in the magazine *Die moderne Wohnung und ihre Ausstattung* (The modern dwelling and its equipment): "For economic, social and hygienic reasons, the new aesthetics that are essential for our apartment requires smooth and white plaster on walls and ceiling," and that ornament is itself a "disease."[38] The idea was to infuse cities with the sanitary aesthetic of white, where "cleanliness reigns."

The late eighteenth-century call for clean, smooth, simple, unornamented, white forms to counter disease by reformers like John Howard – that was itself a conscious echo of plague emergency architecture since the fourteenth century – were now implicitly understood as anti-bacterial.[39] The very word "modern" now implied the removal of microbes.

1 Louis Pasteur, "Conference faite aux 'Soirées scientifiques de la Sorbonne,' le 7 avril 1864," in *Oeuvres de Pasteur* vol. 2 (Paris: Masson, 1922), 332. Originally published in *Revue des cours scientifics* (April 23, 1864): 257–64.

2 Pasteur, "Conference faite aux 'Soirées scientifiques de la Sorbonne,' le 7 avril 1864," 345.

3 John Tyndall, "On Haze and Dust," *Nature* 1 (January 27, 1870): 339–42.

4 John Tyndall, "The Optical Deportment of the Atmosphere in Relation to the Phenomena of Putrefaction and Infection," *Proceedings of the Royal Society of London* 166 (1876): 39. Tyndall later claimed not having known that Ehrenberg had already imagined "the tiny creatures floating in the atmosphere as clouds" in 1838. Christian Gottfied Ehrenberg, *Die Infusionsthierchen als vollkommene Organism* (Leipzig: L. Voss, 1838), 525.

5 Arthur Downes, "Researches on the effect of light upon bacteria and other organisms," *Proceedings of the Royal Society of London* 26 (1877): 488–500.

6 Bruno Latour, *The Pasteurization of France* (Cambridge, MA: Harvard University Press, 1993).

7 David S. Barnes, *The Great Stink of Paris and the Nineteenth-Century Struggle Against Filth and Germs* (Baltimore, MD: Johns Hopkins, 2006), 2.

8 "Health and the House-Builder," *The Builder* 39 (October 16, 1880): 462–63.

9 Previously, architectural magazines were reporting on the generalized threat of germs rather than specific pathogens. An 1876 issue of *The Architect*, for example, reports on a recent speech that compares the relative dangers of "noxious germs" in the air and the water in causing contagious disease. C. W. Merrifield, "The Sanitary Administration of Towns," *The Architect* (September 16, 1876): 170. The original speech concluded with an extensive discussion of the uncertainty of how to counter the "living germs" in both water supply and sewage deposits when scientists have yet to identify which germs cause disease, noting that "it is not every germ that we need to be afraid of: the greater part of them, probably, are innoucus." "Address by C. W. Merrifield," in *Report on the Forty-Sixth Meeting of the British Association for the Advancement of Science* (London: John Murray, 1877), 217.

10 Emille Vallin, "La surveillance sanitaire des maisons," lecture at congress on the advancement of science in Rouen, published in *Revue d'hygiène et de police sanitaire*, 5 (1883): 627.

11 Rudolf Emmerich, "Die Verunreinigung der Zwischendecken unserer Wohnungen in ihren Beziehungen zu den Infectionskrankheiten," *Zeitschrift für Biologie*, 18 (1882): 253–382, 371.

12 Emmerich, "Die Verunreinigung," 317.

13 Emmerich's mentor, Max Joseph von Pettenkofer, had founded the science of hygiene, being the first university professor in the field in 1865 and was a prominent opponent of germ theory. He accepted the existence of bacteria but credited the environment for the transmission of disease more than the microorganism, particularly the polluted soil underneath buildings. In a sense, Emmerich's research found a new form of soil, even more polluted, inside the structure of buildings, endearing him to von Pettenkofer, who published it and promptly offered him a university position. On von Pettenkofer's influential role in using scientific analysis of the relationship between bodies and buildings to propel change in the built environment, see Didem Ekici, "The Physiology of the House: Modern Architecture and the Science of Hygiene," in *Healing Spaces, Modern Architecture, and the Body*, eds. Sarah Schrank and Didem Ekici (Abingdon: Routledge, 2017), 47–64.

14 M. Alsbero, "Ein Krankheitsherd in unseren Wohnungen," *Frankfurter Zeitung* (April 10, 1883): 1–2.

15 Adolf Kessler patented a system with a brick oven constructed on the building site to sterilize the incoming filler matter immediately before use so that all "harmful organisms and germs are thoroughly destroyed." Kessler's 1892 book on the invention repeats the need to sterilize building materials since they are inevitably "filled with countless germs, often with pathogens" that "are a source of infection for the whole household." Adolf Kessler, *Theorie und System der Deckenfüllmaterialien-Disinfektion* (1892), 25.

16 Arthur R. Leeds, "The Filtration of Water," *The Engineering Record* (May 23, 1891): 406.

17 François de Chaumont, "Sanitary Science and Preventive Medicine," *The Builder* (September 26, 1886): 468. Three years earlier, Chaumont had edited the latest edition of the two-volume *A Manual of Practical Hygiene* that extensively analyzed the health of the built environment. The 1883 edition repeated the skeptical miasma-inspired line of the 1878 edition that Chaumont edited after the death of the original author: "At present there seems no reason to think that common (putrefactive)

bacteria and *vibriones* are in themselves hurtful, but they indicate the existence of putrefactive organic matter, which is a danger," while adding the sentence: "But there may be, and probably are, forms of *bacteria* which are more dangerous." Edmund A. Parkes and Francois Chaumont, *A Manual of Practical Hygiene*, vol. 1 (New York: William Wood & Company, 1883), 71. The successive editions from 1864 to 1905 reflect the gradual bacterial turn.

18 Percy Faraday Frankland, *Our Secret Friends and Foes* (London: Society for the Promotion of Christian Knowledge, 1893). Likewise, *The Book on Practical and Healthy Homes*, published in Leipzig 1891, which symptomatically begins with a sixty-two page illustrated chapter on "our invisible enemies" – bacteria – giving detailed protocols for disinfecting buildings where germs "settle," embraces most microbes: "We can ultimately be indifferent to the millions and billions of non-pathogenic bacteria; they are everywhere, swirling in every speck of dust, and would soon find their way through even the cleanest false floor. From a hygienic point of view, we only need to ensure that pathogenic bacteria do not enter the false floor or, if they do, that they are destroyed." C. Falkenhorst, *Das Buch von der gesunden und praktischen Wohnung* (Leipzig: Ernst Keil, 1891).

19 Pasteur, "Conference faite aux 'Soirées scientifiques de la Sorbonne,' le 7 avril 1864," 342.

20 Selina Cook, "*Mothers and daughters. A manual of hygiene for women and the Household*," (New York, Fowler & Wells, 1884), 71.

21 Douglas Galton, "Warming and Ventilation," in *Our Homes, and how to Make Them Healthy*, ed. Shirley Forster Murphy (London: Cassell, 1883), 494. Galton was an expert in the sanitary reform of hospitals who had worked closely with Florence Nightingale.

22 Richard W. Hayes, "The Aesthetic Interior as Incubator of Health and Well-Being," *Architectural History*, no. 60 (2017): 277–301.

23 The original design in white bricks without paneling or ornamentation was rejected by the Metropolitan Board of Works as "like a dead-house" until Godwin added some minimal abstracted ornament. E. W. Godwin, "The Designing of Studios," talk at the Architectural Association, published in *The Architect* (March 8, 1879): 146.

24 Helen Campbell, "Household Art and the Microbe," *House Beautiful* 6, no. 5 (October 1899): 218–19. "Enter the microbe. Is he a modern invention purely, or has he been with us since creation ended its work and man began his? ... His real discovery waited the microscope, the biologist, the chemist, the modern physician equipped with forms of learning and with appliances of healing that would have sent him to the stake three hundred years ago. In the mean time the microbe, unknown and thus in undisputed possession, led a career of phenomenal activity, all civilized life being under absolute if unconscious submission to his dominion, and arranged for his special delight and perpetual reproduction.... Where beauty at its highest dwells, he has no place."

25 "Boldly, the Touring-Club has exposed something still unheard of in France: a hotel room that looks like a hospital room. It is in the hospital that the rules of hygiene are best practiced ... never, at any price, rugs fixed with nails or screws! They are a paradise for bacteria. No more of that. No fabric on the walls; it would absorb odors as well as microbes and retain them. Ugh! No wallpaper. Under its inevitable blisters, terrible bacilli would beat the drum and rally, ready to pounce on the unfortunate traveler. On the walls, paint, whether with whitewash or oil. And the paint clear, white, so you can easily follow the steps of a bug if by chance it sneaks into the hygienic nest where it must never penetrate." Pierre Giffard, "La Chambre Blanche," *Revue Mensuelle de Touring Club de France* (September 1900): 385–87.

26 *Type de chambre d'hôtel – hygiénique* (Paris: Touring-Club de France, 1900). The formula basically transposed Léon-Petit's book describing tuberculosis sanatoria design to the formula for a hotel room. E. P. Léon-Petit, *Le Phtisique et Son Traitement Hygienique* (Paris: Félix Alcan, 1895). It also echoes Léon-Petit's recommendation for the room of a tuberculosis patient at home: "The ideal of the patient's room would be a vast cell with bare, smooth walls and sparse furniture, devoid of those charming but useless ornaments that make any disinfection impossible." E. P. Léon-Petit, "Les Convulsions de l'enfance," *L'Hygiène usuelle: organe médical de la famille* 4, no. 7 (April 1, 1898): 101.

27 When reprinting the protocol in its own report, the Exposition jury noted that the Touring-Club protocol for hygienic hotel rooms could be "a kind of code or manual" for guiding not just the bedroom and bathroom of houses but all spaces. See "Chambre et cabinet de toilette hygiéniques pour les hotels, d'après le Touring-Club," in *Rapports du Jury*

International, Troisime Partie – Groupe XVI (Paris: Imprimerie Nationale, 1900), 321–28.

28 The detailed formula was widely discussed in medical publications after Gustave Rives presented it at the Tenth International Congress on Hygiene and Demography in Paris in August 1900. Gustave Rives, "La Chambre d'hótel au point de vue de l'hygiène," in *Xe Congrès International D'Hygiène et de Démographie a Paris en 1900* (Paris: Masson, 1900), 348–60.

29 A. T., "Chronique," *L'art décoratif* 25 (October 1900): 41. The Touring-Club's campaign to reform hotels was understood as a simultaneously medical and aesthetic project to ultimately transform all spaces. At the end of 1903, the Touring-Club completed its conversion of a Paris building into its own headquarters, including an exhibition space to permanently display model hygienic rooms, installations, and furniture. In fact, the whole building was renovated according to the same principles. Gustave Rives removed many internal walls to admit "air, light, life." All hanging, molding and ornament was removed and every surface from cellar to attic (except the striped marble around the grand stairs) was "coated with a uniformly white, glossy paint." This "immaculate shade" of white was portrayed as producing a "crisp," "simple," "fresh, healthy, and cheerful overall effect." The office of the club president was symbolically "all white, quite simple – too simple perhaps ... sacrificed to Ripolin." G. Davin de Champolos, "Notre nouveau domicile," *Revue Mensuelle de Touring Club de France* (February 1904): 49–51. Popular magazines like *Le Monde illustré* referred to the "immaculately white tone" of the building.

30 "Brutstätten der Bakterien im Haus," *Wiener Illustrierte Zeitung*, no. 2564 (August 20, 1892): 215–16.

31 Otto Wagner, *Moderne Architektur: seinen Schülern ein Führer auf diesem Kunstgebiete* (Vienna: Verlag von Anton Schroll & Co., 1902), 160.

32 Wagner, *Moderne Architektur* (1896 edition), 95.

33 Leopold Bauer, *Verschiedene Skizzen, Entwürfe und Studien. Ein Beitrag zum Verständnis unserer modernen Bestrebungen in der Baukunst* (Vienna: Verlag von Anton Schroll & Co., 1899), 24.

34 Adolf Loos, "Die Plumber," *Neue Freie Press* (July 17, 1898). Translated by Jane O. Newman and John H. Smith in *Spoken into the Void* (Cambridge, MA: MIT Press, 1982), 49.

35 Hermann Muthesius, *Stilarchitektur und Baukunst : Wandlungen der Architektur im XIX. Jahrhundert und ihr heutiger Standpunkt* (Mülheim: K. Schimmelpfeng, 1902), 52. Translated by Stanford Anderson as *Style-Architecture and Building-Art* (Los Angeles: Getty, 1994), 80.

36 Hermann Muthesius, *Das englische Haus* (1904). Translated by Dennis Sharp as *The English House* (New York: Rizzoli, 1979).

37 Hermann Muthesius, *Wie baue ich mein Haus?* (Munich: F. Bruckmann, 1919).

38 Joseph August Lux, *Die moderne Wohnung und ihre Ausstattung* (Vienna: Vienna Verlag, 1905), 31. Lux presented all the arguments for hygienic interiors: white walls, lack of decoration as the new decoration, all bedrooms treated as sick rooms, cleaning protocols, etc.

39 "From a regard to the health of the patients, I wish to see plain white walls in hospitals, and no article of ornamental furniture introduced." John Howard, *An Account of the Principal Lazarettos in Europe: With Various Papers Relative to the Plague, Together with Further Observations on Some Foreign Prisons and Hospitals, and Additional Remarks on the Present State of Those in Great Britain and Ireland* (London: J. Johnson, C. Dilly and T. Cadell, 1791), 57.

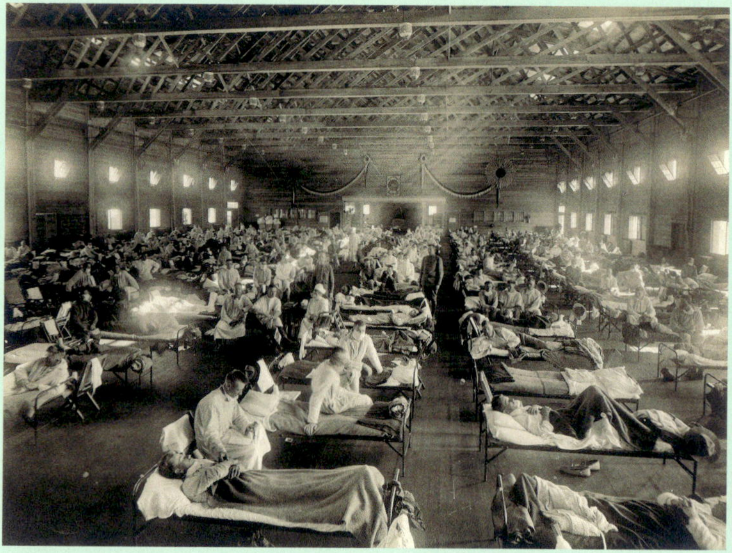

1 Influenza patients at Camp Funston, Fort Riley, Kansas, during the early days of the 1918–1919 flu pandemic

Microbial pandemics continued to ravage the twentieth century, particularly affecting marginalized communities – the laboring urban poor living in crowded, unventilated, humid interiors, without healthcare – who were further marginalized by the diseases. The first half of the twentieth century was dominated by tuberculosis, responsible for one in four deaths globally. But TB was not alone. The 1918 flu pandemic is estimated to have killed between fifty to one hundred million people globally, and more people more quickly than any other disease in history. Yet it was largely forgotten until COVID-19. Like all pandemics, COVID made visible the invisible city – not just the invisible urbanism of hyper-social microorganisms but the invisible urbanism of inequities, hidden workers, and uneven access to care and empathy.

HOUSEHOLD BACTERIOLOGY

If all architecture produces disease, architects have paradoxically always presented their work as healthy, both a form of prevention and cure. Vitruvius devoted a large part of his *Ten Books on Architecture* to the question of health, giving detailed instructions on how to determine the healthiness of a proposed site for a city by returning to the ancient method of sacrificing an animal that lives there and inspecting its liver to make sure it is "sound and firm." He discusses Hippocrates' theory of the four humors, and emphasizes the direction of the winds and the sun in the setting and design of a building. Too much of one humor enfeebles and "impairs the fluids of the human body."[1] In reverse, he argued that those who are unwell can be cured through design, rebuilding the system of those "exhausted by disease," including tuberculosis.[2]

Paradigms of health evolve, and each paradigm implies a different architecture and a different politics. Cities represent a kind of accumulation of theories of disease from ancient times to the present. Disease is the real designer of cities. If the microbial pandemics of the nineteenth century brought us the infrastructure we still have today in our cities – clean water and sewage systems, urban parks, etc. – tuberculosis revolutionized architecture, particularly domestic architecture. As the American doctor and specialist in the disease William Osler put it in 1904, "The problem of tuberculosis is a home problem."[3] Domestic space is a theater for the staging of contagion:

> In an immense proportion of all cases the scene of the drama is the home; on its stage the acts are played, whether to the happy issue of a recovery or the dark ending of a tragedy.... The battlefield of tuberculosis is not in the hospitals or in the sanitaria but in the homes, where practically the disease is born and bred.[4]

Osler had been committed to the microbial theory of tuberculosis ever since Robert Koch's discovery of the bacillus in 1882, and became increasingly convinced that the home itself was a huge factor in its spread and effects. **[5]** For early-stage patients, he recommended the "open air" cure offered by sanatoria, particularly

2 Naval Training Station, San Francisco, 1918: Drill Hall repurposed as emergency influenza ward

3 5500-bed COVID-19 field hospital at the IFEMA Madrid, March 22, 2020
4 COVID-19 makeshift hospital inside the Belgrade Fair, Serbia, March 24, 2020

the one run by his friend Dr. Edward Trudeau at Saranac Lake in the Adirondack Mountains. For those who could not "take advantage" of Trudeau's sanatorium, Osler wanted to bring its logic to urban dwellings, changing the domestic space of patients through a system of visiting district nurses. An "intelligent woman" would give instructions on how to handle the patient's sputum to avoid infecting other members of the household, along with advice on diet; rest in the sun and air on porches, balconies, or the yard during much of the day (offering rolling furniture provided by a charity); and sleeping with the windows open.[5]

Osler was building on an established practice. Already in 1859, visiting nurses in England, following Florence Nightingale's

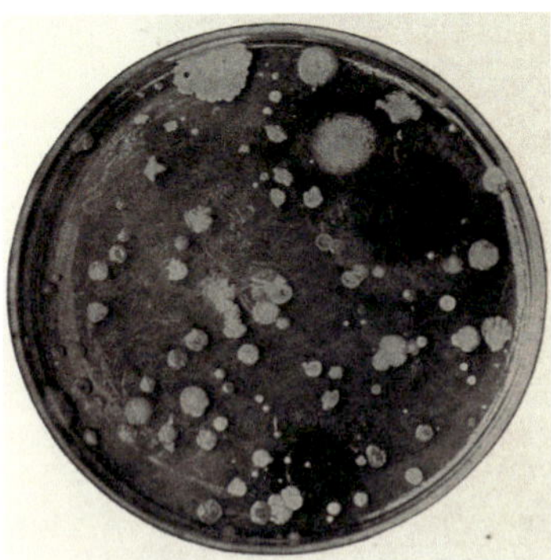

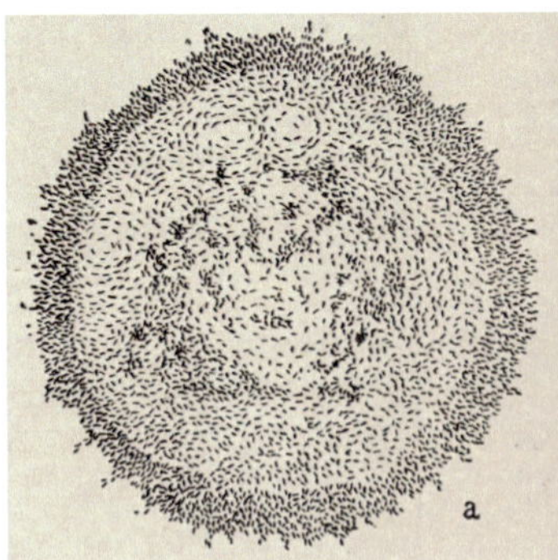

5 Robert Koch looking into the microscope, 1900

6 Bacteria grown in petri dish immediately after bed making, illustration from S. Maria Elliott, *Household Bacteriology*, 1904

formulas, recommended removing wallpaper and draperies from a sick person's room, whitewashing the walls, scrubbing the floors, opening the windows, and replacing old furniture with just a clean bed and simple chair.[6] Nurses were modernizing interiors before modern architects were born. By the turn of the century, the house was a health machine where microbes were increasingly the focus – a domestic sanatorium.

If the house was a battlefield, the woman became a combination of military commander, scientist, and doctor. The house was her laboratory, kept scrupulously clean of dirt, dust, and, above all, germs. Women were advised by home economics founders like scientists Ellen Richards and Sophronia Maria Elliott to leave out

7 Colony of rod-shaped bacilli seen in dust garden, from *The House Beautiful*, April 1905

8 Lysol advertisement, from *The Ladies' Home Journal*, September 1922

petri dishes to see if any bacteria had survived their cleaning routines. **[6–7]** With these exercises in "household bacteriology," a magnifying glass or preferably a microscope was recommended as a standard domestic tool. Eliott's 1904 book and associated articles in *House Beautiful* provided images of bacterial and fungal colonies so the housewife–bacteriologist knew what to look for.[7] Pathogens of tuberculosis and typhoid fever are highlighted as "murderers" within the millions of otherwise harmless, or even "helpful" microbes.

From the late 1880s, countless advertisements in popular magazines featured multiple ways of killing germs in homes with chemicals developed for hospitals, such as Lysol, sometimes depicting microscopes, petri dishes, and the dreaded microbes themselves.[8] **[8]** The microscope was the ultimate way to see a building, and the housewife was armed with a new arsenal of chemicals, materials, and technologies. Nightingale's argument that houses should use the same sanitary strategies as a hospital was realized.

THE ARCHITECTURE OF ESCAPE

From the mid-nineteenth century, a new architectural typology emerged: the sanatorium. Sanatoria were located away from cities in the mountains, seaside, and countryside, where patients spent most of the day outdoors. The paradoxical idea of the

9 Advertisement for Dr. Brehmer's sanatorium, Görbersdorf, from *Über Land und Meer: Allgemeine illustrierte Zeitung,* October, 1879

sanatorium is that it is a building meant to be minimally occupied, since buildings themselves incubate and exacerbate diseases. It is an architecture to escape architecture.

The first sanatorium for open-air treatment was the Heilanstalt für Lungenkranke (Healing Place for the Lung-Sick) established by doctor Hermann Brehmer in Görbersdorf, Silesia (present-day Poland) in 1854. **[9]** He had suffered from tuberculosis while a student of botany and claimed to have recovered in the Himalayas. This made him believe in "immune places," where tuberculosis did not exist and where patients with the disease could be cured with altitude, fresh air, exercise, and nutrition.[9] Returning to Berlin, he switched to medicine and wrote the controversial thesis *Tuberculosis primis in stadiis semper curibalibus* (Tuberculosis is always curable in the early phases) in 1853, based on the observations of pathologist Karl von Rokitansky that healed tubercles were found in 90 percent of all autopsies.[10] In 1857 Brehmer published the book *Die chronische Lungenschwindsucht und Tuberkulose der Lunge* (The laws of healing of chronic tuberculosis of the lungs), which was largely ignored, except for a negative review in a Viennese medical journal.[11] The idea that TB could be cured was anathema at the time.

There is no evidence that Brehmer knew about George Bodington, a country doctor in England who had already advocated a regime of open air, exercise, and nutrition in 1836. Bodington

10 George Bodington, "White House" for the treatment of TB, Sutton Coldfield criticized doctors for thinking there was no cure and for requiring patients to remain in rooms closed off from the supposedly bad air outside, forced to "breathe over and again the same foul air contaminated with the diseased effluvia of their own persons."[12] He argued that urban dwellings only foster and accelerate the disease. He rented a three-story country house in the small town of Sutton Coldfield, which he called the "White House," **[10]** for treating tuberculosis patients, taking advantage of the "dryness, mildness, and purity of the air":

> To live in and breathe freely the open air, without being deterred by the wind or weather, is one important and essential remedy in arresting its progress; – one about which there appears to have generally prevailed, a groundless alarm lest the consumptive patient should take cold.[13]

Bodington's 1840 book documented the case histories of a number of successfully cured patients in his establishment. Nevertheless, the leading medical journal *The Lancet* sarcastically dismissed it, writing that it was not even worth "expending any portion of our critical wrath on his crude ideas and unsupported assertions."[14] *The British and Foreign Medical Review* was equally scathing, accusing Bodington of "utter ignorance of the pathology, therapeutics and the English language."[15] The preferred treatment at the time was confinement in closed rooms, bloodletting, leeches, emetics, purgatives, and mercury-based medications – methods which Bodington claimed were weakening patients and killing far more than they were curing. Discouraged by the reviews, Bodington abandoned the field of tuberculosis treatment and opened an asylum for the mentally ill, but still sent his book to the University of Erlangen in Bavaria in 1843 and was awarded a doctorate in medicine. He was only retroactively recognized by *The Lancet* for anticipating "by many years the modern views of the treatment of phthisis" in his obituary in 1882.[16]
In retrospect, the vehement reaction of the British medical establishment is surprising. Fresh air, diet, and exercise are all crucial elements in the ancient Greek miasma theory that remained a dominant paradigm in the nineteenth century. The Greco-Roman physician Claudius Galen, who elaborated Hippocrates' founda-

tional theory of bad air, was already prescribing dry, high-altitude, fresh air for tuberculosis in the second century, and Ibn Sina (Avicenna) claimed to have cured consumption that way in the eleventh century. The ancient Indian Vedas of around 1500 BCE also gave the same advice and described the disease as infectious. Even within England, Bodington was echoing the much-read doctor Thomas Sydenham, who argued in the mid-seventeenth century that tuberculosis was curable with exercise in the open air and well-aired beds at night.[17] A number of eighteenth-century doctors had similarly prescribed the "air-bath," but most nineteenth-century English doctors were convinced that the problem was "hereditary," albeit exacerbated by the environmental conditions of the industrial city.

Tuberculosis was so endemic in the mid-nineteenth century that it was paradoxically treated as a fact of life rather than a disease that could be cured. Edwin Chadwick's massive report on the effect of the built environment on the health of the laboring poor in 1842 recognized the effect of buildings on tuberculosis but consciously focused on epidemics like typhus and cholera – rather than "the mass slaughter" by tuberculosis which was responsible for around a third of all deaths in England at the time.[18] There was a kind of deep-seated fatalism about the disease.

Benjamin Ward Richardson, who was a physcian in the Royal Infirmary for Diseases of the Chest in 1856, blamed buildings for both producing the disease and killing those with it. He prescribed the outdoors and exercise, opening up rooms, sleeping with the windows open, minimal furniture in the bedroom, and no one other than the patient in the room. He published the prescription as a set of rules in *Sanitary Review and Journal of Public Health,* the journal he had recently founded, and then as a book on "the hygienic treatment":

> In a cozy room the consumptive is bound never to live, nor in any one room indeed for great lengths of time. So long as he is able to be out of doors, he is in his best and safest home. In the fields, on the hills, wherever the fresh air vivifies, where plants look most vigorous, and animals frisk about in the joy of health, the consumptive draw in his choicest medicine, there dissolve and throw off most freely, the germs

of his disease, and there repair most easily the tissues he has lost.[19]

For Richardson, the combination of outdoor life and indoor ventilation offered both cure and prevention. He cited a 1829 paper by an American doctor making similar recommendations and referred to Bodington's book in admiration. Symptomatically, it is here that he argues that the prehistoric move of humans indoors is the very source of disease:

> Nomadic tribes, living mainly out of doors, or covering themselves in from the rain and wind in canvas tents, take and require but little care in regard to ventilation, since they interfere not with atmospheric laws. But when men begin to erect stone walls, to hedge themselves in from the atmosphere with impermeable barriers, and to pollute their confined dwellings with their own emanations, the matter is reversed. Supreme nature is defied, and the defiants pay the forfeit always visited on such delinquency.[20]

Having diagnosed the sickness of the interior, the doctor becomes a kind of architect that treats buildings. Richardson goes on to make a lengthy analysis of the extended history of ventilation in buildings, including recent mechanical systems, but ultimately

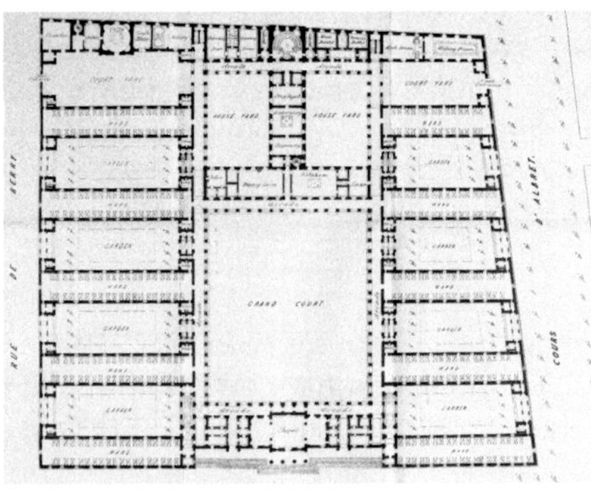

11 The perforated plan of the highly ventilated eighteenth-century Bordeaux Hospital, a model for air and light for Dr. Richardson

endorses the "natural" principal "to admit air into dwellings as freely as light" with large openings. He takes the model of hospital wards with large open windows on both sides and transfers it to the house.[21] [11] The interior has to be modernized to open to the exterior. The best treatment for TB is to escape the house, but a new kind of house is imagined that already offers escape. The sanatorium type combines escape from the city and a new architecture of escape.

THE SANATORIUM MOVEMENT

Unlike Bodington in England, Brehmer seemed to be strengthened by the skepticism of the medical establishment in Germany. He started his practice in the mountains of Görbersdorf, where his sister-in-law, Marianna von Colomb – a physician with whom he had collaborated on some publications – had been running a small hydropathic spa in the area since 1849 based on the Vinzenz Priessnitz hydrotherapy method. [12] Brehmer adopted the method as part of his therapeutic regime. [13] At first, he had only a couple of TB patients who lodged in the village, but over time he developed a following and a few sympathetic doctors sent him patients. After treating around twenty of them, he took over the existing spa building in 1859 and opened a sanatorium through the support of the celebrated naturalist and explorer Alexander von Humboldt, who was a cousin of Marianna von Colomb, as well as the scientist and professor of medicine Johan Lucas Schöenlein, who had coined the word "tuberculosis" in 1839. Humboldt was also convinced that tuberculosis didn't happen in high altitude and had praised Brehmer's book, writing on June 26, 1857:

> You were able to describe from the perspective of geography and natural history how the composition of the ground, the air, and style of life influence the pathological states as well as the interactions of so many forces to be given account of in complex organisms. Your work, which I had the pleasure of pointing out to my learned friend Schöenlein, has the additional quality – rare today in medical writings – of a charming quality of exposition and description.[22]

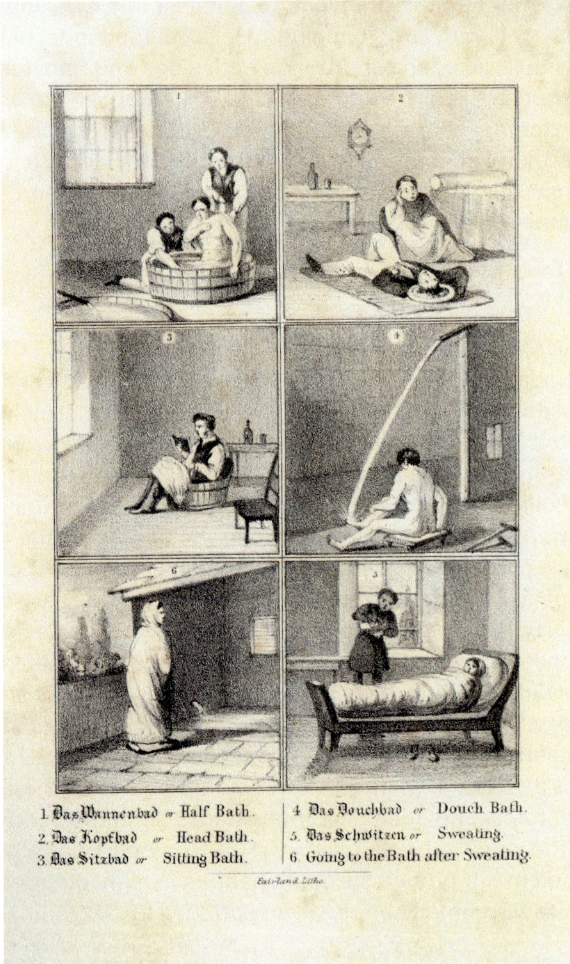

12 Frontispiece of R. T. Claridge, *Hydropathy as Practiced by Vincent Priessnitz at Grefenberg, Silesia, Austria*, 1842

13 Hydrotherapy at the sanatorium *Lebendige Kraft*, full body wrap by Dr. Maximilian Bircher-Brenner, Zurich, 1910

14 Dr. Brehmer's 1862 sanatorium building in Görbersdorf

Brehmer built a substantial *Kurhaus* (cure house) in 1862, designed by the Hanover-based architect Edwin Oppler. [14] It was a neo-Gothic building with well-ventilated rooms opening onto balconies, shafts to remove foul air, and eventually a system to change the air five times an hour in the dining room. Each patient had their own room and there were no carpets to attract dust. There was also a series of pavilions located in the 120-hectare forested property through which patients had to ascend a steep three hundred meters each day to receive a thirty-second ice-cold forest shower (*die Walddusche*) from water blasting down from five meters above them – supervised by Brehmer in case there were objections to the freezing water. [15] By 1869 the sanatorium had treated 958 patients, reporting that less than 5 percent of them had died there. As its reputation grew it kept expanding, with a second *Kurhaus* wing added in 1878, enabling 330 patients to be in residence.

One of Brehmer's patients in 1868, Dr. Peter Dettweiler, who had contracted tuberculosis as a surgeon in the army, became his assistant after recovering in Görbersdorf. In 1876 Dettweiler opened his own sanatorium, Heilanstalt Falkenstein,

15 Dr. Brehmer's sanatorium and mountainside estate

16 Dr. Dettweiler's Falkenstein sanatorium, 1875, colored wood engraving after a drawing by J. J. Kirchner

17 *Liegehallen* in Dettweiler's Falkenstein sanatorium

a large five-story building made of white stone and plaster facing southwest to catch the sun in the Tanus Mountains, near Frankfurt am Main. [16] Dettweiler was less committed to the idea of altitude and shifted the emphasis from strenuous exercise to light exercise, rest, diet, sun, and the air. Treatment was centered on resting chaises, specially designed by Dettweiler, where patients lay most of the day side-by-side, summer and winter, in *Liegehallen* – open-air porches on the building with glass sides for shelter and pavilions on the grounds that could revolve, with flaps to block the wind. [17]

The Dettweiler chaise and *Liegehallen* became the symbol of the TB cure, from Davos to the Adirondacks, [18–19] as his sun–air–rest–diet regime was a major influence on the rapidly expanding sanatorium movement. In 1895 there were already thirty-five major state and private sanatoria in Germany alone.[23] Between 1897 and 1901, forty-six new sanatoria were added and by 1905, Robert Koch, who was skeptical about the sanatorium rate of cure, estimated in his Nobel Prize lecture for discovering the tuberculosis bacillus, that the number of sanatoria in Germany had reached one hundred.[24] The sanatorium movement

18 Rondack Combination Couch and Chair, advertisement for used Saranac cure chairs

extended itself across Europe, Canada, the United States, Latin America, India, and Australasia.

Another key figure in the sanatorium movement was doctor Edward Trudeau. He too was diagnosed with the disease in 1873 while living in New York City and went to a tiny village in the Adirondacks to spend his last days in a place he loved.[25] To his surprise, he recovered but relapsed each time he returned to the city. In 1876 he moved permanently with his family to Saranac Lake and started a practice there, treating a few patients sent from the city by colleagues and lodged in the village. Influenced by Brehmer and Dettweiler, Trudeau set up his own "sanitarium," the Adirondak Cottage Sanitarium at Saranac Lake in 1885. The first cottage was the Little Red Cottage, a modest one-room wood-frame building with a porch where Trudeau treated two sisters who had been factory workers in New York. **[20]** Trudeau volunteered his services and fundraised to cover the cost of the sanatorium for those who could not afford it. Eventually the sanatorium had thirty-five so-called "cure cottages," and people from the village turned their houses into boardinghouses for consumptives by adding "sleeping" porches and glass-enclosed

19 Men rest on cure chairs on a porch, Saranac Lake

20 The Little Red cottage, Trudeau Adirondack Sanatorium, 1884

21 Tents for the treatment of tuberculosis patients in Ray Brook Sanatorium, Saranac Lake, ca. 1909

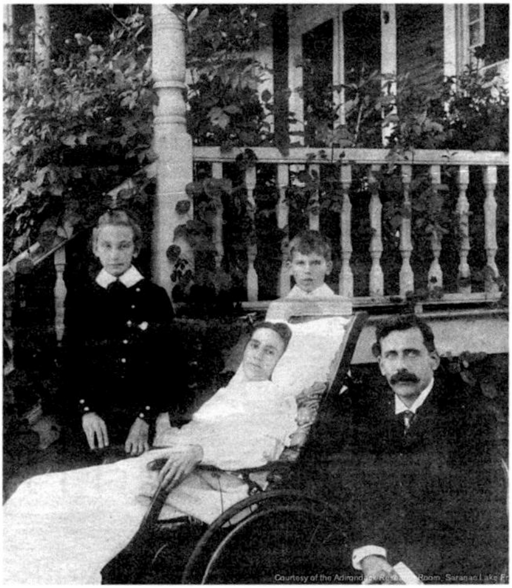

22 A family outside the Noyes Cottage, Saranac Lake

23 "Lunger" tent for a tuberculosis patient, desert near Tucson, Arizona,1906

24 Barlow Sanatorium, Los Angeles, 1927

25 City of Hope, Los Angeles, ca. 1925

26–27 Tent colony, Nordrach Ranch Sanatorium, Colorado Springs, 1906

verandas for fresh-air treatment. By the 1920s, there were 166 cure cottages in Saranac, many of which were built by families who had moved there accompanying a sick family member, along with rows of tents. **[21–22]** Saranac became known as the "Magic Mountain" of the United States as many artists, authors, poets, scientists, and physicians went to the area for the cure.[26]

Unlike European sanatoria, which tended to be centralized institutional buildings, many American sanatoria grew out of tent colonies under the auspices of physicians who often had moved to the area to treat their own health problems. If Saranac Lake was the center of the cure on the East Coast, Arizona, Colorado, and southern California were even bigger destinations. **[23]** Tucson advertised itself as a health site practically from its founding in 1877, with ads in popular and medical magazines such as *Ladies Home Journal* and *Journal of the American Medical Association*.[27] The Southern Pacific Railroad connected Arizona to the transcontinental railroad in 1880, accelerating the arrival of patients from all over the US.[28] Colorado called iself "the world's sanatorium" in 1891, and by 1900 one third of its population had originally come for the cure. The Chamber of Commerce of Colorado Springs advertised that "the atmosphere is absolutely aseptic and free from all germs."[29] Southern California likewise promoted itself as "The Sanatorium of the World," attracting multitudes of "health seekers" through the trans-

28 Modern Woodmen Sanatorium, Colorado Springs, postcard, ca. 1910

continental railroad and contributing enormously to urban development. Once again, disease shaped cities – particularly Los Angeles. A doctor from New York with tuberculosis, W. Jarvis Barlow, moved west in 1895 looking for a cure, first to Colorado and then to California where he founded the Barlow Sanatorium in Los Angeles in 1902. The sanatorium started as a cluster of cottages, and later a large building was added to the campus with Spanish arches providing shade for the outdoor cure. **[24]** Countless sanatoria sprouted up and kept expanding. The Los Angeles Sanatorium, founded by the Jewish Consumptive Relief Association in 1913 with two canvas cottages, grew quickly into a little suburban town and renamed itself "The City of Hope." **[25]**

Cities competed for patients and were transformed by them. Grids of atomized tents, huts, and cottages formed a veritable American urbanism in the image of dispersed individualism that was eventually combined with some concentrated buildings. **[26–29]** Brehmer, Dettweiller, and Trudeau – three doctors who had been tuberculosis patients themselves – had shaped two types of building to escape unhealthy buildings: an architecture to escape architecture and cure its effects.

29 Jewish Consumptives' Relief Society, Lakewood, Colorado, ca. 1930, founded in 1904 as a grid of tent cottages eventually supplemented with a terraced building

1 Vitruvius didn't just apply the theory of the four humors, the dominant medical theory of the time, but adjusted it to develop his own architecturally based theory of health or health-based theory of architecture. He argued that objects can be combinations of the four elements in different proportions rather than just of two as in the original medical theory. "Commentary: Book 2," in Vitruvius Pollio, *Vitruvius: Ten Books on Architecture*, eds. Ingrid D. Rowland and Thomas Noble Howe, trans. Ingrid D. Rowland (New York: Cambridge University Press, 1999), 178.

2 Vitruvius refers to curing both "consumption" and "phthisis," the two diseases in ancient Greek medicine that were finally understood to be the same disease and unified under the name "tuberculosis" in 1839.

3 William Osler, "The Home in its Relation to the Tuberculosis Problem," *Medical News* 83, no. 24 (December 12, 1903): 1105.

4 Osler, "The Home in its Relation to the Tuberculosis Problem," 1105–6. The name sanatorium comes from *sanare* (to heal). At first, the word "sanitarium" (from *sanitas*, health) was also used, but then "sanatorium" prevailed. Sanitarium became more common in the US, as in the original name of Edward Trudeau's treatment center.

5 William Osler, *The Principles and Practice of Medicine* (New York: D. Appleton, 1892), 250. J. S. Ames, "The Work of District Nurses among Tuberculous Patients in Baltimore," *The American Journal of Nursing* 4, no. 9 (1904): 671–73.

6 *Organization of Nursing: An Account of the Liverpool Nursing Training School, with an introduction and notes by Florence Nightingale* (Liverpool: A. Holden, 1865), 47.

7 Sophronia Maria Elliott, *Household Bacteriology* (Chicago: American School of Household Economics, 1904). The book was one of the volumes of a highly influential set on home economics and parts of it were serialized in *House Beautiful*. Sophronia Maria Elliott, "Household Bacteriology," *House Beautiful* 17, no. 4 (March 1905): 37–39, 48–49; "House Bacteriology," *House Beautiful* 17, no. 5 (April 1905): 49–58; "House Bacteriology," *House Beautiful* 18, no. 6 (November 1905): 55–57.

8 Lysol was developed in Hamburg in 1889 during a cholera epidemic and used for disinfection in hospitals, but almost immediately started to be promoted internationally for disinfection in the home to prevent the spread of bacteria and eliminate household odors.

9 There is doubt about whether Brehmer actually went the Himalayas. Peter Warren, "The Evolution of the Sanatorium: The First Half-Century, 1854-1904," *Canadian Bulletin of Medical History* 23, no. 2 (2006): 463.

10 Warren, "The Evolution of the Sanatorium": 462.

11 Hermann Brehmer, *Die chronische Lungenschwindsucht und Tuberkulose der Lunge. Ihre Ursache und ihre Heilung* (Berlin: Verlag von Enslin, 1857). Brehmer aimed his book to a popular audience. In addition to a general skepticism about Brehmer's claims, the review condemns the book for conveying detailed medical research to a general public. *Wiener medizinische Wochenschrift*, no. 3 (Janurary 16, 1858): 40–42.

12 George Bodington, *An Essay on the Treatment and Cure of Pulmonary Consumption* (London: Longman, Orme, Brown, Green, and Longmans, 1840), 2. Bodington argued that people living and working in the fresh air rarely get the disease, so city dwellers need to be in the same healthy conditions, spending much of the day outdoors regardless of the weather, and having the round-the-clock supervision of the therapeutic regime.

13 Bodington, *An Essay*, 6.

14 "Review of Mr. Bodington on Consumption," *The Lancet* (July 11, 1840): 575.

15 "It is, in fact, an elaborate advertisement to make known to all concerned, that the author has 'taken a large house near his own residence, for the reception of patients,' ... it betrays an utter ignorance of pathology, of therapeutics, and of the English language." "Bibliographical Notices," *The British and Foreign Medical Review*, (October, 1840): 549.

16 "Obituary," *The Lancet* (March 11, 1882): 417.

17 Thomas Sydenham, "Epistolary Dissertation, 1681," in *The Works of Thomas Sydenham, M.D Vol. II* (London: Sydenham Society, 1850), 107.

18 Tuberculosis accounted for 27.9 percent of all deaths in the last six months of 1837. *First Annual Report of the Registrar-General* (1839), 166. Chadwick's report acknowledges that overcrowded unventilated dwellings and dust seem to play a role "in producing or aggravating other tendencies to consumption." Edwin Chadwick, *Report into the Sanitary Condition of the Labouring Population of Great Britain* (London: Her Majesty's Stationary Office, 1842), 195. But it says that trying to understand the causes of "the immense mass of mortality occasioned by that disease, would be beyond the time or

means allowed for the present inquiry." Chadwick, *Report*, 105.

19 Benjamin Ward Richardson, *The Hygienic Treatment of Pulmonary Consumption* (London: Churchill, 1857), 8. Richardson was not referring to germs in the sense of microbes, but to the causes of the disease. In fact, Richardson would be one the most outspoken critics of the germ theory, arguing that if the theory was correct there would only be germs in the world since everyone infected by the germ should be killed by them. Benjamin Ward Richardson, *The Diseases of Modern Life* (London: Macmillan, 1876), 87. After Koch's discovery of the bacillus, Richardson remained skeptical about germs, but could accept the explanation that individuals have different predispositions to be affected by germs – whether heredity or environmental – a position that Koch too finally adopted.

20 Richardson, *The Hygienic Treatment of Pulmonary Consumption*, 91.

21 Richardson, *The Hygienic Treatment of Pulmonary Consumption*, 111–12. A key source for Richardson's formula, and associated architectural prescription, was the surgeon John Roberton's recently published celebration of the completely perforated plan of the Bordeaux Hospital with its floor-to-ceiling windows and set of guidelines for hospital interiors, finishes, and furnishings. Roberton italicized his concluding principle, which Richardson echoed: "*The air must flow through it in correspondence with the natural movements of the atmosphere without.*" John Roberton, *On the Defects with Reference to the Plan of Construction and* Ventilation *of Most of Our Hospitals for the Reception of the Sick and Wounded* (Manchester: 1856). The model of doctors designing ventilation systems for buildings in the name of health was already established, as, for example, with one of Richardson's examples, Dr. David Boswell Reid's "natural" ventilation system for the British Houses of Parliament, designed between 1840 and 1846, operational between 1847 and 1848. In fact, the architects of the building opposed the hiring of a doctor and their design had to be completely reworked to accommodate a network of ducts. Henricht Schoenefeldt, "The Historic Ventilation of the System of the House of Commons, 1840–52: Revisiting David Boswell Reid's Environmental Legacy," *The Antiquaries Journal*, no. 98 (2018): 245–95.

22 Alexander von Humboldt, letter to Hermann Brehmer, June 26, 1857, cited in Hermann Brehmer, *Die chronische Lungenschwindsucht und Tuberkulose der Lunge. Ihre Ursache und ihre Heilung* (Berlin: Adolph Enslin, 1869), IV. Quoted in Daniela Vaj, "Medical geography and phthisic immunity in the high altitudes: The origins of a Therapeutic hypothesis," *Revue de Géographie Alpine* 93, no. 1 (2005): 36. As a Prussian State official, von Humboldt was able to facilitate the permission for Brehmer to turn the spa into a sanatorium.

23 Twenty-five state sanatoria and ten private ones were surveyed in a large illustrated book for the 1899 German congress on fighting tuberculosis in Berlin. *Deutsche Industrie und Technik bei Einrichtung und Betrieb von Sanatorien und Krankenhäusern* (Berlin: Das Rothe Kreuz, 1889).

24 Robert Koch, "The current state of the struggle against tuberculosis," in *Nobel Lectures, Physiology or Medicine 1901–1921* (Amsterdam, London, New York: Elsevier Publishing Company, 1967), 175. Eva Eylers, "Planning the Nation: The Sanatorium Movement in Germany," *The Journal of Architecture* 19, no. 5 (2014): 674.

25 "During the entire journey I had felt gloomy forebodings as to the hopelessness of my case, but, under the magic influence of the surroundings I had longed for, these all disappeared and I felt convinced I was going to recover." Edwin Livingston Trudeau, *An Autobiography* (Garden City, NY: Doubleday, 1916), 80.

26 Sixty-four of the hundreds of cure cottages still extant in Saranac Lake are listed in the National Register of Historic Places. Philip Gallos, *Cure Cottages of Saranac Lake*, (Historic Saranac Lake, 1985). Robert Taylor, *Saranac: America's Magic Mountain* (Boston, MA: Houghton Mifflin, 1986).

27 Gizem Sivri, "Desert Fever: Harvesting the Sun, Colonizing the Land," *Sick Architecture* (e-flux Architecture, 2020).

28 Gregg Mitman, *Breathing Space: How Allergies Shape our Lives and Landscapes* (New Haven, CT: Yale University Press, 2012), 94.

29 "Colorado Springs, The City of Sunshine" brochure of Colorado Springs Chamber of Commerce, circa 1890, Colorado Springs Pioneers Museum. The same text was used in advertisements in medical journals, such as *The Canadian Journal of Medicine and Surgery* in 1903.

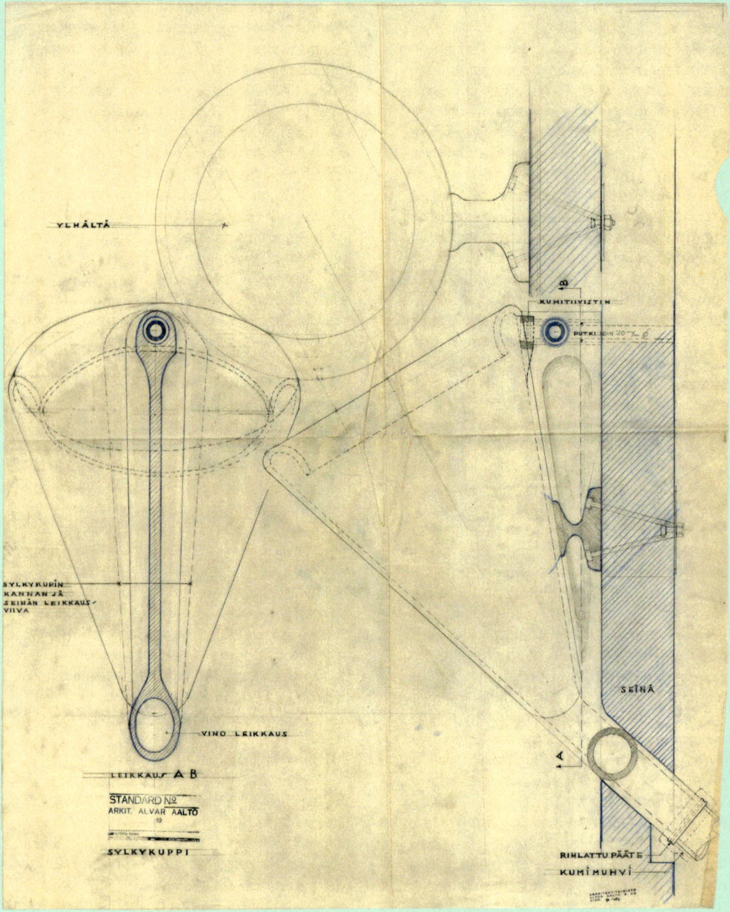

1 Alvar and Aino Aalto, detail drawing of spitting sink at Paimio Sanatorium

The announcement of Robert Koch's discovery of the tuberculosis bacillus in 1882, covered extensively by the international press, provoked a momentary crisis in the emerging sanatorium movement. If TB was contagious, surely a concentration of highly infectious patients in a building presented a risk to less severe cases, caretakers, visiting families, and those living in the area. The sanatorium quickly found ways to not only absorb bacteriological thinking and adapt to it, but to accelerate with it. Buildings, furnishings, infrastructure, and maintenance were consciously reshaped by microbes.

ENTER THE MICROBES

Hermann Brehmer, who had founded the first, and what was still the largest, sanatorium high in the mountains of Silesia in 1854, modified the building and its maintenance to control the movements of microbes immediately after Koch's discovery. His sanatorium started disinfecting its wastewater and adopted the Heidelberger Tonnen system to isolate its sewage in barrels. Patients had their own numbered linen, and all linen and clothing were regularly disinfected with specialized equipment – as were the walls and floor of the rooms between patients. Hygiene practices were taken to another level.

In widely reported subsequent studies by Koch's associates Ernst Schill and Bernhard Fisher, the bacillus could survive 187 days in dried spit, which confirmed the sanitary reform movement's longstanding fear of dust. The threat was magnified by the follow-up study of another associate, George Cornet, that used the dust taken from the walls, floors, and furniture of hospitals, workplaces, and homes, long after sick people had been there, to produce tuberculosis in rabbits. He took samples where no direct spitting had occurred to show that the bacillus travels in the air before settling.[1] With the assumption that tuberculosis was transmitted by inhaling dust, and with bacillus spores coming back to life in the warmth and moisture of the body, buildings were understood as lethal vectors of disease. In other words, TB was transmissible human to human via the building.

Brehmer set up a sophisticated bacterial laboratory in its own building on the sanatorium's grounds to confirm Koch's results and carry out his own research, publishing a lengthy book on his findings in 1885.[2] He changed his protocols and only released seemingly cured patients when their sputum tested negative for the bacillus after five weeks of testing. The memorial book published on Brehmer's death in 1889 symptomatically begins with an obituary by his long-term colleague, the influential hygienist and bacteriologist Carl Flügge, who would soon show that the bacillus can be spread in minute droplets propelled into the air by coughing.[3]

Peter Dettweiler, in his sanatorium at Falkenstein near Frankfurt, also quickly adapted to Koch's microbial theory, seting up a bacteriological lab and changing his protocols and building technologies. He had already published a paper on the bacillus in 1883, and a book the following year explored the enigma of why the tuberculosis bacillus was likely inhaled by everyone yet not everyone gets infected. His theory implicated buildings. While Koch concentrated on infection, Dettweiler and Brehmer underlined the role of the built environment, particularly hygiene and air, in both the transmission of the bacillus and people's predisposition toward it.[4] Living in unsanitary conditions increases the chances of being infected and weakens the immune response. Dettweiler's book argued that the disease could be eradicated, or at least dramatically reduced, if spit never touched buildings.[5] The microbes needed their own spatial system separate from the one for patients.

Dettweiler intensified the cleaning and disinfection of all surfaces of his sanatorium and placed 250 spittoons around the grounds, emptying them daily into a new closed sewage system with a disinfection shaft leading to isolated tanks near the forest. He worked with technicians to develop a glass pocket spit-flask that patients (whether in the institution, the streets, or at home) would constantly carry with them to catch their sputum. **[2]** A patient could use one hand to flip the spring-loaded lid open and spit directly into the tunnel that prevented spillage outside. The screwcap on the bottom made for easy cleaning and sterilization by heat or steam. The final design was made with blue cobalt

2 Peter Dettweiler, "Blauer Heinrich" ("Blue Henry")

glass to disguise its contents to others. The flask was often hidden behind a handkerchief when used to avoid stigma. Dettweiler presented the flask at the eighth International Congress of Medicine in 1889 in Wiesbaden, in an attempt to start a "small social revolution" that was widely reported in the medical and popular press.[6]

More than half a million of Dettweiler's sputum flasks, which became known as "Der Blaue Heinrich" ("the Blue Henry"), were commercially produced by Noelle & Co. in Lüdenscheid. They were ubiquitous in sanatoria, and even made their way into literature. In the Berghof, an imaginary sanatorium in Davos, Switzerland, where Thomas Mann set his famous 1924 novel *The Magic Mountain*, the main character, Hans Castorp, is introduced to the device by his sick cousin: "Most of us here have one; it even has a nickname, very jolly," but doesn't disclose the name, as if a secret. Later, as another character excuses himself from the dinner table, Frau Stöhr remarks: "Poor thing. He'll soon be drawing his last breath. Once more he has to go out for a meeting with the Blue Henry."[7]

On the other side of the Atlantic, just as the first cure cottage of his sanatorium in Saranac Lake was completed, Edward Trudeau traveled to New York in 1885 to learn how to stain the tuberculosis bacillus from a doctor that had just learned it in Koch's lab. He quickly set up a bacteriological laboratory in one of the rooms in his own cottage to duplicate Koch's experiments and test his own patients. **[3]** One of the first experiments was to inject the bacillus into ten rabbits, keeping half of them inside a damp, dark, closed space with insufficient food and letting the other half run around outside.[8] Only one of the indoor rabbits survived while all the outdoor rabbits recovered, as was Trudeau's own experience. As William Osler's medical textbook put it, the urban poor suffer the same fate as the confined rabbits.[9]

Trudeau's experiment echoed Jean-Antonine Villemin's pivotal 1865 demonstration that tuberculosis is infectious, producing disease in rabbits by injecting material from infected humans into them.[10] Villemin had observed that soldiers stationed in barracks for a long period had a much higher rate of tuberculosis than those in the fields. Not only is every occupied room filled with human-associated microbes in the air and dust –

as Pasteur had just demonstrated so publicly with a theatrical lecture in Paris the year before – but rooms magnify the possibility of being infected.

THE MAGIC MOUNTAIN

Davos was the epicenter of the modern cure phenomenon in Europe. By 1910 there were as many as twenty-six sanatoria and forty-six hotels catering to the disease. It had started when a country doctor in the alpine village, Alexander Spengler, noticed the lack of tuberculosis patients in the area and how villagers descending to the lowlands for work would get the disease and improve when returning. He opened a *Kurhaus* in a modest hotel, offering open-air high-altitude treatment, in 1865. It attracted increasing numbers of patients and eventually a sponsor, the businessman Willem Jan Hoelsboer, whose wife was a patient of Spengler. They opened a spa hotel in 1868, which was soon joined by a series of smaller hotels and pensions with similar programs.

3 Dr. Edward Trudeau in his Saranac Lake laboratory, 1894

The first modern sanatorium in Davos was the Schatzalp, **[4]** built between 1899 and 1900 by Hoelsboer, and the only sanatorium identified by name in *The Magic Mountain*. It was a collaboration between a doctor, Spengler's son Lucius, and two young architects from Zurich, Otto Pfleghardt and Max Haefeli, with the engineer Robert Maillart working for François Hennebique, who had pioneered reinforced concrete construction.[11] The first building in Switzerland to be constructed of concrete and steel, the Schatzalp became the model for the modern sanatorium.**[5]** It had steam floor heating, a flat roof with internal drainage, electrical lighting, and the latest mechanical ventilation system. Three hundred meters above Davos, the sanatorium was connected to the city by its own electrical funicular. **[6]** The most advanced medical treatment coincided with the most advanced technology in architecture and engineering.

The architecture of the Schatzalp is brutally modern in its horizontality and abstraction. With its one-hundred-meter-long façade, its four levels of terraces facing south, and its endless corridors, the building is like an ocean liner floating on the mountainside. **[7]** All parts are subordinated to the terraces as therapeutic spaces, dimensioned for a patient reclining in a specially designed chaise longue, a version of Dettweiler's chaise, from 7:00 a.m. to 10:00 p.m., in winter and summer. **[8–9]** The terraces of the patients rooms formed "a kind of second open air

4 Schatzalp Sanatorium, Davos, façade rendering, from *Heilanstalt für Lungenkranke, Sanatorium Schaltzalp Davos*, prospectus, ca. 1901–1902

5 Schatzalp Sanatorium, Davos, from *Sanatorium de la Schatzalp pour le traitment des affections pulmonaires, Davos Platz*, prospectus, ca. 1900

6 Schatzalp connected by funicular to Davos, 300 meters below, from *Sanatorium de la Schatzalp pour le traitment des affections pulmonaires, Davos Platz*, prospectus, ca. 1900

room," according to the original publicity brochure, which also celebrated the "simple and uncluttered" style of the building.[12]

The technological and aesthetic modernity of the building is reinforced by its microbial paradigm. The modern architecture of the new therapeutic typology is held in place by the portable architecture of the sputum flask, the bacteriological laboratory on the ground floor where the sputum is analyzed, and the disinfection rooms in the basement. The building's simple, washable furniture, largely white walls, electrical lighting, mechanical ventilation system, and linoleum floors were all understood as antimicrobial. The nineteenth-century prescription of hygienic protocols and smooth white surfaces was now rationalized and exaggerated by microbial control to produce a polemically white health machine, inside and out.

More radical than any built sanatorium to date was an unrealized project of 1902 made by doctor Karl Turban in collaboration with the Zurich-based architect Jaques Gros, in which every detail was designed to "prevent the spread of infectious agents." Turban had contracted tuberculosis while working as an assistant of Robert Koch in Berlin, and opened a Davos sanatorium in 1889

7 Schatzalp Sanatorium, Davos, postcard, ca. 1900

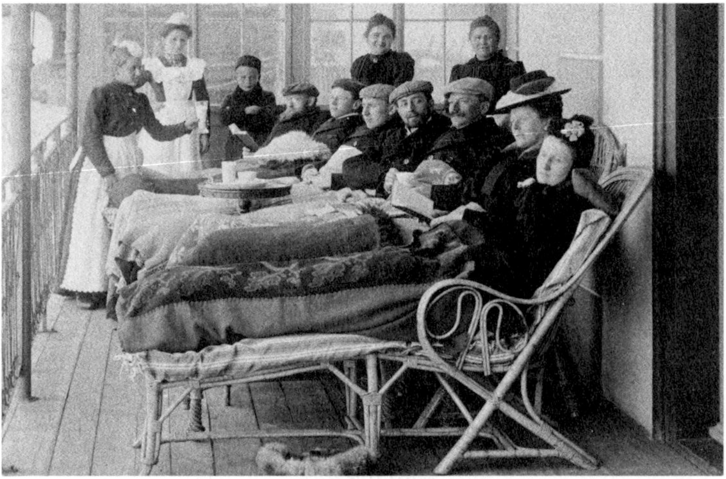

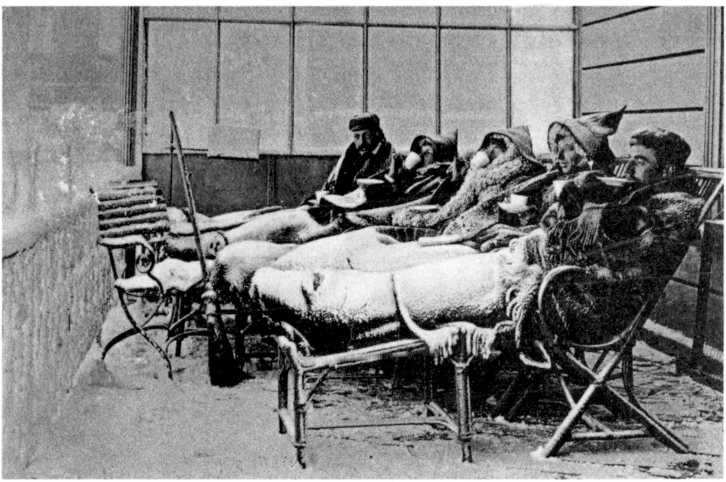

8 *Liegekur* (lying cure) on the terrace of the Villa Pravenda, Davos, ca. 1900

9 *Liegekur*, Davos, postcard, ca. 1910

that was the first to impose Dettweiler's strict protocols on the mountain. His influential set of guidelines for constructing sanatoria, published in 1893, argued against balconies in favor of opening patient rooms to the sun and air with floor-to-ceiling French doors with a guard rail.[13] Turban and Gros went further with this idea in "Open Air Everywhere," their 1902 design-competition entry for a sanatorium in England for one hundred people. Turban presented the design in the medical journal *Tuberculosis* as entirely buildable, giving all the details of construction, furnishings, finishes, technologies, and the inputs of engineers, furniture makers, and manufacturers.[14] It was intended as a prototype for all future sanatoria, adjustable to any location and climate.

The model project consisted of ground-floor communal spaces under multiple floors of naturally ventilated patient rooms all lined up to face south, with the toilets on the north side and technical spaces for disinfection and the bacteriological labs concentrated further behind. Instead of terraces, the entire façade is made of mobile glass panels set into a thin iron structure. Hypothetically, all of the glass could be moved away to fully

10 Karl Turban, mobile window system for sanatorium competition, 1902

expose every space to the outdoors. Each patient room has "movable glass walls" that can be folded vertically and horizontally or away to the side entirely to turn the room into a "loggia" that is neither indoors nor outdoors. [10–11] Wooden flaps set into the metal window frames allow for adjustable shading in the curtainless rooms when needed. The glass walls on the ground floor can slide down on tracks into the basement to completely open the communal spaces to the outside – an anticipation of the descending glass in Mies van der Rohe and Lilly Reich's Tugendhat House of 1927, a house that was explicitly understood by the clients as a health instrument and likened by Fritz Tugendhat to a sanatorium.[15] The fixed and revolving *Liegehallen* on the grounds in front of the building, sheltered from the wind by the wings of rooms angled a little inwards, have adjustable horizontal canvas awnings and vertical shutters for sun and wind. [12–13] The whole project operates as an adjustable antimicrobial instrument.

Inside there are no moldings and all corners between floors, walls, and ceiling are rounded to prevent dust accumulation. [14] Floors of the patient rooms are made of Euböolith, a new material applied as paste, that "makes the penetration of infectious substances impossible," and there is "bacilli-resistant" Ripolin paint on the seamless smooth washable walls, ceilings, window frames, and minimal metal furniture. All the other spaces are lined in washable tiles. Even the stone staircases have a "hygienic"

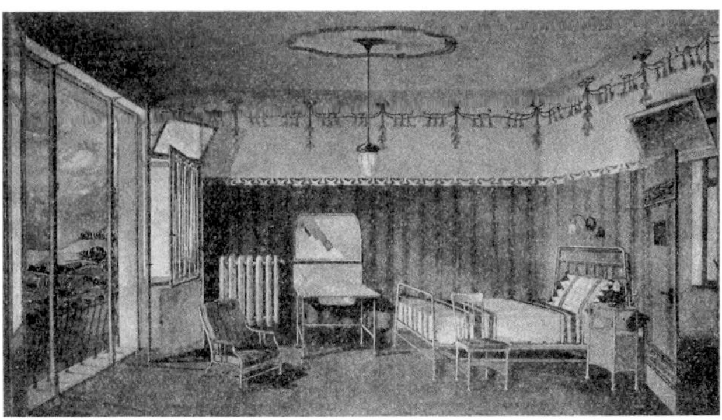

11 Karl Turban, patient room for sanatorium competition, 1902. Interior design by A. Dietler

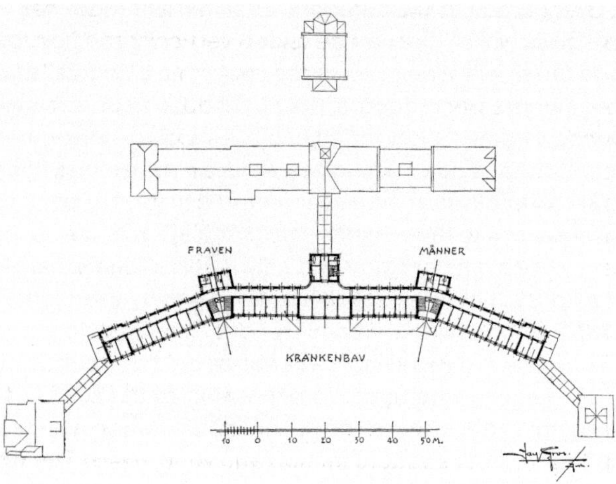

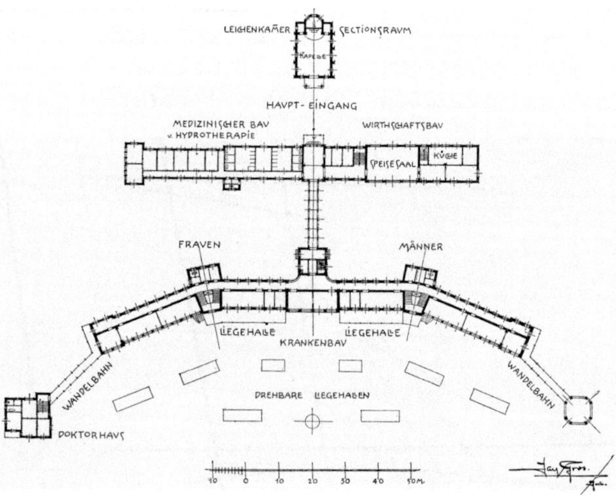

12–13 Karl Turban, plans of ground-floor common rooms and upper-floor patient rooms for sanatorium competition, 1902

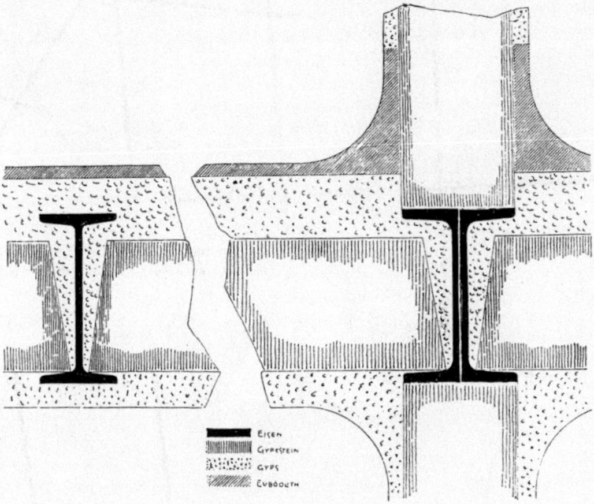

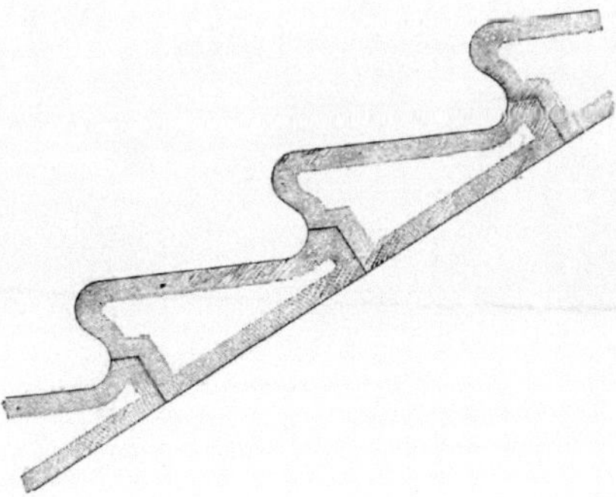

14 Karl Turban, detail of curves where floors and ceilings meet walls for sanatorium competition, 1902

15 Karl Turban, detail of "hygienic stairs" for sanatorium competition, 1902

16 Josef Hoffmann, Purkersdorf Sanatorium, Vienna, dining room, 1905–1906

17 Josef Hoffmann, Purkersdorf Sanatorium, electromechanotherapy room, 1905–1906

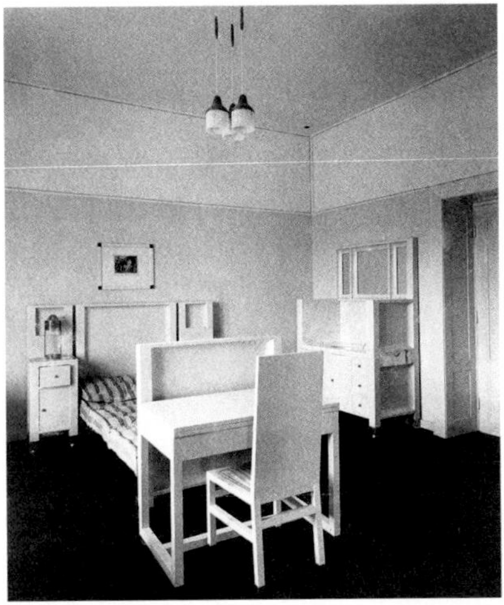

design with curves to resist dust. [15] Every element throughout the building and its furnishings is "disinfectable." Turban describes in detail the need for "spitting discipline"; the systems for controlling sputum, sewage, and wastewater; and the protocols for disinfecting sputum flasks, furniture, and rooms.

Josef Hoffmann's Purkersdorf Sanatorium outside Vienna of 1903 also incorporated the antimicrobial aesthetic into every space. Again, the building exemplified the alliance of modern architecture with medicine and technology. Its washable tiles, Hennebique construction in reinforced concrete and iron (the first in Austria), and electricity, were all considered part of its hygienic program.[16] [16] Electricity was not only used to illuminate – considered more hygienic than gas – and ostensibly displayed with visible cables, but was also used for all kinds of experimental therapies, including electric massage machines and electric baths and chairs for strengthening the nerves. [17] At the time it was built, critic Ludwig Hevesi described the Purkersdorf as "the naked Hoffmann building," whose walls were lined with white porcelain tiles – "a white-painted or white-tiled 'washable world.'"[17]

18 Josef Hoffman, Purkersdorf Sanatorium, patient room, 1905–1906

Critics hailed the building as one of clarity and truth. The success of the institution owed enormously to the modernity of the architecture. "Modern" was becoming a new and sophisticated taste among the bourgeoisie and the intelligentsia, who were supposed to dine around a single white table (as a kind of talking cure), sleep in spartan white rooms, and subject themselves to regimes of treatment in white spaces. **[18]** The association of cubic white forms with mental and physical health was already strong enough for architecture to act as an effective placebo.

This idea also made its way into literature. Thomas Mann's short novel *Tristan*, written in 1903, was set in an imaginary sanatorium, the Einfried, "a long, white, rectilinear building," "warmly recommended for lung patients" but also "for patients of all sorts": "sufferers of gastric disorders ... people with defective hearts, paralytics, rheumatics, nervous sufferers of all grumblings." When one of the patients, Herr Kloterjahn's wife, ask another one, "Why are you in Einfried really? ... What cure are you taking, Herr Spinell?" He answers:

> Cure? Oh, I'm having myself electrified a bit. Nothing worth mentioning. I will tell you the real reason why I am here, Madame. It is a feeling for style ... Obviously people feel one way among furniture that is soft and comfortable and voluptuous, and quite another among the straight lines of these tables, chairs and draperies. This brightness and hardness, this cold, austere simplicity and reserved strength, Madame – it has upon me the ultimate effect of an inward purification and rebirth.[18]

"Style"– modern architecture and furniture – is the true cure of whatever ails Herr Spinell. The antimicrobial campaign had shaped an aesthetic that was believed to be therapeutic, and therefore was.

THE HORIZONTAL CLIENT

Alvar and Aino Aalto's Paimio Sanatorium in Finland of 1929–1933 exemplifies this fusion of antimicrobial techniques and a new aesthetic. [19] Its clean-lined bedrooms, void of ornament, were designed to minimize surfaces where dust could accumulate, with the intersection of floor and wall beneath the window curved to stop dust build-up. [20–21] The floor in linoleum, understood as antimicrobial, was a calming blue in the patient rooms and bright canary yellow in the circulation spaces "to evoke sunny optimism even in cold, cloudy days."[19] The building was equipped with furniture and sanitary fittings designed by the architects, including chairs whose back was angled to facilitate breathing and expectoration, sinks designed to reduce splashing, and spittoons to minimize sound. [22] Even door handles were carefully designed not to catch the sleeves of the doctors' white coats. But the building's main equipment was the top-floor terrace, [23] seven stories above the forested landscape, where patients were wheeled out for regular doses of fresh air and sun in lounge chairs specially designed by Aino Aalto. [24]

The sanatorium was a trans-scalar design. Concerns in the neighboring town about contagion through sputum led to an independent water supply, a modern biological purification plant, and specialized circuits for moving, testing, and disposing spit. Each room had a sputum basin connected to a specialized drainage system isolated from the main wastewater system. Specially designed sputum mugs were transported on wheeled tables to a dedicated "sputum lift" that took them to the basement where the sputum was routinely tested in the lab, and the mugs sterilized. [25]

Tuberculosis made modern architecture modern. It is not that modern architects made modern sanatoria. Rather, sanatoria modernized architects. Alvar Aalto was a neoclassical architect before, in his words, his "conversion to functionalism" with his 1927 competition entry for a tuberculosis sanatorium at Kinkomaa, Finland – an unrealized project of horizontal lines and wide terraces for curing that anticipates Paimio.[20] [26] For the Aaltos, the sanatorium was not architecture in the service of medicine but a form of medicine in its own right – a medical instrument:

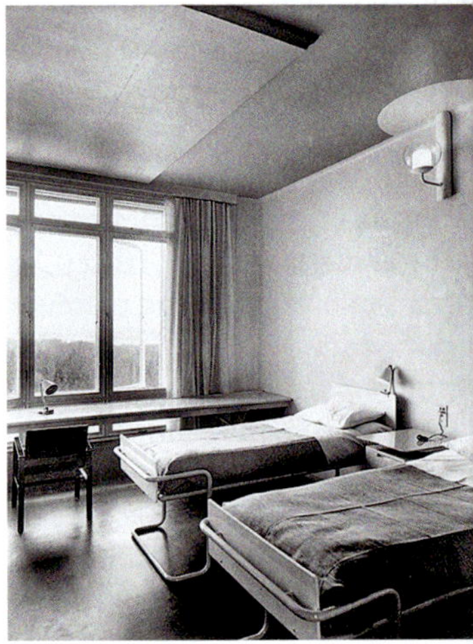

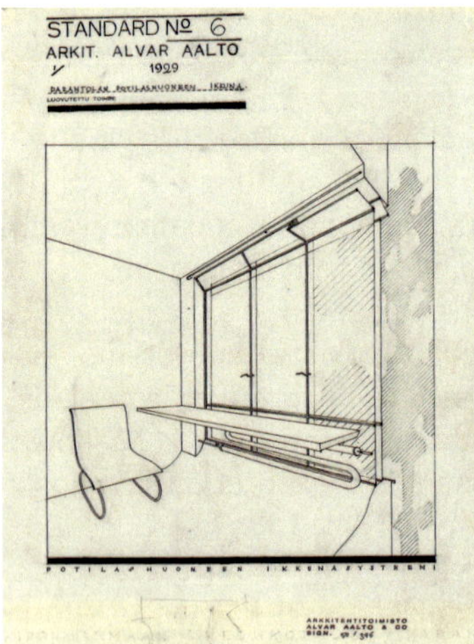

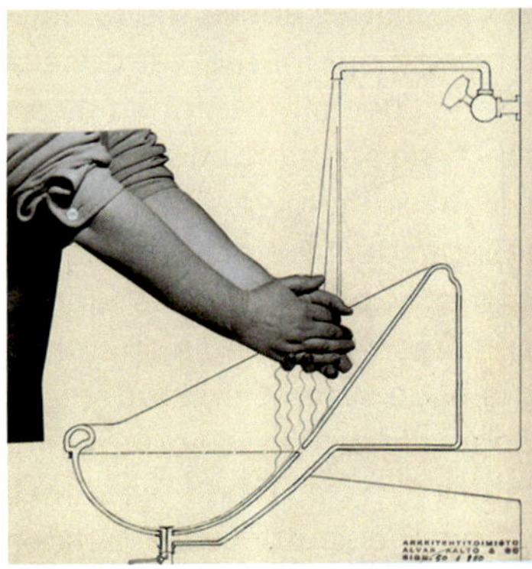

19 Alvar and Aino Aalto, Paimio Sanatorium, exterior view with sundeck balconies, 1932

20 Alvar and Aino Aalto, Paimio Sanatorium, patient room, 1933

21 Alvar Aalto, Paimio Sanatorium, drawing of curved floor under window, 1929

22 Alvar Aalto, Paimio Sanatorium, noiseless sink, 1932

23 Alvar and Aino Aalto, Paimio Sanatorium, the upper sun terrace with patients taking the fresh-air cure, ca. 1933

24 Aino Aalto lying on the terrace of Paimio Sanatorium in the lounge chair she designed, ca. 1934

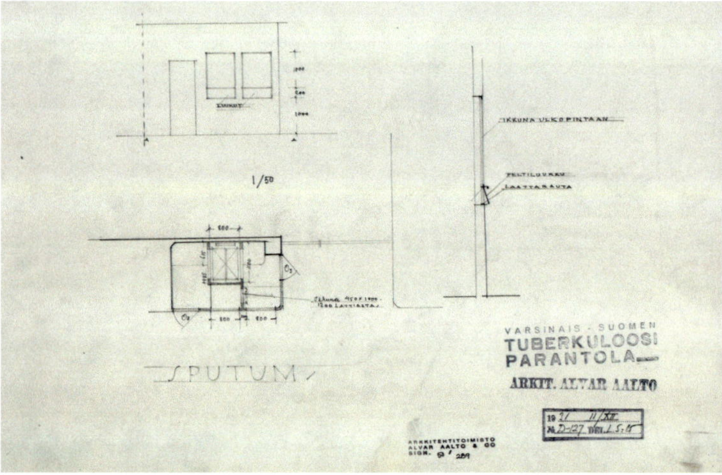

25 Alvar and Aino Aalto, Paimio Sanatorium, sputum lift, 1931

26 Alvar Aalto, Kinkomaa Tuberculosis Sanatorium, competition entry, 1927

> The main purpose of the building is to function as a medical instrument ... The room design is determined by the depleted strength of the patient, reclining in his bed. The color of the ceiling is chosen for quietness, the light sources are outside of the patient's field of vision, the heating is oriented towards the patient's feet, and the water runs soundlessly from the taps to make sure that no patient disturbs his neighbor.[21]

Alvar Aalto himself had been sick at the time of the competition for the building and claimed that having to lie in bed for an extended period of time had been crucial to his understanding of the problem.[22] Architecture was always conceived for the vertical person, but here was a client permanently in the horizontal. The whole design of the room and the building had to change accordingly. All architecture had to change. **[27]**

The vertical person goes back to the treatises and manuals of architecture that from the Renaissance to modern architecture have always been centered on the upright, athletic, healthy, white, male figure – from Leonardo da Vinci to Le Corbusier. This is a myth that excludes most of humanity, not to mention all other species. Even for those few who fit this heroic ideal, how long does it last? It is hard to understand how such a narrow view of humanity could have survived through so many centuries. The Aaltos claimed, "the architect should always design for the person in the weakest position." This means designing for everyone. The human is a very fragile creature that needs to be kept at an internal temperature of 36–37 degrees Celsius, and architecture is a protective cocoon for this vulnerable figure who spends most of its life in the "weakest position": as a baby or when old, sick, breaking a leg, pregnant, dying, etc. The Aaltos' proposition, born in the sanatorium, is the road not taken toward an architecture for diverse abilities.

Thomas Mann writes in *The Magic Mountain* of the sanatorium as a "horizontal manner of life." The "horizontal reigned" as patients "take up the horizontal," rhythmically "exchange the horizontal without for the horizontal within," only to finally "take up the horizontal for good," in death. Patients are not just taking the horizontal as "horizontallers" but they are themselves "horizontals":

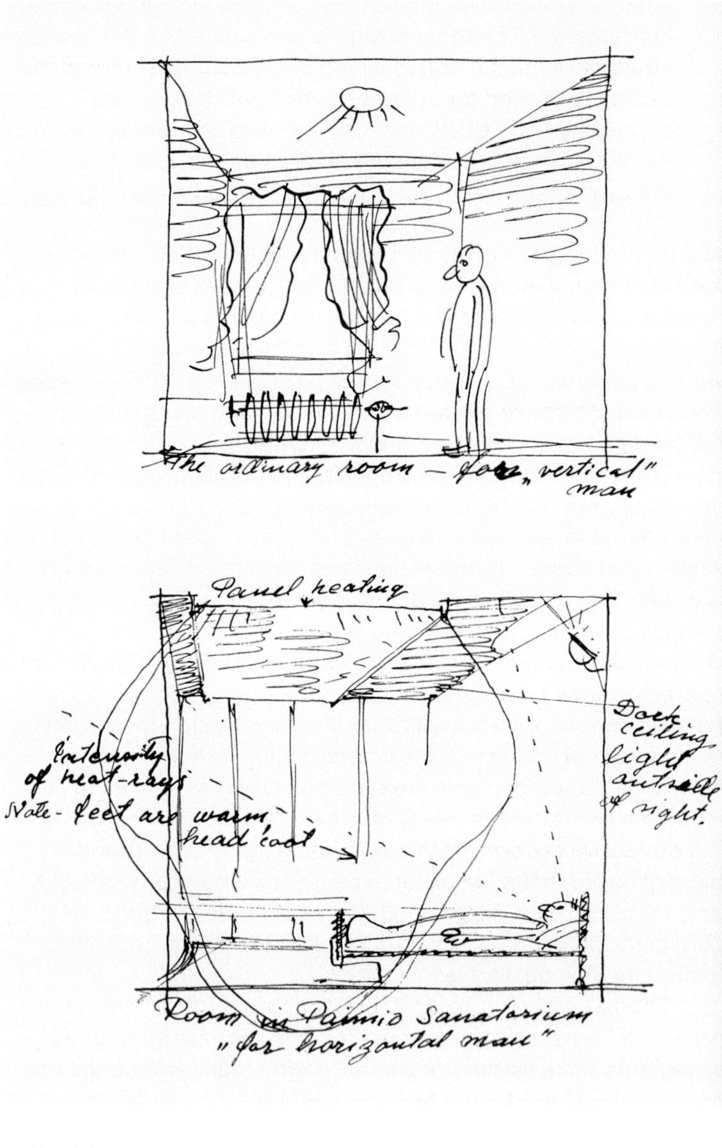

27 Alvar Aalto, drawings of an ordinary room for a "vertical" person and a room in Paimio Sanatorium for a "horizontal" person, 1940

> "You don't play here, do you?" asked Hans Castorp. "I'm not allowed to," replied Joachim. "We have to lie down, always lie down ... Settembrini always says we live horizontally – he says we are horizontals.[23]

The relentless horizontality of modern architecture is a response to the horizontality of the occupant – the tuberculosis convalescent lying on the chaise and the psychoanalytic patient on the couch. These were the paradigmatic clients of modern architecture. As Erich Mendelsohn put it in 1923, "Modern man, amidst the flurry of his fast moving life, can find equilibrium only in the tension-free horizontal."[24] The sanatorium aesthetic was itself medicinal, able to transform any building into a form of therapy. Why else did the reclining chaise of the TB patient migrate into all homes? Think of all the lounge chairs and daybeds of modern architecture: Le Corbusier and Charlotte Perriand, Aino Aalto, Marcel Breuer, Jean Prouvé, Eileen Gray, Mies van der Rohe and Lily Reich, Bruno Mathsson... All the way down to Charles and Ray Eames' nap chair for Billy Wilder. The Dettweiler chair became everybody's chair. Everybody is a "horizontaller."

1 George Cornet, "Die Verbreitung der Tuberkel bacillen ausserhalb des Körpers," *Zeitschrift für Hygiene* 5 (1889): 191–331.
2 Hermann Brehmer, *Die Aetiologie der chronischen Lungenschwindsucht, vom Standpunkt der klinischen Erfahrung* (Berlin: August Hirschwald, 1885). The lab was one of the best in Germany and was used by other scientists.
3 Carl Flügge, "Nachruf von Hermann Brehmer," in *Mittheilungen aus Dr. Brehmer's Heilanstalt für Lungenkranke in Görbersdorf - Neue Folge* (Wiesbaden: J. F. Bergmann, 1890), vii–xxxi.
4 Peter Dettweiler, *Die Behandlung der Lungenschwindsucht in geschlossenen Heilanstalten mit besonderer Beziehung auf Falkenstein* (Berlin: George Reimer, 1884). Koch reacted critically to the argument at the time, but eventually accepted the idea that humans have different predispositions to be overwhelmed by the bacillus, and that this predisposition can be affected by the environment.
5 Dettweiler, *Die Behandlung der Lungenschwindsucht*, 100.
6 Peter Dettweiler, "Ueber ein *Taschenfläschchen* für Hustende," *Therapeutische Monatshefte*, 3 (1889): 216. Dettweiler recalls that his first designs in 1884 had been unsuccessful because the technicians he worked with were not up to the task.
7 Thomas Mann, *Der Zauberberg* (1924) (Berlin: G. B. Fisher, 1965), 11, 83.
8 Edward Trudeau, "Environment in its Relation to the Progress of Bacterial Invasion in Turbuculosis," *Transactions of the American Clinical and Climatological Association* (1887): 131–36.
9 "A patient confined to the house – particularly in the close, overheated, stuffy dwellings of the poor, or treated in a hospital ward – is in a position analogous to the rabbit confined to a hutch in the cellar; whereas a patient living in the fresh air and sunshine for the greater part of the day has chances comparable to those of the rabbit running wild." William Osler, *The Principles and Practice of Medicine* (New York: D. Appleton, 1892), 250.
10 Jean-Antoine Villemin, "Cause et nature de la tuberclose," *Bulletin de l'Académie Impériale de Médecine*, 31 (1865): 211–16.
11 The Schatzalp is considered the first large building by Robert Maillart who was at the time an employee of Francois Hennebique. Pfleghardt and Haefeli went on to design the Queen Alexandra Sanatorium, another iconic sanatorium of Davos, critically acclaimed by Sigfried Giedion. Daniel Korman, *Discovering Early Modernism in Switzerland – The Queen Alexandra Sanatorium* (Basel: Birkhäuser, 2023). See also, Tim Altenhof, "Inhabiting the Atmosphere: The Architecture of the Queen Alexandra Sanatorium," *Journal of the Society of Architectural Historicans* 82, no. 3 (2023): 314–34.
12 Lucius Spengler and Edward Neumann, *Sanatorium de la Schatzalp pour le traitement des affections pulmonaires: Davos-Platz*, publicity brochure (ca. 1900).
13 Karl Turban, "Normalien für die Erstellung von Heilstätten für Lungenkranke in der Schweiz (1893)," in *Tuberkulose-Arbeiten 1890–1909 aus Dr. Turbans Sanatorium Davos: Bei Anlass des zwanzigjährigen Bestehens der Anstalt* (Davos: Davos-Platz, 1909), 234–43. Turban presents the "basic principles" of sanatoria design, including: site; orientation; communal space; volume of air in patient rooms; windows; smooth, undecorated, washable surfaces; linoleum floors; curved corners; absence of upholstery, carpets, and curtains; outdoor lying rooms; mechanical systems; cleaning and disinfection protocols; "spitting discipline"; etc.
14 Karl Turban, "Entwurf für die Errichtung eines Tuberkulose-Sanatoriums in England," *Tuberculosis – Monatsschrift des internationalen Centralbureaus zur Bekämpfung der Tuberkulose,* 2 (1903): 324–47. Having argued against terraces, Turban would belatedly add them to his original sanatorium building.
15 Fritz Tugendhat had been sick at the time of the commission of the house and defended it to a critic from the journal *Die Form* who had questioned if it was possible to live in the house, by praising it and comparing it with a sanatorium in Davos. Fritz Tugendhat, "Letter to the Editor," *Die Form* 6, no. 11 (November 1931): 438. In response to Justus Bier, "Kann man im Haus Tugendhat wohnen?," *Die Form* 6, no. 10 (October 15, 1931): 392. See Beatriz Colomina, *X-Ray Architecture* (Zurich: Lars Müller Publishers, 2019).
16 About Purkersdorf, see the detailed study by Leslie Topp, "The Purkersdorf Sanatorium and the Appearance of Science," in *Architecture and Truth in Fin-de-Siecle Vienna* (Cambridge: Cambridge University Press, 2004), 63–95.
17 Ludwig Hevesi, "Neubauten von Josef Hoffmann. Purkersdorf. Hohe Warte. Brüssels," in *Altkunst-Neukunst: Wien 1894–1908* (Vienna: Carl Konegen, 1909), translated and

reprinted in English in Peter Vergo, *Art in Vienna, 1898–1918* (London: Phaidon, 1975), 135.

18 Thomas Mann, *Tristan* (Berlin: S. Fischer, 1903). Translated by H. T. Lowe-Porter in *Death in Venice and Other Stories* (New York: Modern Library, 1992), 374.

19 *Alvar Aalto: Das Gesamtwerk / L'oeuvre complète / The Complete Work*, eds. Karl Fleig and Elissa Aalto, vol. 1 (Basel: Birkhäuser, 1963).

20 Göran Schildt, *Alvar Aalto: The Complete Catalog of Architecture, Design and Art* (New York: Rizzoli, 1994), 68. See Colomina, *X-Ray Architecture*.

21 Alvar Aalto, from a lecture in Italy describing Paimio, 1956. Schildt, *Alvar Aalto*, 68–69. Text in the Aalto Archives.

22 Aalto doesn't specify the illness but spending an extended period of time on the horizontal in that period likely meant tuberculosis.

23 Mann, *Der Zauberberg*, 68.

24 Erich Mendelsohn, "Dynamics and Function" (1923), in *Programs and Manifestoes on 20th-Century Architecture*, ed. Ulrich Conrads (Cambridge, MA: MIT Press, 1971), 72.

1 Willi Baumeister, poster for the Werkbund exhibition *Wie Wohnen? Die Wohnung* (How will we live? The dwelling), Stuttgart, 1927

Microbes were both the literal and metaphorical basis of a new architecture and urbanism in the twentieth century. To produce the idea of modern architecture as healthy, nineteenth-century architecture was demonized as nervous, unhealthy, and literally filled with disease, especially the bacilli of tuberculosis. Decorative excess was itself treated as an infection. Modernizing architecture was firstly a form of disinfection, a purification of buildings leading to a health-giving environment of light, air, cleanliness, and smooth white surfaces without cracks or crevices where contagion might lurk.

HOME SANATORIUM

Modern architecture was produced under emergency conditions. Throughout the nineteenth and first half of the twentieth century, millions were dying of tuberculosis every year all over the world, with deaths strongly correlated with poverty. Architects, many of whom had suffered from the disease or had relatives and friends die from it, offered buildings as a prophylactic. The strategy of sanatoria distant from the unhealthy city migrated into the city as a form of prevention in housing, schools, and other public buildings. The sanatorium became the model of all architecture for healthy everyday life – understood as a form of continuous defense against microbes. Modern architecture is a medical project. **[2]**

The most influential exhibition in the campaign to promote modern architecture, the Weissenhofsiedlung in Stuttgart, a housing estate built for the Deutscher Werkbund exhibition *Die Wohnung* (The dwelling) in 1927 – which was intended as a showcase of new and affordable housing solutions for the city – was in many ways a health exhibition. **[3]** The model estate included twenty-one buildings (detached houses and apartment buildings) designed by leading avant-garde European architects including Mies van der Rohe, who was in charge of the overall project with Lilly Reich. Mies did the master plan and chose the architects: Peter Behrens, Victor Bourgeois, Le Corbusier,

2 Pierre Chareau, open-air room in Robert Mallet-Stevens' Villa Noailles, Hyères, ca. 1926

Richard Döcker, Josef Frank, Walter Gropius, Ludwig Hilberseimer, Pierre Jeanneret, Jacobus Johannes Pieter Oud, Hans Poelzig, Adolf Rading, Hans Scharoun, Adolf Schneck, Mart Stam, Bruno Taut, and Max Taut.

A remarkable group of women architects were also involved. Else Oppler-Legband, a member of the Deutscher Werkbund, designed some interiors for Behrens, even if they were not realized in the end. Marlene Moeschke-Poelzig collaborated with Hans Poelzig, even if she is usually excluded from the project's credit. And Lilly Reich worked closely with Mies during the entire process, even if her contributions are likewise mostly under-represented.[1] Reich was responsible for five major rooms in the *Die Wohnung* exhibition hall in the center of the city (including the *Glasraum* and the *Linoleumraum*, in collaboration with Mies), and designed the interior and furniture of Apartment 9 in Mies' housing block.[2]

The sociologist, doctor, and home economist Erna Meyer, who had published the year before the bestseller *Der neue Haushalt – Ein Wegweiser zu wirtschaftlicher Hausführung* (The new household – A guide to economical housekeeping), was also involved in the exhibition.[3] She curated the household section of *Die Wohnung*, which included a range of hygienic model kitchens, some by Grete Schütte-Lihotzky, designer of the ground-breaking *Frankfurter Küche* of 1926, and two on which Meyer

3 Weissenhofsiedlung, Stuttgart, postcard, 1927

herself collaborated with Hilde Zimmerman.[4] [4] More extraordinary, every architect involved in the Weissenhofsiedlung was provided with guidelines on the design of kitchen and utility areas that had been prepared by the Stuttgart Housewives Association and Erna Meyer. Oud and Schneck were among the only architects who took these recommendations seriously, and their kitchens were published by Meyer in the Werkbund journal *Die Form*.[5] [5] Oud's kitchen was often compared with Schütte-Lihotzky's *Frankfurter Küche*.

While the exhibition organizers put emphasis on new materials and technical solutions – steel and reinforced concrete structures, mass production – every project explicitly or implicitly presented itself as providing health. Richard Döcker, who had been building his tuberculosis sanatorium in Waiblingen since 1926, was the site architect in charge of overseeing construction of the model estate. The orientation of the settlement, perched on the edge of a hill to catch the sun, already resonates with the sanatorium tradition. Willi Baumeister's poster *Wie Wohnen? Die Wohnung* (How will we live? The dwelling) announcing the exhibition is symptomatic. [1] Instead of showing what modern

4 Erna Mayer and Hilde Zimmerman, *Stuttgart Küche*, Weissenhofsiedlung, Stuttgart, 1927

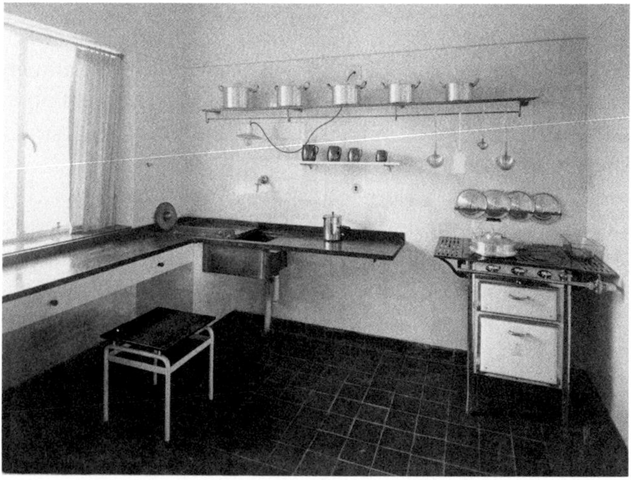

architecture should be, it shows what it shouldn't be: a picture of a dark nineteenth-century interior – full of fabrics, bric-a-brac, ornamental detail, closed in and unventilated – is crossed out with thick red lines, reminiscent of marks made on the houses of the infected during plagues.[6]

Peter Behrens made the health call explicit, even if he had not initially been invited to participate. He wrote a plaintive letter to Mies van der Rohe, his former employee, in 1926, soliciting his involvement and using health as his rationale:

> One hears so much of the Werkbund exhibition in Stuttgart. I understand that the execution and organization are in your hands. I would like to enquire whether it might not be possible to put my idea of a Terraced Block into practice there.... If ever this type of Terraced Block is translated into reality, I believe that it can do a great deal for the health of the people.[7]

Behrens wanted to bring stepped terraces of sanatoria to the modern house, insisting on the prevention and cure of tuberculosis.

5 J. J. P. Oud, kitchen of House 8, Weissenhofsiedlung, Stuttgart, 1927

Eventually invited to participate, his entry in *Bau und Wohnung*, the catalog of the exhibition, asserts that traditional dense housing blocks are "hotbeds of disease" and presents drawings of his earlier housing project for Vienna of 1924, a building with stepped terraces from the ground to the roof and almost continuous windows facing the sun:

> Years ago, I attempted to construct a multi-story building that could be suitable for preventing or promoting the cure of the main common diseases. To be effective against tuberculosis, it appears necessary that every apartment, even in a multi-story building, be provided with a large open-air space. It is no less necessary to ensure that all dwellings have thorough ventilation. The roof garden-like open spaces must have enough depth to allow beds and other reclining furniture to be easily brought outside and back into the apartment.[8]

Behrens further argues that "a cure is provided" to those "suffering from tuberculosis, or those predisposed to it," by a "hygienically

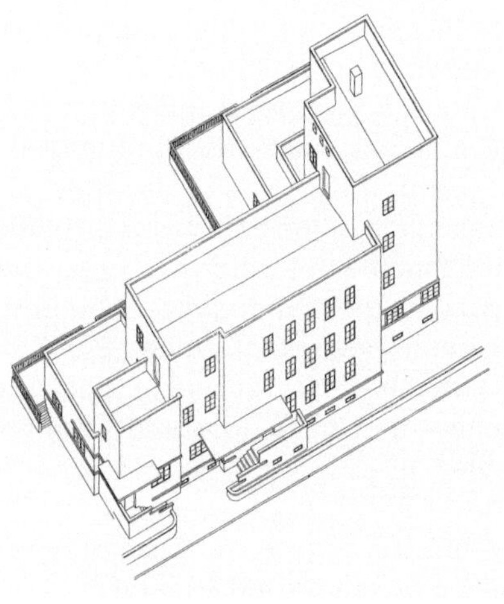

6 Peter Behrens, axonometric of terrace housing for the Weissenhofsiedlung, Stuttgart, 1927

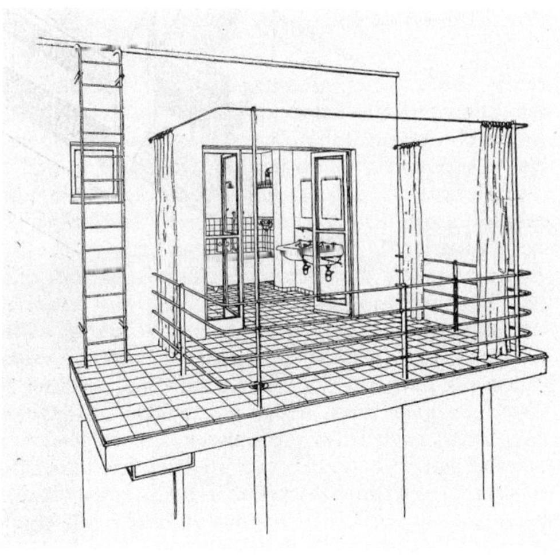

7 Walter Gropius, house in the Weissenhofsiedlung, Stuttgart, 1927

8 Adolf Schneck, house in the Weissenhofsiedlung, Stuttgart, 1927 modern" design that resists "the dangers of infection" through fresh air, hygiene, separation of sick from healthy, and by making individual sleeping places with sliding walls.[9] [6]

While Behrens was the only architect involved in the exhibition to make health his calling card, almost all the houses in the Weissenhofsiedlung offered terraces and open-air rooms, some described as "sunrooms" that can be closed off with curtains for the cure. [7] Adolf Schneck's house, for example, had a large terrace to which the bathroom could be fully opened, offering an "air bath" to promote health. [8] He wrote: "For modern people, daily exposure to fresh air and sunlight is essential for the preservation of their health and physical and mental strength."[10]

Similarly, the living room on the upper floor of the semi-detached houses of Le Corbusier and Pierre Jeanneret was convertible at night into sleeping cabins with sliding walls. Foldable, metal sliding beds on metal runners specially designed for this purpose were hidden in closets during the day. Le Corbusier claimed inspiration in passenger trains, but it is hard to forget the movable beds of sanatoria and the imperative to sleep with open windows for the cure. The house is detached with pilotis from

9 Woman exercising on terrace of Richard Döcker's house, Weissenhofsiedlung Stuttgart, 1927

the "humid ground where disease breeds," as Le Corbusier puts it. Richard Döcker's house had a large roof terrace featuring a shower with hot and cold water and a wall bar for gymnastics. **[9]** It was open to the living room and the bathroom, which was dimensioned to serve as another exercise space. Photos of the Poelzig house show the typical TB chaise laying on the terrace, pointing again to the tuberculosis patient as a client of modern architecture. The small balconies in the row houses of Oud (a true working-class scheme, unlike most houses in the settlement) were dimensioned to allow a movable bed to stick outside for the open-air cure.

Even the furniture was "healthy." The tubular steel cantilever chair was first presented at the Weissenhofsiedlung. In preparation for the exhibition, Mart Stam showed Mies his gas tube cantilever chair concept, recently developed for his pregnant wife. **[10]** Inspired by Stam's design, Mies realized the cantilevered Weissenhof chair in collaboration with Lily Reich.[11] The chair is quintessential hygienic, with smooth metal tubes without joints for dust to gather, minimal contact with the floor, and easy access for cleaning the floor. It suspends the sitter in the air which flows all around. Its clean lines, its modernity, resonate with the project of cleanliness.

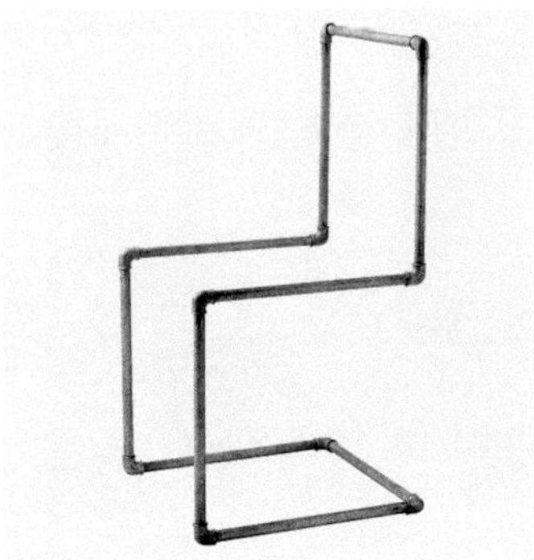

10 Mart Stam, cantilever chair, first prototype, 1924

TERRASSENTYP

It was not just modern architects but also critics and historians such as Sigfried Giedion who were advocating life in a sanatorium. Take, for example, his little 1929 book *Befreites Wohnen* (*Liberated Dwelling*), subtitled *Licht, Luft, Oeffnung* (*Light, Air, Opening*), which could otherwise serve as the slogan of sanatoria. [11] Between the covers of a book about the modern house, more than half of the illustrations are dedicated to hospitals and sports: Richard Döcker's sanatorium in Waiblingen (1926–1928), Bernard Bijvoet and Jan Duiker's Zonnestraal Sanatorium (1925–1931), sanatoria in Davos such as the Queen Alexandra by Pfleghardt and Haefeli (1907–1909), [12] mountain lodges, seaside resorts, sports stadiums, images of gymnastics, sunbathing, and tennis. By the time the reader finally gets to the houses, the few that Giedion included appear to have been turned into home sanatoria, with convalescents resting on long chairs on terraces (as in a picture of a Max Haefeli house in Zurich of 1928 [13]) or gyms, as in Marcel Breuer's bedroom for Piscator in Berlin (1927–1928), André Lurcat's rooftop gym on the Guggenbühl House in Paris (1926–1927), and Richard Döcker's terrace with

11 Cover of Sigfried Giedion, *Befreites Wohnen: Licht, Luft, Oeffnung*, 1929

12 Otto Pfleghardt and Max Ernst Haefeli, with engineer Robert Maillart, Queen Alexandra Sanatorium, 1909

13 Max Ernst Haefeli, house on Wasserwerkstrasse, with patient on the terrace, Zurich, 1928 exercise equipment in the Weissenhofsiedlung (1927). Giedion was not the only one advocating life in a sanatorium. Another influential book of that time, Döcker's *Terrassentyp* of 1929, [14] follows the development of the terrace in modern architecture, from the sanatorium to the home, starting with Döcker's own sanatorium in Waiblingen [15] and proceeding to Zonnestraal, Davos, [16] and beyond, delineating a seamless transition from the terraces of sanatoria to those of modern houses.[12] Diagrams show the penetration of sun rays in modern sanatoria and in modern terrace houses alike. [17] The book concludes with a series of photographs of domestic terraces furnished with exercise equipment, as in Döcker's Weissenhofsiedlung house, Le Corbusier's terraces, and the terraces of Robert Mallet-Steven's Villa Noailles (1923–1927) in Hyères. The book conveys a sense of the medical innovation in sanatoria being steadily domesticated into houses, with Döcker insisting that "our era urgently demands the hygienic design of life" ("*hygienische Gestaltung des Lebens*"). A lengthy essay by the chief physician of Waiblingen, Dr. Poehlmann, confirms the medical benefits of the terrace system – an architectural prescription.

14 Cover of Richard Döcker's *Terrassentyp*, 1929

15 Richard Döcker, sanatorium in Waiblingen, from *Terrassentyp*

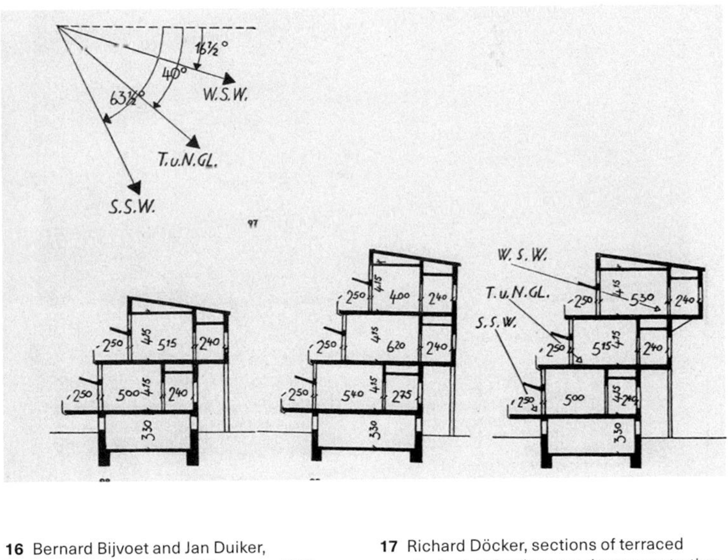

16 Bernard Bijvoet and Jan Duiker, Zonnestraal Sanatorium, Hilversum, 1927

17 Richard Döcker, sections of terraced sanatoria showing improved sun penetration

Yet the history of medical terracing is longer and not a straightforward line from sanatorium to home, from doctors to architects. It was more like a oscillation between the two, with housing projects sometimes ahead and sometimes behind. The first design for a terraced tuberculosis sanatorium was made by the art nouveau architect Paul Hankar, who worked with a group of doctors in 1896 to design a model sanatorium in a forest outside Brussels. **[18]** The unrealized project, which was supposed to be part of the 1897 World's Fair in Brussels, was a three-storied "bar" building facing south with long lines of identical patient rooms opening onto stepped terraces connected to a multi-story metal rotunda for additional exposure to the air and sun. The all-white minimalist building stripped of all the ornament typical of art nouveau, and the attachment of its metal structure and technical spaces to the back of the bar, evokes an industrial building – a machine for health. **[19]**

Seemingly unaware of Hankar's project, David Sarason, the head physician at a Hamburg sanatorium, who had been trained by Robert Koch, worked on a stepped-terrace concept for the 1902 design competition for a sanatorium in England. He immedi-

18 Paul Hankar, perspective of tuberculosis sanatorium project for Kraainem, brochure, 1897

19 Paul Hankar, main façade of tuberculosis sanatorium project for Kraainem, 1897

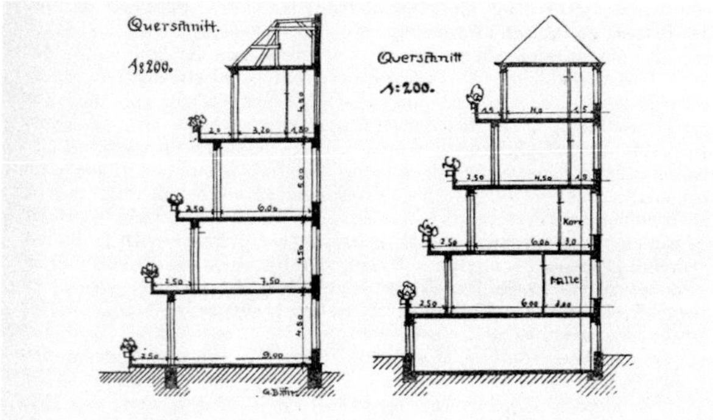

ately started promoting the concept at medical conferences, such as the first International Tuberculosis Conference in Berlin, and patented it with very rudimentary drawings—claiming it provided “sun and air baths” for tuberculosis patients in hospitals and sanatoria but was also ideal in private houses.[13] **[20]** At the fourteenth International Congress on Hygiene and Demography of 1907 in Berlin, Sarason argued that the new building type could even “attack the entire tuberculosis problem at its root” by forming entire “garden city” neighborhoods for the working classes, where they could bathe naked for hours in the air and sun, “for there is no doubt that the lack of adequate housing and fresh air must be held primarily responsible for the destructive power of tuberculosis.”[14] By then, Sarason was working with the Berlin architect Gustav Bähr on designs in reinforced concrete for stepped-terraced sanatoria, housing, and sanatoria that could be converted to housing, exhibiting the drawings and models to acclaim under the name of “open-air houses” (*Freilufthäuser*) in a public exhibition in Washington DC held in association with the sixth international tuberculosis conference in 1908 and again in the International Exhibition on Hygiene in Dresden in 1911.[15] When the designs were finally published in a 1913 book, the very last lines argued that every house should be a sanatorium.[16]

Architects Henri Sauvage and Charles Sarazin were the first to realize the terracing idea for preventative health in a gleaming

20 David Sarason, section of terraced sanatorium and terraced hospital, 1907

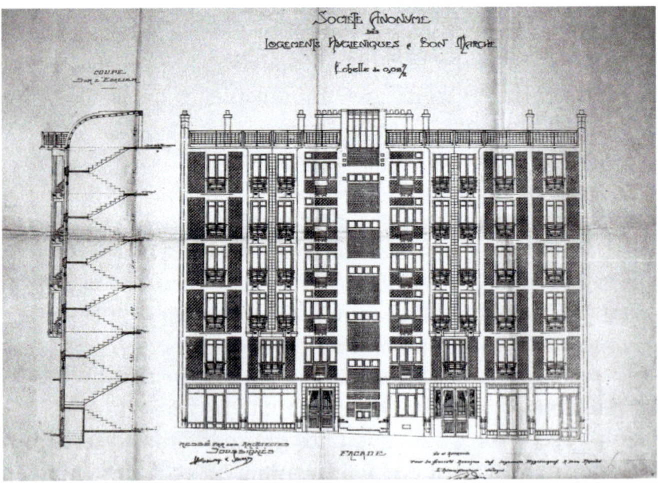

21 Henri Sauvage and Charles Sarazin, terraced residential building clad in glazed white ceramic tiles, 26–28 rue Vavin, Paris, 1912–1913

22 Sauvage and Sarazin, original all-glass façade (clear and glass block) for "hygienic" workers' housing building, 7 rue Tretaigne, Paris, 1903 housing project that looked like a piece of an ocean liner inserted into rue Vavin in Paris in 1912.[17] **[21]** The architects had formed a "hygienic housing" society (Société des logements hygiéniques à bon marché) with fellow architects in 1903 in response to the 1902 Paris building law that called for architects to admit more sunlight and air into the housing for the poor – characterized by French sanitary reformers as "diseased" and acting as "nests of microbes," even "microbe factories."[18] Their first project in 1903 on rue Trétaigne was for an exposed reinforced concrete building with an all-glass façade and communal roof terrace for maximizing sun. **[22]** It was considered too extreme by the building authorities and was constructed with less glass, but had a solarium on the roof. The architects wanted to avoid the unwelcoming "impression of hospitalization," and to "differentiate this building from a sanatorium."[19] Yet the building had the Ripolin-painted surfaces that had been standard in hospitals and sanatoria since the turn of the century, along with smoothly curving intersections of floor, wall, and ceiling surfaces to facilitate cleaning, the absence of added ornament to collect dust, and large operable windows for light and air.

The building on rue Vavin, inside which Sauvage set up his own studio, was a manifesto to antimicrobial hygiene, with its layers of terraces lined with shiny white ceramic tiles stepping back from the street.[20] All rooms opened onto 2.25-meter-deep terraces, with planting at the edges to produce hanging gardens. The building received a lot of attention in the popular and architectural press and was featured as a "revolution in the art of building" in two full pages of *L'illustration*, with diagrams showing how both the apartments and the street receive so much more light and air than those of conventional buildings.[21] Unique here is Sauvage's idea that these stepped terrace buildings contribute not just to the health of inhabitants but also the people outside them – the health of the city. **[23]**

It was not until 1917 that Tony Garnier made the first project for a terraced sanatorium, a massive project to treat five thousand patients in eight three-story structures facing south on a hillside outside Lyon – all connected by train to a large "Institut Bacteriologique."[22] **[24]** Voluminous patient rooms, with almost five-meter-high ceilings, allowed an adjustable louvered glass

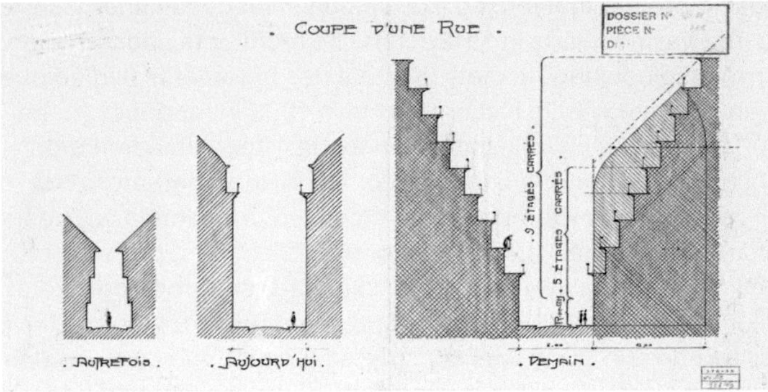

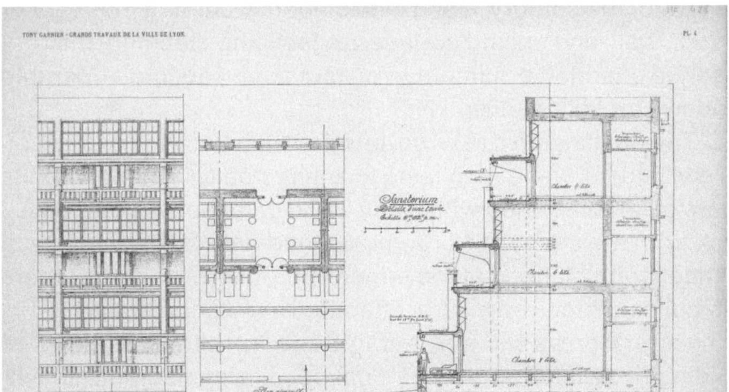

23 Henri Sauvage and Charles Sarazin, comparison of medieval, contemporary, and future streets published in *L'illustration*, March 21, 1914

24 Tony Garnier,Sanatorium Franco-Américain, façade, plan, and section, 1917, from Tony Garnier, *Les grands travaux de la ville de Lyon*, 1921

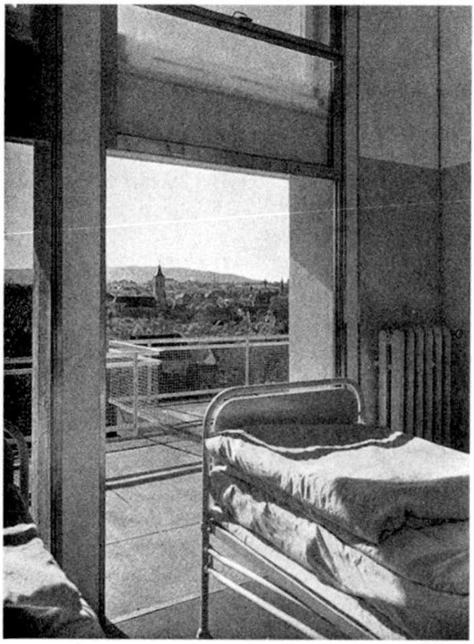

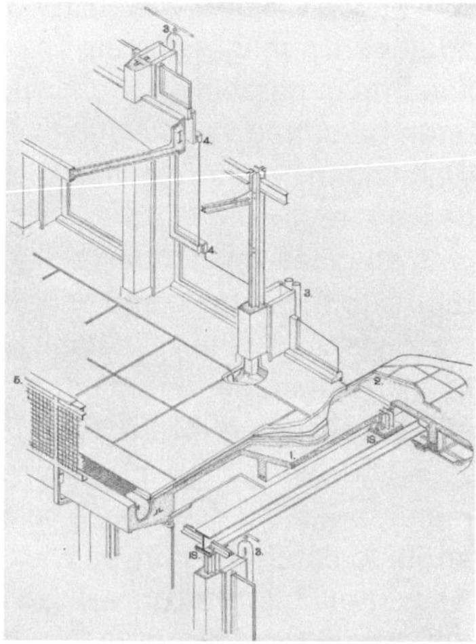

25–26 Richard Döcker, sanatorium in Waiblingen

27 Richard Döcker, axonometric of Waiblingen sanatorium terrace system wall above the doorway to the terraces to flood the rooms with additional sunlight and air. The drawings show horizontal daybeds lined up in parallel on the terraces, "mobile curtains," and an open balustrade to facilitate ventilation. Döcker presented his Waiblingen sanatorium as a biological evolution of this unrealized project, replacing Garnier's French doors to the terraces with all-glass walls that slide up to completely open the patient rooms to the outside and enable the beds to be directly pulled out.[23] **[25–26]** The terrace itself is drawn as a sophisticated medical instrument in reinforced concrete and glass, with its sliding windows, angled awnings, and integrated drainage. **[27]**

The sanatorium modernized architecture. The building ultimately adjusted itself into a solar device, stacking itself at a steep angle to catch the sun, as with Marcel Breuer and Gustav Hassenpflug's 1929 unrealized competition project for an eleven-hundred-bed sanatorium for Elberfeld in Germany that made its own mountain, or rather a mountain range heading into the horizon, with stacks of six to nine floors stepping back, propped up by only a few very thin columns and with all-glass façades.[24] **[28–29]** Their project is directly echoed in Le Corbusier and Pierre

28 Marcel Breuer and Gustav Hassenpflug, unrealized competition project for a 1100-bed sanatorium for Elberfeld, Germany, 1929

29 Model of Breuer and Hassenplug sanatorium project

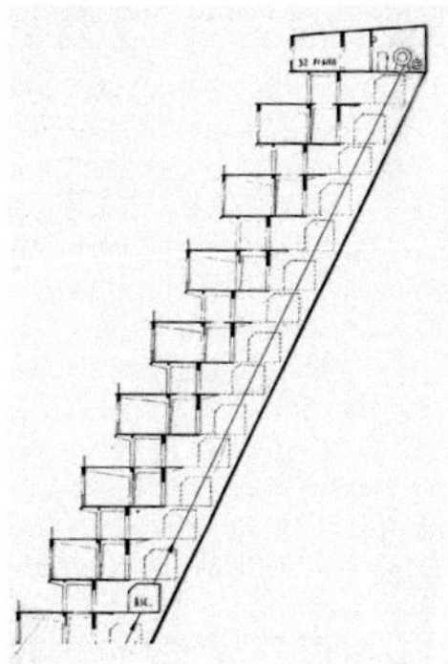

Jeanneret's 1933 Lotissement Durand-Oued Ouchaia, a housing project for Algiers with four stepped buildings of three hundred apartments each in an open landscape, understood as an escape from the tuberculosis-ridden historic Casbah. [30] More radical was Nicola Visontai's 1934 project for a sanatorium in the Italian Alps, a building that took advantage of a much steeper angle of the mountainside and featured an elevator moving up diagonally behind the stacked patients' room. [31]

In these unrealized projects of the early 1930s, architects dreamed of buildings angling themselves to the sun to heal fragile bodies, challenging the definition of architecture. It is as if architecture itself took the cure.

30 Le Corbusier and Pierre Jeanneret, Lotissement Durand-Oued Ouchaia, housing project for Algiers, 1933

31 Nicola Visontai, project for a sanatorium in the Italian Alps, 1934

1 In fact, Mies and Reich rented an apartment in Stuttgart and lived there together as a couple for the first and last time.
2 Reich was responsible for the design and organization of the exhibition rooms no. 1, 4, 5, 6, and 7. Hall 4 and 5, the *Linoleumraum* (Linoleum Hall, for the company Deutsche Linoleum-Werke A-G), and the *Glasraum* (Plate-Glass Hall, for the company Verein Deutscher Spiegelglasfabriken GmbH) were designed in collaboration with Mies.
3 Erna Meyer, *Der neue Haushalt – Ein Wegweiser zu wirtschaftlicher Hausführung* (Stuttgart: Franckh'sche Verlagshandlung, 1926). The book went into twenty-nine editions in just two years, and soon after into forty. It was widely translated and read by architects and the lay public.
4 Grete Schütte-Lihotzky's model kitchen was designed for the low-income housing estates designed by Ernst May and considered to be the first European realization of the efficient kitchen. Susan Henderson, "The New Woman's Home, Kitchens, Laundries, Furnishings," in *Building Culture: Ernst May and the New Frankfurt Initiative, 1926–1931* (New York: Peter Lang, 2013), 143–202.
5 Erna Meyer, "Das Küchenproblem auf der Werkbundausstellung," *Die Form* 2, no. 10 (1927): 303.
6 Another poster for the exhibition, designed by Karl Ludwig Straub, shows a collage of modern interior images from the houses and an aerial view of the Weissenhofsiedlung.
7 Letter of Peter Behrens to Mies, October 6, 1926. Mies van der Rohe Archives, MoMA, New York. Quoted in Karin Kirsch, *The Weissenhofsiedlung: Experimental Housing Built for the Deutscher Werkbund, Stuttgart, 1927* (New York: Rizzoli, 1989), 176.
8 Peter Behrens, "Terrassen am Hause," in Deutscher Werkbund, *Bau und Wohnung* (Stuttgart: Akad. Verlag Dr. Fr. Wedekind & Co, 1927), 17.
9 Behrens, "Terrassen am Hause."
10 Adolf Gustav Schneck, "Für den modernen Menschen ist das tägliche Luftund Lichtbad zur Erhaltung seiner Gesundheit, seiner körperlichen und geistigen Kräfte eine Notwendigkeit." "Haus Schneck," *Die Form* 2, no. 9 (1927): 268.
11 Sergius Ruegenberg, who had worked in Mies' office recalls: "Mies came back from Stuttgart in November 1926 and talked about Mart Stam and his idea for the chair. We had a drawing board on the wall, and Mies drew the Stam chair on it, right-angled, starting from the top. He also added the sleeves and said: 'Ugly, so ugly with those sleeves. If he had at least rounded it off – that would be nicer' and sketched an arc. – Just a bow from his hand on the Stam sketch made up the new chair." Unpublished tape recording in TECTA's archives. Mart Stam was eventually given the copyright for his design of the cantilever chair.
12 Richard Döcker, *Terrassentyp* (Stuttgart: Fritz Wedekind, 1929).
13 David Sarason, "Construction of Hospitals, Sanatoriums, or Other Buildings," US Patent 736,158 (August 11, 1903).
14 David Sarason, "Ein neues Bausystem für Krankenanstalten und Wohnhäuser," *Bericht über den XIV. internationalen Kongress für Hygiene und Demographie*, vol. 4 (Berlin: Verlag von August Hirschwald, 1908), 567–73.
15 David Sarason, "'Freilufthäuser' ein neues Bauprinzip für Krankenanstalten und Wohngebäude," *Hygienische Rundschau* 19, no. 16 (1909): 974–96. Sarason won a gold medal in Washington "for models and plans showing new and interesting principles in house construction in its relation to the prevention of tuberculosis." *Transactions of the Sixth International Congress on Tuberculosis*, vol. five (Philadelphia, PA: William F. Fell Company, 1908), 265. On the response to the Dresden exhibit, see Christina K. M. Flototto, "Neues Bauen and Hygiene: A mutually profitable relationship investigated in relation to the medical doctor Friedrich Wolf." Ph.D. diss. (University of Edinburgh, 2003): 54–55.
16 Dr. Noel Bardswell, "Ein Freiluftsanatorium im Betriebe," in David Sarason, *Das Freilufthaus. Ein neues Bausystem für Krankenanstalten und Wohngebäude* (Munich: J.F. Lehmanns Verlag, 1913), 122. Bardswell was the director of the sanatorium built on the basis of the 1902 competition. Both Sarason and Turban felt that their entries had deeply influenced the sanatorium that was built.
17 Sauvage and Sarazin's first drawings of stepped housing were done in 1907. Sauvage was likely aware of Sarason's argument and Pierre-Louis Laget suggests that he may have seen the drawings of Hankar's sanatorium project because he was based in Brussels at the time they were exhibited. Pierre-Louis Laget, "L'invention du système des immeubles à gradins. Sa genèse à visée sanitaire avant sa diffusion mondiale dans la villégiature de montagne et de bord de mer," *In Situ: Revue des patrimoines*, no. 24 (2014). See also, Rodrigo Almonacid Canseco, and María Pura Moreno Moreno, "El Terrassen Typ de Richard Döcker: del origen helio-terapéutico

de las terrazas al uso preventivo y estético en los nuevos tipos de la arquitectura moderna." In *Arquitectura para la salud y el descanso: 1914–1975*, (Pamplona: Escuela Técnica Superior de Arquitectura Universidad de Navarra, 2022): 143–154.
18 Ann-Louis Shapiro, *Housing the Poor of Paris, 1850–1902* (Madison: University of Wisconsin, 1985).
19 Edmond Uhry, "Logements Hygiéniques a Bon Marché de Rapport," *L'art décoratif: revue de l'art ancien et de la vie artistique moderne* 6, no. 2 (1904): 129, 132.
20 Sauvage and Sarazin patented the terraced housing idea in 1912, using drawings of the rue Vavin design. Henry Sauvage and Charles Sarazin, "Système de constructions," French Patent 439,292 (July 10, 1912).
21 F. Honoré, "La Maison a Gradins," *L'illustration* 72, no. 3708 (March 21, 1914): 220–21.
22 Tony Garnier, "Sanatorium franco-américan (1917)," in Tony Garnier, *Les grands travaux de la ville de Lyon: études, projects et travaux executes* (Paris: Massin, 1921).
23 Döcker includes Garnier and Sarason as early variations in an evolutionary sequence of ten ever-higher-performing sections through stepped sanatoria with his own Waiblingen as the sixth variation and his "ideal" design for a four-story sanatorium propped up on thin legs as the ultimate step. Döcker, *Terrassentyp*, 60–63. Sauvage and Sarazin's stepped buildings are not included in the sequence, presumably because they are housing rather than sanatoria, yet Döcker symptomatically doesn't include them in the housing section of the book either.
24 The thin columns seem to be inspired by Döcker's just-published "ideal" sanatorium section.

1 Alexander Fleming studying mold cultures in his laboratory, 1955

Modern architecture inserted itself into the newly palpable microbial world as a prophylactic cocoon, shielding from threatening bacteria and viruses. Its visual rhetoric of smooth white surfaces, reflective floors, furnishings, and fittings conveyed its antimicrobial ambition. Modern buildings were an active antibiotic that could both cure and prevent disease.

PROPHYLACTIC SPACE

It was not until 1928 that the first modern antibiotic, penicillin, was accidentally discovered by Alexander Fleming when he observed that *penicillium* mold stopped the growth of bacteria – unknowingly reactivating an ancient knowledge. **[1]** Imhotep, the Egyptian architect of the stepped pyramid of Djoser at Saqqara of 2600 BCE, a doctor, and the author of the oldest known medical treatise, had already applied moldy bread (penicillin) to skin infections. **[2]** Plants and fungi with antibacterial properties have been central to the ancient and ongoing health practices of many Indigenous communities and are now closely studied as alternatives to antibiotics in the age of antimicrobial resistance.

Before penicillin was (re)discovered there was already an antibiotic attitude toward buildings. Modern architecture channeled this antibiotic approach. Le Corbusier obsessed about bacteria. He quoted counts of bacteria per cubic meter in the air, describing himself as a bacteriologist, and architecture and city planning as laboratory work. In *Precisions*, 1930, he writes:

2 Imhotep, ca. 2667–2600 BCE

> In 1922 I tried to delve into an analysis, I did some laboratory work. Isolating my microbe. I watched it develop. The biology of my microbe appeared in indisputable clarity. Certitudes acquired; diagnosis. Then, by an effort of synthesis, I drew up the fundamental principles of modern city planning.[1]

The historian of modern architecture must be a bacteriologist too. Sigfried Giedion wrote:

> It is not enough for a physician to know that a body is attacked by a disease. Even if he is not a bacteriologist, he must push his research into usually invisible realms, he must have a modest knowledge of bacteriology, he must know when the organism was attacked and how the tuberculosis spread. Likewise, the historian cannot dispense with the microscope. He cannot relent in tracing the theme to its origins. He has to show when an idea first appears; how quickly or slowly it spreads or disappears. He cannot confine himself to mechanization alone any more than the doctor can to bacteria. He must take psychic factors into reckoning, for often they exert a decisive influence.[2]

In *La ville radieuse* (*The Radiant City*) of 1935, Le Corbusier dismisses the "natural ground" as a "dispenser of rheumatism

3 "History. Historic Paris, tubercular Paris," illustration from Le Corbusier's *The Radiant City*

and tuberculosis" and declares it to be "the enemy of man." He insists on detaching the house, with the help of pilotis, from the "wet, humid, ground, where disease breeds," and on using the roof as a garden for sunbathing and exercise.[3] To reinforce the point, he used pictures taken from medical texts as architectural illustrations, showing the lungs and their inner workings, while giving architectural illustrations medical labels, as when a photograph of an old part of the city is labeled "Historic Paris, tubercular Paris." **[3–5]**

The book develops a concept of "exact respiration" whereby the indoor air is continually circulated and cleaned, "made dust free, disinfected ... and ready to be consumed by the lung."[4] One by one, it presents the characteristic features of modern architecture – pilotis, roof garden, glass walls, and clean air – as medical devices, and the overall effect is that of a sanatorium devoted to both a preventive and reactive cure. Once again, there is no line between sanatorium and domestic architecture.

Modern architecture was only modern as long as it was free of bacteria. What had been experimented on in sanatoria became part of everyday architecture. Even the client was understood as a patient. Aalto claimed when designing Paimio that the architect had to design for the person in the "weakest position" – the tuberculosis patient had become the model for modern architecture. In other words, sickness was no longer seen as the exception but

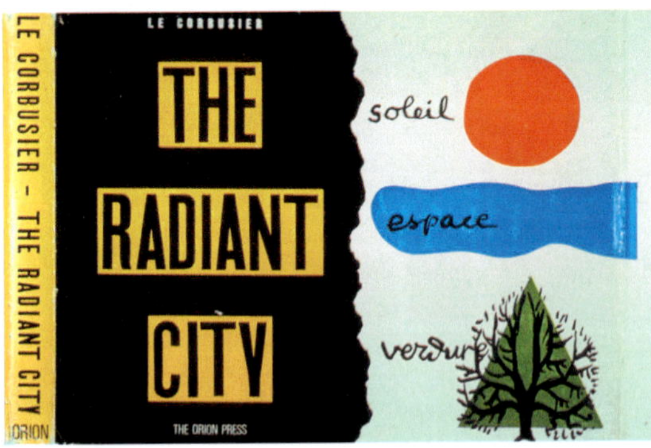

4 Cover of Le Corbusier, *The Radiant City*, English translation of *La ville radieuse*, 1967

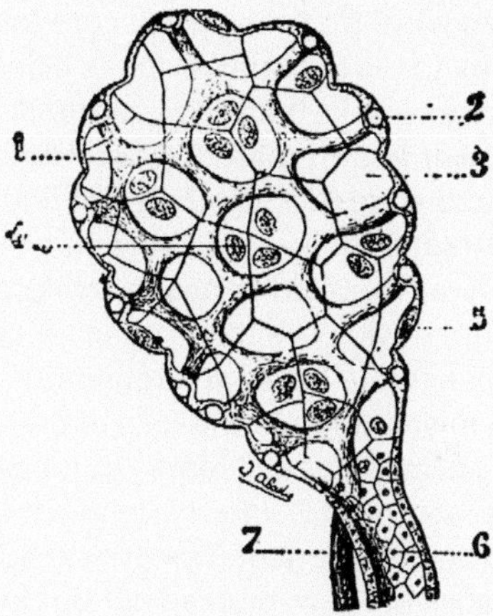

as the norm – and varying degrees of sickness define the human condition. The modern subject has multiple ailments, physical and psychological, and architecture is a protective cocoon not just against the weather and other outside threats but, in modernity, about internal threats: psychological and bodily ailments. The specialized furniture of Paimio, for example, became ordinary everyday pieces for the modern house. If the cantilevered birch-wood Paimio chair was designed to open the chest of the patient, allowing them to breathe easier, soon enough that chair became everybody's chair. **[6]** Likewise with the rest of the furniture specially designed for the sick in Paimio: "The sanatorium needed furniture which should be light, flexible, easy to clean and so on. After extensive experimentation in wood, the flexible system was discovered ... to produce furniture which was more suitable for the long and painful life in a sanatorium."[5] A workshop was set up and in 1935, barely two years after completing Paimio, Alvar and Aino Aalto founded Artek, a furniture company with "the ambition to support and nourish human beings' physical and psychological wellbeing."[6] The sanatorium, which they symptomatically called a "collective dwelling-house," incubated a new form of domesticity.[7]

5 Medical illustration of pulmonary lobule, from *The Radiant City*

SURVIVAL THROUGH DESIGN

Modern architecture went from being the cure for tuberculosis to being an apparatus for its prevention. In the Open Air School in Amsterdam, [7] for example, built between 1927 and 1929 and designed by Jan Duiker and Bernard Bijvoet – the architects who had designed and were building the Zoonestraal Sanatorium in Hilversum, near Amsterdam, at the same time – principles of light, air, and sun were applied to healthy children. The building is conceived as a light device like those used for light therapy in the 1920s. Likewise in the USA, the architectural features of the cure cottage in sanatoria at the turn of the century would soon spread to the private house: sleeping porches, for instance, became common in southern California, where many TB-afflicted people had gone to seek treatment. The private house took on other characteristics of the public sanatorium, including large windows, clean surfaces, and clean lines – meaning the absence of ornament, of draperies, of carpeting, of encumbering objects. White walls were not only considered sanitary but were believed to have a positive impact on the mental health of the inhabitants, their effect the equivalent of a rest cure. In other words, the ideology of modern architecture was present in North America before the official representatives of the European avant-garde arrived.

As the European avant-garde started to emigrate to the USA, this tradition combined with that of high modernism in projects such as Rudolph M. Schindler's Schindler–Chace House of 1921–1922, Schindler's Lovell Beach House of 1925–1926, and Richard Neutra's Lovell "Health" House of 1928–1929 – all of which included sleeping porches and sleeping lofts. [8–9] Neutra included sleeping balconies outside every bedroom in projects into the late 1930s and 1940s, such as the 1939 house for Dr. Scioberetti in Berkeley.

Neutra writes about the architect being a kind of physician and about the special role of the house in the development of an architecture attuned to biology. His famous Lovell Health House in Los Angeles was a doctor–architect collaboration with Dr. Philip Lovell, a naturopath and drugless practitioner who thought all diseases had a dietary origin. Lovell arrived in California and opened a practice in downtown Los Angeles in 1924. His theories of diet, exercise, sun therapy, nudism, and open-air sleeping,

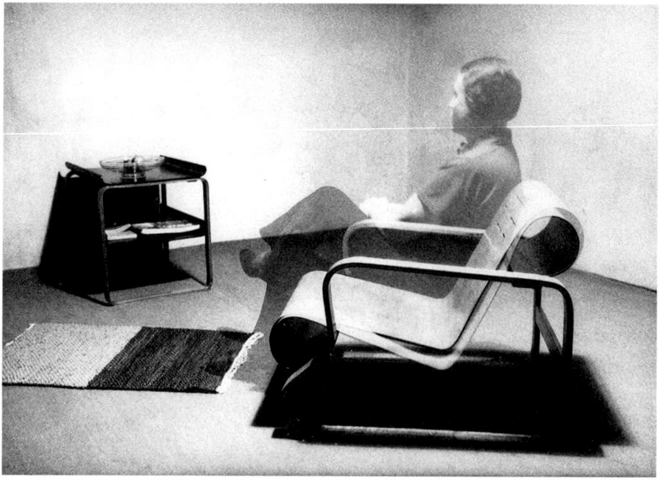

6 Aino Aalto sitting on a Paimio chair

7 Bernard Bijvoet, Jan Duiker, Open Air School for Healthy Children , Amsterdam, 1927–1930

8 Rudolph M. Schindler, Lovell Beach House, Newport Beach, 1925–1926

9 Richard Neutra, Physical Culture Center for Philip Lovell, Los Angeles, 1927 which were disseminated in his column for the *Los Angeles Times* entitled "Care of the Body" (the publisher of the newspaper, Harry Chandler, was one of his patients), were very influential. The Health House is organized around a full regime of sun, air, exercise, fasting, and diet strategies. It was a demonstration house for Lovell's theories, with en-suite sleeping porches outside every room, "nude sun bathing opportunities" throughout the house, "hydrotherapy equipment" and "marathon showers" in the bathroom, which was also equipped with a "built-in enema fixture with various douches and nozzle devices, thermostatically controlled."[8] The house had a swimming pool, basketball court, and playground facilities for the children. The windows were made of Vitaglass to allow in UV rays. **[10]** Lovell opened the house to the public for two weekends, announcing it in his "Care of the Body" column, with a photograph of the house, a description, and a map showing how to get there.[9] Around fifteen thousand people showed up, and Neutra himself gave the tours. **[11]**

Lovell saw in modern architecture a model for health, a mechanism for reconstructing the human: "When we learn to build our bodies with the same careful precision and the same scientific accuracy with which the modern builder constructs his houses," we finally will become healthy.[10] Neutra, on the other hand, saw architecture as a "branch of preventive medicine." Influenced by Lovell's theories of drugless health, he was proud of resisting what he called the "drugs of ornamentation" in the design of the house, avoiding the "corpulent excesses of ornament and curvature."[11] Neutra had his own theories on the relationship between health and architecture, and wrote extensively about it. In *Survival Through Design* of 1954, for example, he argues that the survival of the human species depends on having designers focus on "physiological space." Design operates for Neutra at the intersection of biology and psychology as a therapeutic defense against the "disastrous effects" of all the accumulated conditions of modern life. He writes about how the "warm, moist air practically stationary, saturated with airborne bacteria, and recirculated through many lungs, had made tuberculosis endemic," and of the need for design to address both "pathology, the manifest spreading of disease," and psychological comfort, what he calls "nervous health."[12]

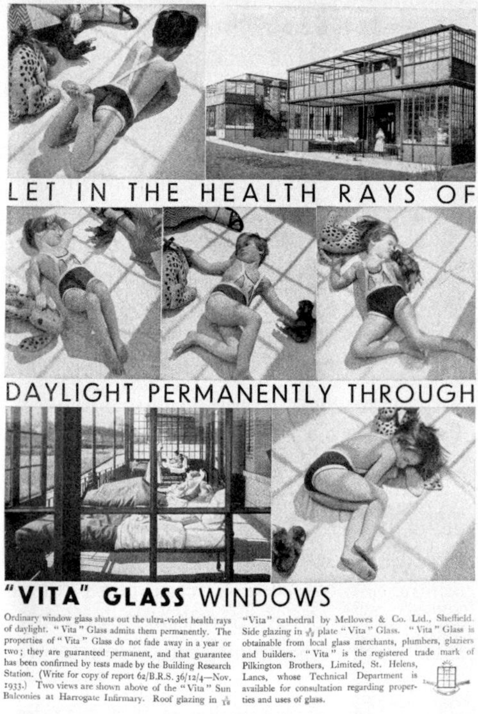

10 Vitaglass advertisement, from *The Architectural Review*, January 1935

11 Richard Neutra pointing to the Lovell House, Los Angeles 1928–1929

For Neutra, mental and physical health are always intertwined. He insists, for example, that the success of his own tropical classroom designs in Puerto Rico from 1944 to 1945 is not just that “airborne bacteria no longer hover in the classroom” and “expectoration dries promptly, quickly diminishing in contagiousness.”[13] **[12]** It is equally in the calming and delightful sensation of cool air passing across the skin as the large fold-up doors extend the possible classroom space.[14] Neutra also designed TB clinics in Puerto Rico, claiming that their spatial organization not only resisted contagion but also conveyed the danger of contagion to the public, which ultimately had more of an effect in resisting contagion. Antibiotic architecture creates a separation from pathogens, but also, and more importantly, conveys that separation:

> T.B clinics ... are always provided with separate entrance and waiting space, both for safety against contagion itself and perhaps *even more for upholding a popular consciousness of this danger*. Such a consciousness is a valuable educational product won by hard effort. It will be effective in combating the spread of the disease.[15]

Neutra himself had tuberculosis and spent a year in a sanatorium in Switzerland before emigrating to the USA. His brother, a doctor, had tuberculosis from the age of nineteen and eventually died from the disease. Several of Neutra’s clients had tuberculosis – Howard Bald, for example, was brought to Los Angeles at the age of eight to be cured. The modest Bald House has an all-white interior and a living room that opens onto a screened porch.

12 Richard Neutra, rural school in Puerto Rico, 1943

Southern California was, in fact, tuberculosis central. Many people migrated there for "the cure" – as did modern architecture. Even the great critic of modern architecture, Esther McCoy, originally came to California to recover from TB.

The battle against bacteria continued after the second world war, when antibiotics were already available. In 1944 the California journal *Arts & Architecture* addressed the question "What is a House?," arguing that the fully industrialized postwar house should be sprayed with chemicals every six months to make it "totally free of all insects." **[13–14]** Furthermore, electronic devices should continuously remove bacteria from the air, and sterilization lamps should be used to kill bacteria in water, food, and on any surface.[16] **[15–16]** The postwar house was still at war, just now with bacteria.

The main reference here is Buckminster Fuller, a notorious germophobe, whose 1927 Dymaxion House was a sterilization chamber filled with antibacterial devices and isolated from any possible contagion from the ground, neighbors, or even shared plumbing. The "sanitary" house had no doorknobs because they transfer germs efficiently, or pipes, since they have "been respon-

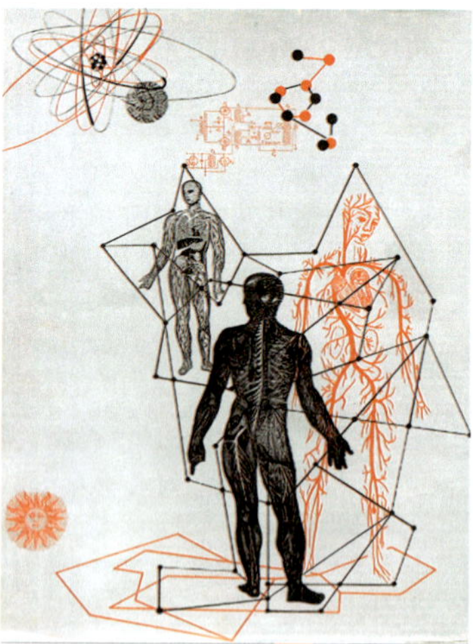

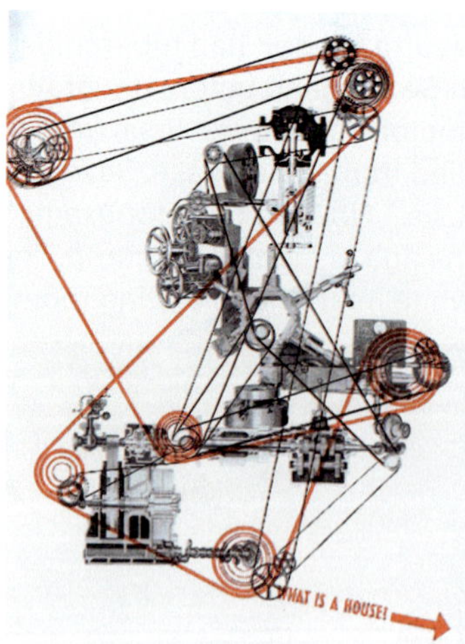

13–14 "What is a House?," *Arts & Architecture*, July 1944

sible for breeding most of all the infectious bacteria heretofore entering human abodes."[17] **[17]** The design goal is "preventative pathology" against the diseases "bred" by housing, "the multi-millions who die from dirt in cracks in housing annually."[18]

Fuller took architectural hygiene to another level. He was obsessed with cleanliness as the basis of physical and mental health – insisting on the shared origin of the words "sane" and "sanitary." The very basis of thinking clearly is "the ability to cope with filth-bred fungi and bacteria and their ravaging."[19] All Fuller's prototypes for industrialized houses were extensions of a combined toilet–bathroom unit molded out of a single curving surface with no corners for microbes, and new systems for deep-cleaning the body.[20] To refine and manufacture the unit, Fuller took a research position at the American Standard Sanitary Manufacturing Company, the largest manufacturer of sanitary fittings in the USA in 1931. His 1932 list of the "universal requirements" of shelter included "intestinal" and "pore cleansing," and the bathroom unit was meant to feature a high-pressure fog gun to "scavenge" into every pore of the skin to remove contamination. Professional magazines like *Architectural Record*

14

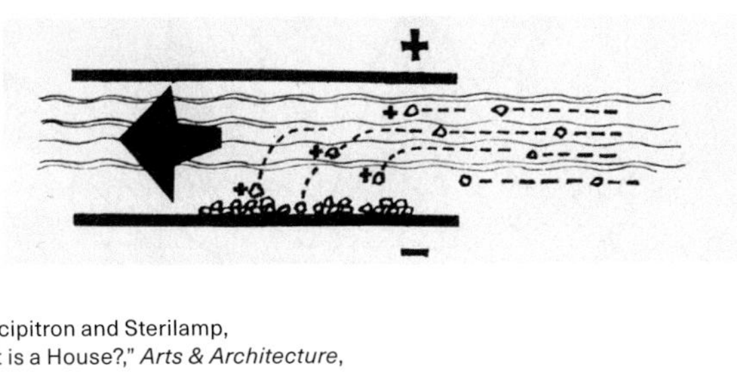

15–16 Precipitron and Sterilamp, from "What is a House?," *Arts & Architecture*, July 1944

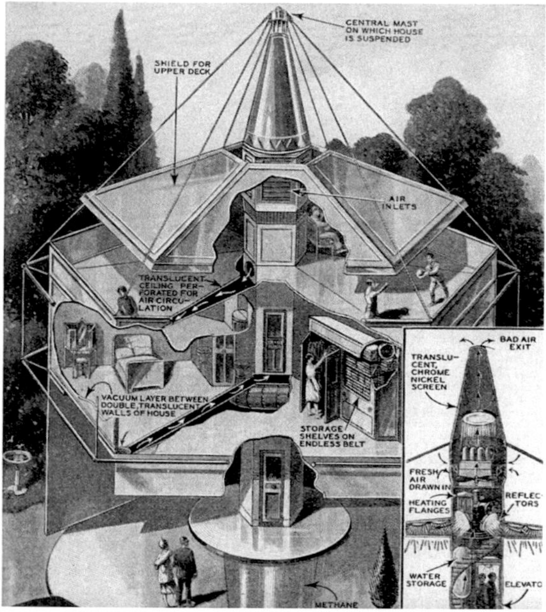

17 Buckminster Fuller, Dymaxion House, from *Modern Mechanix and Inventions*, September 1932

18 Buckminster Fuller alongside Dymaxion House model, 1929

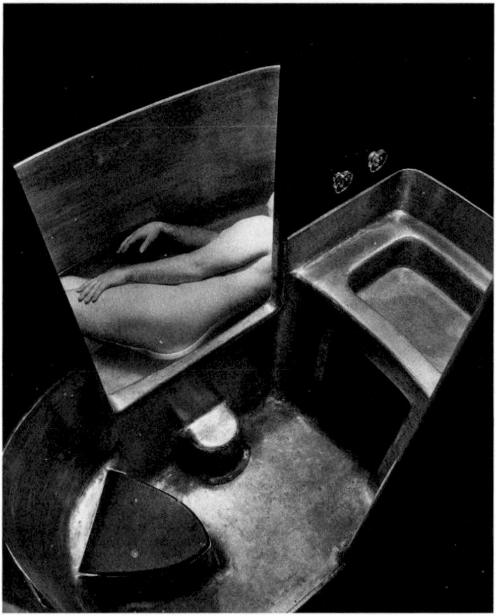

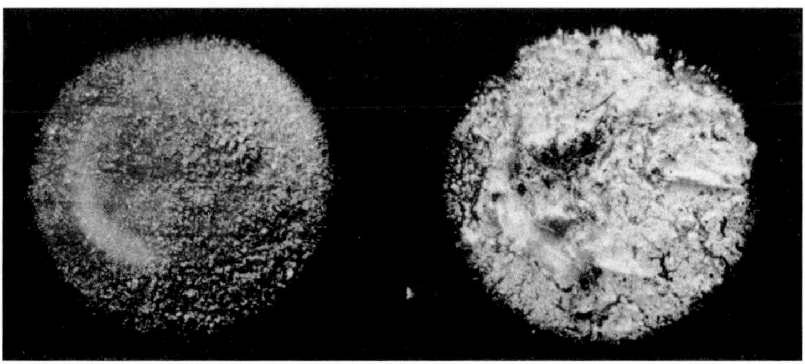

19 Buckminster Fuller inside Dymaxion bathroom, 1937

20 Microscope images of dirt in the pores of Fuller's architecture students and popular magazines like *House Beautiful* presented Fuller's naked cleansed body cocooned in the 1937 version of his bathroom unit. **[19]** Fuller himself published microscope images of the dirt that needed to be blasted out of the pores of his architecture students and recommended sleeping without clothing or bed coverings to enable the purified air of his house to "reach the pores of the body." **[20]** As shown in the first models of the "germ-proof" house, the ideal occupant of modern architecture is naked, experiencing the true comfort of the absence of bacteria. **[18]** Symptomatically, Fuller updated his universal requirements of dwellings in 1949 to include "Interception and neutralization of bacteria by isolation of, – or by direct elimination."[21]

This battle was not just waged in the USA. Alison and Peter Smithson claimed that the 1956 House of the Future – an exhibition house built as a 1:1 structure for the *Ideal Home Exhibition* in London – was completely antibacterial. The whole house is a hyper-clean space, a kind of molded space capsule entered through a decontamination system.[22] **[21]** Towels are considered a microbial hazard, so the shower in the bathroom also functions as a drier, with nozzles for both water and warm air.

21 Alison and Peter Smithson, House of the Future, entrance, 1956

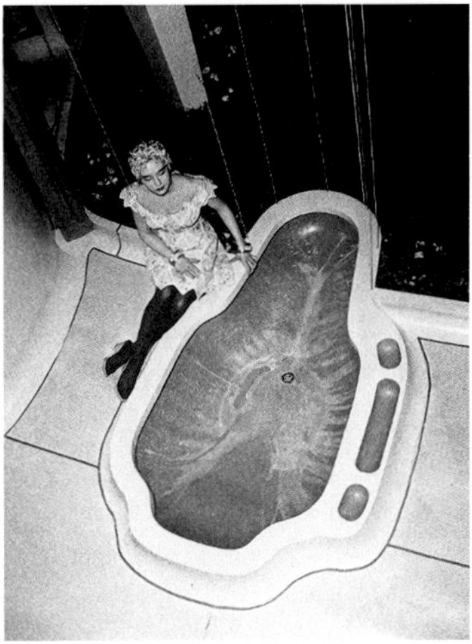

22–23 Alison and Peter Smithson, House of the Future, bathtub (left), 1956

24 Alison and Peter Smithson, House of the Future, kitchen with packaged food, 1956

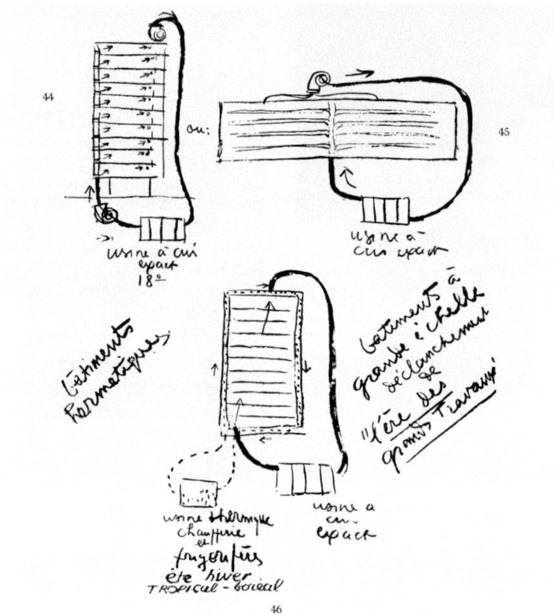

Disposable paper towel dispensers are installed near all water sources. A sun lamp is built into the lavatory wall. The bed has only one fitted nylon sheet because the controlled temperature of the house eliminates the need for bacteria-ridden bedclothes. All smooth plastic surfaces are rounded to avoid dust and facilitate cleaning, **[22–23]** and “all the food is bombarded with gamma rays, an atomic byproduct to kill bacteria.”[23] **[24]**

Yet antibacterial architecture produces sickness. With Sick Building Syndrome, for example, the air conditioning systems that modern architects celebrated for isolating the clean air inside from the contaminated air outside turned out to be reservoirs and vectors of disease. **[25]** The kind of architecture that was supposed to inoculate its occupants against disease turned against them, as if in a science fiction movie.

25 Drawing by Le Corbusier of the closed loops in his *bâtiments hermétiques* (airtight buildings) that harbor and circulate pathogens, illustration in *Précisions*, 1930

1 Le Corbusier, *Precisions sur un état présent de l'architecture et de l'urbanisme* (Paris: Les Editions G. Cres, 1930): 144. Translation, *Precisions on the present state of architecture and city planning* (Cambridge, MA: MIT Press, 1991), 144. In the preface to the second edition of *Vers une architecture* in 1924, Le Corbusier writes: "We are unhappy living in unworthy houses because they ruin our health.... The house eats away at us in our immobility, like consumption [tuberculosis]. We will soon need too many sanatoria." Le Corbusier, *Towards an Architecture*, trans. John Goodman (Los Angeles: Getty Research Institute, 2007), 94.
2 Sigfried Giedion, *Mechanization Takes Command: A Contribution to Anonymous History* (New York: Oxford University Press, 1948), 5.
3 Le Corbusier, *La ville radieuse* (Paris: Éditions de l'Architecture d'aujourd'hui, 1935). Translation, *The Radiant City* (New York: Orion Press, 1967), 48, 56.
4 Le Corbusier, *The Radiant City*, 48.
5 Alvar Aalto, "The Humanizing of Architecture," *Technology Review* (November 1940): 16.
6 "The Artek Manifesto," (1935) Artek Company, Helsinki. See also, *Alvar Aalto*, vol. 1 (Zurich: Artemis Verlag, 1992), 43, 66.
7 The Aaltos described their sanatorium as a "collective dwelling house" in an undated presentation panel highlighting the main design features of the patient rooms as "the individual part of the residence." Marianna Heikinheimo, *Architecture and Technology: Alvar Aalto's Palmio Sanatorium* (Espoo: Aalto University: 2016), 250.
8 Willard Morgan, "Plumbing and Heating for a Modern Health Home," *Domestic Engineering* (April 5, 1930): 52.
9 Philip Lovell, "Care of the Body," *Los Angeles Times Sunday Magazine* (December 15, 1929): 26.
10 Philip Lovell and Leah Lovell, *Diet for Health by Natural Methods: Together with Health Menus and Recipes; Complete Instructions for the Cure of the Sick Without the Use of Drugs* (Los Angeles: Times-Mirror Press, 1927), 16, quoted in Victoria Jane Solan, "Built for Health" PhD diss. (Yale University, 2004), 140.
11 Richard Neutra, quoted in "Steel Construction with Plaster," *California Plasterer,* 1929, clipping in Neutra archives, UCLA. See Solan, "Built for Health," 145–46.
12 Richard Neutra, *Survival Through Design* (New York: Oxford University Press, 1953), 320, 194.
13 Neutra, *Survival Through Design*, 322.
14 "Tilt-up doors let the agreeably steady breezes move the humid classroom air three-four times every minute, and with it evacuate all airborne bacteria. Perspiration drips no longer, but agreeably dries, cooling the skin." Richard Neutra, *Architecture of Social Concern in Regions of Mild Climate* (São Paulo: Gerth Todtmann, 1948), 54.
15 Neutra, *Architecture of Social Concern*, 124. Italics in the original.
16 Unsigned, "What is a House?," *Arts & Architecture* (July 1944): 32–49. The article was referring to the "Precipitron" and "Sterilamp" devices for removing bacteria from air and surfaces that were manufactured by Westinghouse from the late 1930s and advertised for use in homes in architectural journals during the war.
17 Buckminster Fuller, *Critical Path* (New York: Macmillan, 1981), 212.
18 Buckminster Fuller, Excerpts from address on "Mass Production of Houses in Factories" given at City Club Forum Luncheon, Tuesday, May 28, 1929. Buckminster Fuller Papers, Special Collections, Stanford University, Series 2, Box 21, 4.
19 Buckminster Fuller, "The Music of the New Life: Thoughts on Creativity, Sensorial Reality, and Comprehensiveness," *Music Educators Journal* 52, no. 5 (April – May, 1966): 134.
20 Mark Wigley, *Buckminster Fuller Inc.: Architecture in the Age of Radio* (Zurich: Lars Müller Publishers, 2015).
21 "Universal Requirements of a Dwelling Advantage, Teleologic Schedule" 1949, Serge Ivan Chermayeff Architectural Records and Papers, 1909–1980. Dept. of Drawings & Archives, Avery Architectural and Fine Arts Library, Columbia University.
22 Beatriz Colomina, "Unbreathed Air: 1956," in *Alison and Peter Smithson: From the House of the Future to a House of Today*, eds. Dirk van Heuvel and Max Risselada (Rotterdam: 010, 2004).
23 Alison and Peter Smithson, "The House of the Future," *Daily Mail Ideal Home Exhibition, Olympia, 1956* (London: Times Furnishing, 1956), 99.

1 Representation of a polio victim, Egypt, Eighteenth Dynasty (ca. 1403–1365 BCE)

Antibiotic architecture both reduces human microbial diversity and incubates ever-more-lethal antimicrobial-resistant microorganisms. It weakens the ability to resist the very pathogens it incubates. It is a double health crisis. On the one hand, urbanized humans have already lost half of the microbial diversity of their ancestors, severely compromising their resilience. On the other hand, urbanization is triggering the exponential rise of antimicrobial resistance as a global health challenge that impacts everyone, but disproportionately affects disadvantaged communities, countries, and regions. Deaths associated with antimicrobial resistance are predicted to rise 70 percent in the next twenty-five years to become the single largest global killer.

DISEASES OF CLEANLINESS

Paradoxically, sanitation produced new epidemics. Poliomyelitis, for example, is an ancient and highly contagious disease – an Egyptian tablet from the fourteenth century BCE likely shows the symptoms [1] – but it was never an epidemic until the acceleration of industrialization. Other diseases transmitted by contact with fecal matter like cholera and typhoid fever were dramatically reduced with the new fresh water and sewage systems of the late nineteenth century, but polio exploded. Increased sanitation, sewage, and clean water – along with new cleaner living spaces and separation from the soil – meant that children didn't encounter the polio virus in infancy – when they still had protection from the mother's antibodies and the disease was mild, allowing them to develop immunity. In later childhood, the disease can progress to the more dangerous second stage which affects the central nervous system and leads to paralysis or even death.

Polio was "a disease of cleanliness" which struck the middle-class and rich countries the hardest. Sweden had a polio epidemic already in 1881, and during the 1911–1913 epidemic, 10,000 victims were reported in the small country. Scandinavia had for many years the unfair reputation of being the origin and breeding ground of the disease, but the USA was actually the most affected.[1] The 1916 New York City polio epidemic, which originated in Brooklyn, spread across the city, killing more than 2,000 people over five months. Local newspapers published daily the names and addresses of people with the disease. In an echo of the plagues in fourteenth-century Italy, houses were marked with a notice at the door to keep out and the family was quarantined. Panic ensued. Schools, cinemas, swimming pools, beaches, and other public spaces were closed. Thousands fled New York and entire streets, neighborhoods, and even cities were quarantined, with police posted at railway stations and roads to prevent people who had been exposed from leaving. Nevertheless, the epidemic spread to twenty-seven states, paralyzing twenty-seven thousand and killing seven thousand in a few months, mostly children under the age of five. [2–3]

Polio had been identified as a viral infection in 1908 by Karl Landsteiner and Erwin Popper in Vienna, but nobody knew how it was transmitted and how to treat it. At a popular level, the

old miasma theory and the fresh-air cure were revived, with babies wrapped up to sleep outside, despite repeated statements from doctors that foul air was not to blame. Meanwhile, advertisements argued that soap and antibacterial products, such as Lysol, prevented polio. Sanitary police inspected houses, public spaces were disinfected with chemicals, and streets were scrubbed daily with millions of gallons of water. An epidemic spawned by excessive cleaning was countered with more cleaning. As typical of plagues, a particular group was blamed and violently attacked – in this case, Italian Americans – even though they were not particularly affected. The worst-hit areas were not the inner-city neighborhoods of immigrant and Black communities, but wealthier, whiter, more suburban neighborhoods like Staten Island.

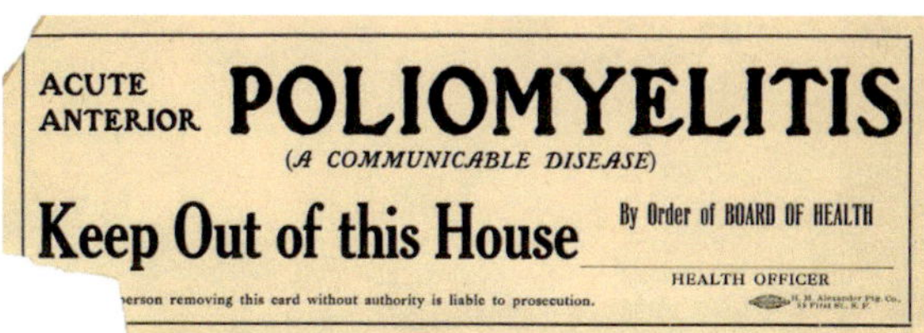
ACUTE ANTERIOR POLIOMYELITIS
(A COMMUNICABLE DISEASE)
Keep Out of this House
By Order of BOARD OF HEALTH
HEALTH OFFICER
...erson removing this card without authority is liable to prosecution.

2 "Keep off this Street," Board of Health warning

3 Board of Health warning, San Francisco, 1910

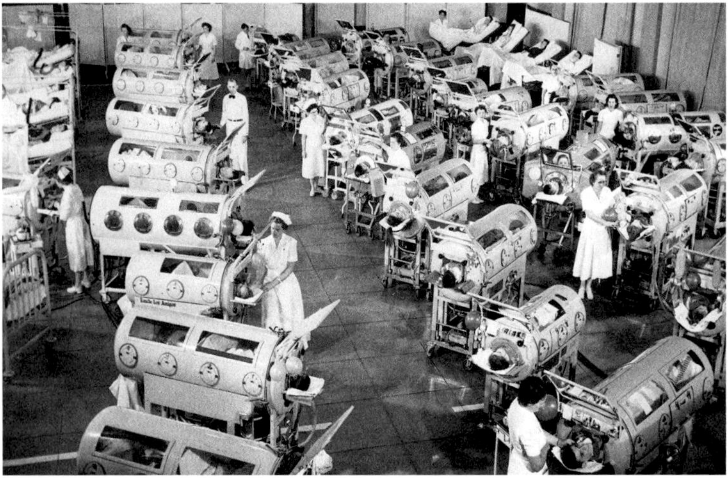

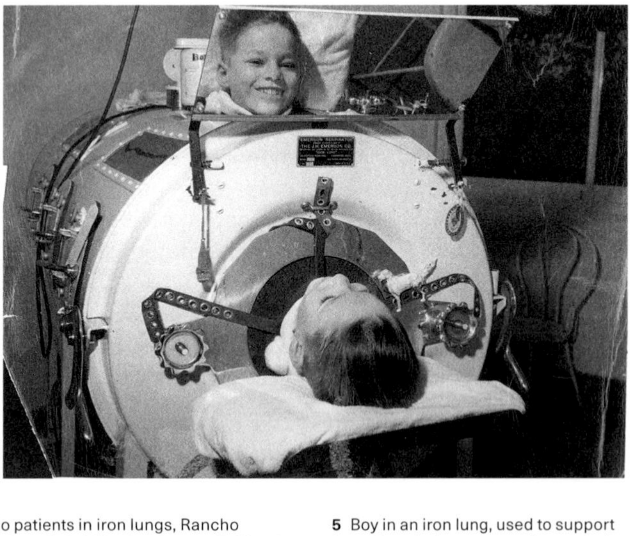

4 Polio patients in iron lungs, Rancho Los Amigos Rehabilitation Center, California, 1953

5 Boy in an iron lung, used to support breathing during acute polio paralysis, ca. 1955

At its peak in the 1940s and 1950s, the terrifying disease paralyzed or killed five hundred thousand people worldwide every year. During the worst outbreak in the USA in 1952, it was again children from richer, more sanitized neighborhoods that were the majority of victims, while children from poorer neighborhoods had more immunity. Vast halls filled with iron lungs – a new architecture that breathed for patients whose respiratory muscles had been paralyzed. Endless coverage in illustrated magazines magnified the fear. **[4–5]** Polio was a mass media event driven by an organism that couldn't be visualized. The "millionth of an inch in diameter" microbe was not seen until the 1952 electron microscope images of doctors Howard Bachrach and Carleton Schwerdt at the University of California, which were immediately front-page news.[2] **[6]** The Salk vaccine became available in 1955, but required multiple shots and a booster every year – a protocol that the middle class was more able to follow.[3] The poor were again left behind, and polio became known as a "disease of the unvaccinated" and poorer countries.

The "hygiene hypothesis" of 1989 proposed that early childhood infections by microbes picked up by contact with other children and the environment are crucial in building up the immune system.[4] Overly clean built environments and behaviors disconnect young children from the microbes essential to building their unique healthy microbial communities, including

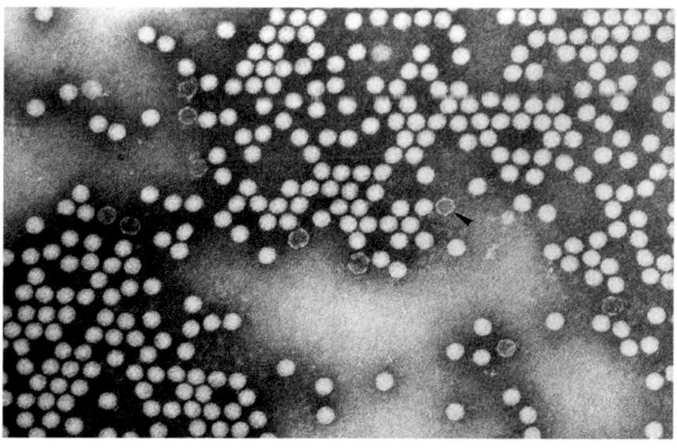

6 Poliovirus type 1 under a transmission electron microscope, 1971

the infections that educate the immune system. The theory was refined by the "old friends hypothesis" in 2003, which argued that the positive effect was not simply from microbial exposure in general, but exposure to specific ancient microbes that co-evolved with humans in the hunter-gatherer phase before the construction of the built environment.[5] Early microbial infections trigger responses that are guided by other microbes that teach the community how to react.

This all-important exposure to both microbial challenges and guidance has to happen during a child's first three years, when its lifelong microbiome and associated adaptive immune system is being formed. The young child learns how to both absorb and survive the world that passes through it. Old friends are not just loyal defenders; they include ancient infections that were common but didn't produce deadly epidemics. Absorbing an old threat acts as a pattern for responding to a new one. The immune system that protects the human doesn't simply distinguish between friend and foe and evict the foes. Rather, it curates a balance of microbes. Survival and health is more about tolerance than intolerance. A resilient organism is able to absorb rather than evict threats. A fragile organism can be undone by its very attempt to evict strangers. Disconnection from the microbial richness of the soil and other species during the crucial first three years of life makes humans fragile. The sanitization of water, spaces, and bodies saved millions of lives but also weakened the species.

THE BIODIVERSITY HYPOTHESIS

The "old friends hypothesis" was in turn refined in 2011 by the "biodiversity hypothesis" that emerged from a remarkable story. After the second world war, Finland ceded half of the largely rural Karelia region of subarctic forests and lake to Russia, with the impermeable iron curtain passing right down the middle. The Russian side remained rural while the Finnish side urbanized rapidly. A massive socio-economic disparity developed with an inversely related health disparity. Since the genetic pool was practically identical, it allowed for a unique case study.

Children in the urbanized Finnish side, living in modern buildings, suffered from an ever-increasing number of allergies and autoimmune disorders while their Russian counterparts didn't. Domestic interiors on the Russian side were much less sanitary – with thousands of times as many living microbes in the drinking water and house dust, and children were much more engaged outside with soil, plants, and animals in forests and farmlands.[6] Their oral, gut, and skin microbiome were around three times more diverse than those of their Finnish counterparts. More specifically, the networks of microbes that activate the genes controlling the immune system were much richer in Russian Karelia.[7] Even on the Finnish side, those children that engaged with a more biodiverse outdoor environment had a richer microbiome and less immune-related disease.

Declining planetary diversity is linked to declining human microbiome diversity and the rise of chronic inflammatory disorders. In framing the biodiversity hypothesis, the scientists studying Karelia argued that the human immune system is unable to adapt to the low microbial diversity in cities.[8] The correlation between urbanization and declining micro- and macro-biodiversity has been confirmed in many other studies worldwide and echoed in the evolution of the human microbiome in deep time. Contemporary urbanized and Westernized humans have around half the diversity of gut microbes of present-day hunter-gatherers, such as the Hazda communities in Tanzania, which have a very similar microbiome to prehistoric communities. Many of the "vanishing microbes" are thought to have co-evolved with the genus *Homo* for millions of years before the emergence of *Homo sapiens*.[9] The loss started with the first permanent settlements but the decline became exponential with industrialization.

The transformation of the gut from the earliest agrarian settlements to industrialized cities is echoed in contemporary migration from non-Western rural settlements to large Westernized cities. A 2018 study of immigrants from Thailand to the United States showed a rapid overall decline in gut microbiodiversity.[10] Some of the disappearing microbes are replaced with new ones. Microrganisms like *Prevotella*, for example, which is associated with digesting a plant-based high-fiber diet, give way to *Bacteroides* that are tuned to processed food, high fat, and sugar. Yet diet alone doesn't entirely explain the shift. Physical, chemical, social, and psychological aspects of urban life also seemed to contribute to the decline. Gut microbiodiversity loss is immediate in recent immigrants and compounded in following generations, which quickly suffer the same immune-related disorders as the rest of the population.

Many of the new microbes associated with urbanization degrade the mucus barrier that forms the sticky line between each human and the world. Mucus is the site of constant curated exchanges between inside and outside. The one-cell-thick epithelial line that is covered by mucus depends on immune regulation circuits that need to be stimulated by a diversity of specific microbes, many of which are now missing. No longer sure how to respond to the world, the border zone becomes intolerant. **[7]** The diseases of urbanization are increasingly diseases of inflammation, the body paradoxically attacking itself by defending itself too much.

Awareness of the relationship between industrialized urban life and mucus has a long history. Doctor Charles Blackley

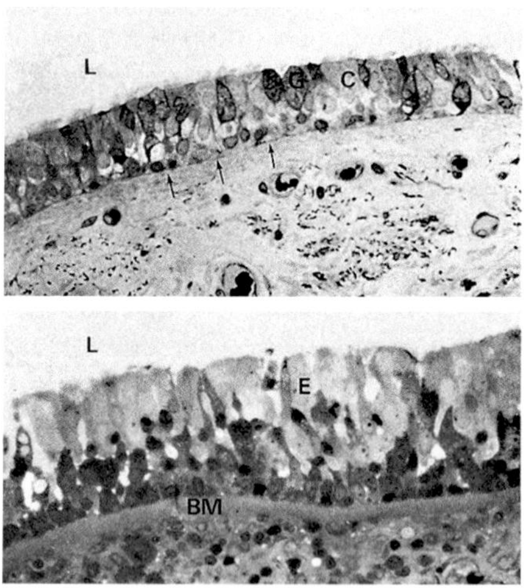

7 Normal bronchial epithelium compared with inflammation of asthma patient in Karelia

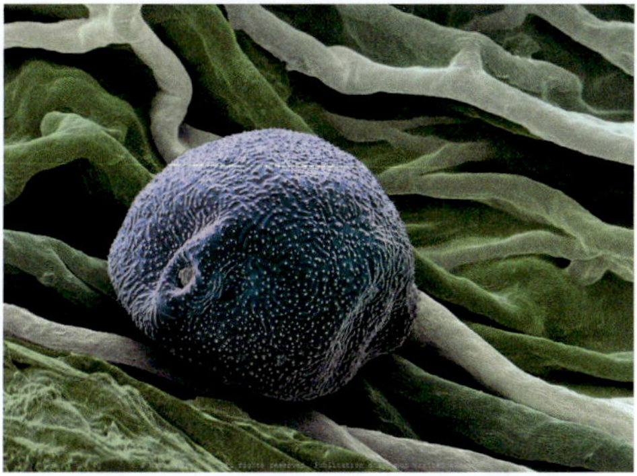

already noted in 1873 that allergies were increasing in urban citizens in rapidly industrializing England and rare for those living in the countryside, who appeared to have immunity through constant exposure.[11] Blackley demonstrated that hay fever was caused by minute particles of pollen in dust. **[8]** Humans had become allergic to the natural world they were separated from. In the twentieth century, they also became increasingly allergic to the built environment and even to themselves. Epidemiologist Martin Blaser treats this immunity crisis triggered by "the silent extinction of microbes" as an accelerating self-perpetuating threat. An overly sanitized environment not only restricts contact with the microbes that have been collaborative companions since prehistory, it also restricts microbial exchanges with other humans – fostering ever-more-rapid microbial loss.[12]

The exact role of the disappearing microbes remains unclear. Maria Gloria Dominguez-Bello and a group of her international colleagues have launched the Microbiota Vault Initiative to preserve microbes that are going extinct. Inspired by the Global Seed Vault in Norway, all the samples are to be stored in a bunker deep in a Swiss mountainside – like a kind of ark – and made available to future researchers.[13] **[9]** The idea is to create a kind of mirror of global microbial diversity in the heart of a mountain as a reservoir for future research. A feces sample donated by an Indigenous hunter-gatherer in the Amazon, for example,

8 Martin Oeggerli, SEM image of birch pollen, a common cause of hay fever

contains microbes already known to be disappearing as well as microbes that have yet to be detectable and might turn out to be crucial endangered companions. Microbiota samples gathered from humans, other animals, food, soil, and the environment around the world by local research collections are brought to the vault where they are isolated from environmental and political fluctuations. The vault facilitates genetic sequencing and the exchange of knowledge among scientists in a collaborative effort to learn more about the roles that microbes play. The goal of this combined biodatabank is to preserve the animal, plant, soil, and food microbiome that may well turn out to be crucial to both human and planetary health.

The project raises many philosophical and ethical questions. Extinction of species is not by definition a crisis of planetary health. On the contrary, the history of life is also the history of successive extinctions that shaped the biosphere, with each mass extinction event followed by a dramatic increase in biodiversity. Furthermore, the implied possibility of rewilding the human and its environments by reintroducing lost microbes is fraught with the risks of all rewilding projects.[14] Reinjecting even one lost species can destabilize a whole ecosystem. The question is less about trying to turn back the clock and more about whether the human will adapt to its own effects or succumb to them.

9 Stool samples stored in Microbiota Vault

For all their extractive and suicidal violence, humans are part of nature. They are ecosystems entangled with other ecosystems. And human impact doesn't simply reduce biodiversity. Take, for instance, topsoil, which is the planet's main reservoir of microbial diversity, hosting a quarter of all microbes. Human activity now plays such a massive role in the composition of soil that it is understood as a "soil forming" force at a planetary scale.[15] Human-made soil has ever-less-diverse microbial communities, yet rising temperatures are releasing ancient microbes from the permafrost – the frozen soil that covers a quarter of the landmass of the northern hemisphere. The consequences of this for planetary diversity and health are unknown. These ancient microbes might be a new threat to human populations, but they could also turn out to be our best friends. The planet itself is a microbial vault.

ANTIMICROBIAL RESISTANCE

Extreme forms of sanitation produce extremophiles. Applying a strong disinfectant to a room kills most microbes but encourages the emergence of resistant species that, without competition, can take over the space. The hyper-sterilized spaces of hospitals, for example, are plagued with pathogens that are resistant to antibiotics. These pathogens don't just survive attempts to kill them, but feed off those attempts. Every chemical, no matter how harsh, is food for some organism. Domestic spaces have increasingly adopted the sterilizing antimicrobial strategies of hospitals and likewise cultivate pathogens. Antibiotic architecture breeds antimicrobial resistance.

Every corner of the planet is infused with antibiotics. Global human antibiotic consumption more than doubled between 2000 and 2023, and is estimated to increase another 50 percent by 2030.[16] Around a third of all antibiotics consumed are infused into the environment through wastewater, where it joins the residue of other antibiotics used in agriculture. More than 70 percent of all antibiotics produced globally are used to promote animal and plant growth, yet much of it ends up being consumed by humans again in an endless cycle. All planetary soil, water, and plants contain traces of antibiotics.[17]

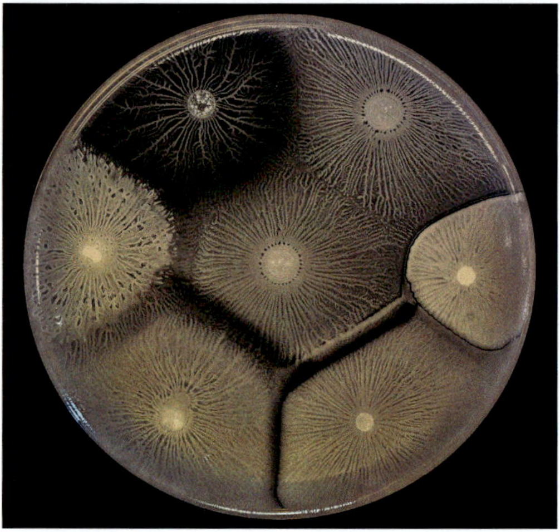

Antimicrobial resistance is a crucial part of the way microbes have interacted for billions of years – not just in competition with each other but also to facilitate collaboration. Symbiotic relationships between species are mediated by antimicrobial signals.[18] Plants, for example, produce an array of antimicrobial molecules to actively curate the bacteria that penetrate their root nodules and process nitrogen into a form the plants can use. The spatial organization of the trillions of microbes in human and most animal guts is similarly regulated by antimicrobials.[19] Antimicrobial molecules structure space. **[10]**

Penicillin, the first modern antibiotic that revolutionized healthcare in the 1940s, is the product of several species of *penicillium* mold that spreads in the air and is found in cool damp environments like soil, decaying vegetation, food, house dust, carpet, dry walls, and water-damaged buildings. **[11]** The fungus releases the chemical to keep rival bacteria at a distance while creating a space to carry out decomposition as a crucial part of the ecosystem. There is a constant dance between its rivals, each adapting to the other, as the mold tries to maintain its own space and bacteria try to occupy it. Humans found the

10 Different strains of *Bacillus subtilis* merge with close relatives but emit antimicrobials to preserve distance from dissimilar strains

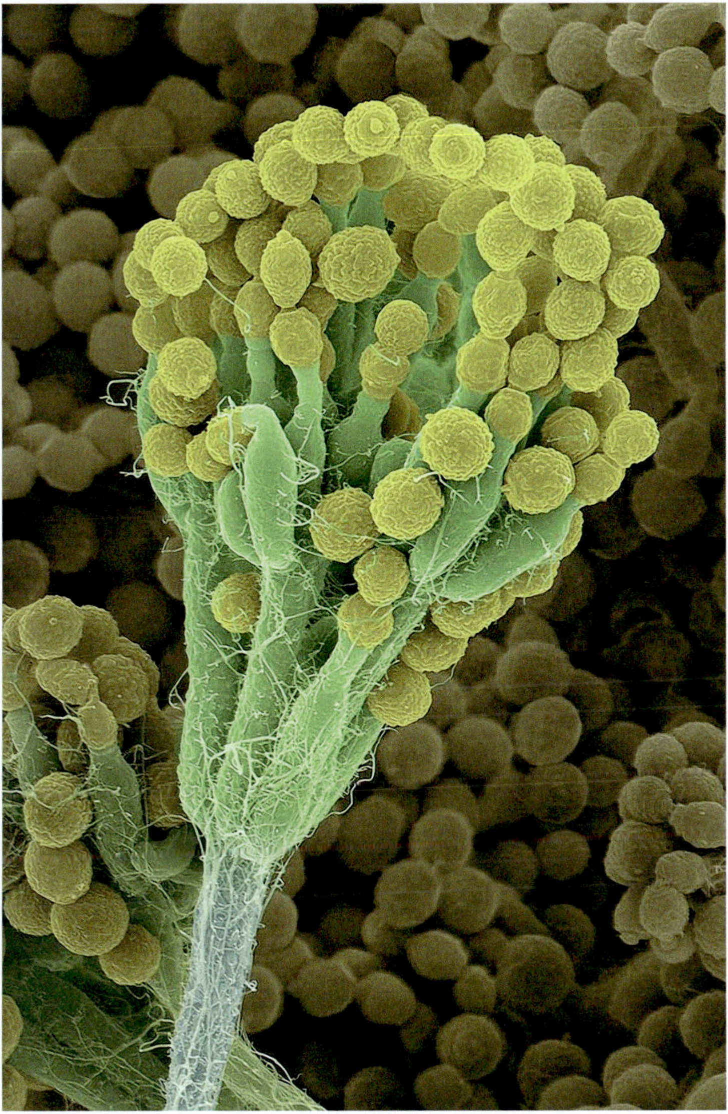

11 SEM image of penicillin-producing mold

species of mold that makes the most antibiotics, made it produce even more by mutating it with X-rays, industrialized that production, and distributed it throughout the environment. Trillions of doses generated from the descendants of one sample found on a cantaloupe have been consumed by humans and farm animals everywhere in the world, with most of the active chemical excreted in urine. It kills a wide range of both beneficial and harmful bacteria in the body and the environment. It continues to create space, and effectively challenges bacteria to mutate in order to enter that space. The first *E. coli* bacteria resistant to penicillin were already seen in 1940, and each new version of the antibiotic has become quickly ineffective against an ever-growing number of pathogens.

Bacteria develop resistance by picking up resistance genes, fragments of DNA that offer a mechanism to survive antimicrobials.[20] These genes can be found far from human contact deep underground, but are more prevalent wherever humans go. In Antarctica, for example, which is regarded as the most pristine environment on the planet, there are very few resistance genes except around research stations.[21] These genes have the signature of the cities the researchers came from. Microbiologist María Mercedes Zambrano describes how buildings, cities, and the territories around them host specific sets of resistance genes.[22] The genes in the air of buildings and public transport are specific to cities, as are those in the wastewater and ultimately most things produced by humans. The quantity of these genes is inverse to the degree of microbial diversity. A study in China, for example, showed that the microbiomes of urban communities are much less diverse than nearby rural communities and exhibit much more virulence and antimicrobial resistance genes.[23] These genes concentrate where humans concentrate but travel in oceans and clouds, moving across and between continents.[24]

Similarly, microplastics shed by cities now infuse the soil, water, and air of the entire planet along with the food chain and products used on bodies and buildings. They are continually inhaled and ingested by humans and most animals, becoming resident in all lung and intestinal tissue. Microplastics are an ideal platform of hosting, generating, and dispersing pathogens and resistance genes.[25] They support biofilms that dramatically magnify the antimicrobial resistance in any environment, and a diversity of adjacent microplastics magnifies it even more.[26] **[12]** Furthermore, climate change is steadily magnifying that resistance.

Antimicrobial resistance has become a signature of human occupation and transformation of the planet. The built environment is its very engine. Resistance radiates outward from buildings, with fewer pathogens and antimicrobial genes found outside of cities, and fewer still in minimally occupied landscapes. But in the end, the built environment encircles the planet – diminishing biodiversity as it spreads and thereby fostering antimicrobial resistance. Buildings and settlements are extended ever more widely through infrastructural networks and systems of extraction into all landscapes, oceans, underground, the atmosphere of the planet, and ever-larger parts of outer space. This expansion into every corner of the biosphere has effectively constructed an ever-more accommodating home for antimicrobial-resistant genes. There is an urgent need for a more biotic architecture.

12 Variety of microbes on a fragment of microplastic collected off of the US East Coast, photo by Erik Zettler

1 John Rodman Paul, *A History of Poliomyelitis* (London and New Haven, CT: Yale Studies in the History of Science and Medicine, 1978), 126.
2 "Polio Virus Definitively Identified and Photographed for First Time," *New York Times* (November 12, 1953), 1.
3 Jonas Salk announced his injectable polio vaccine in 1953 and it was declared safe in 1955 after a trial of over a million children. The oral vaccine developed by Albert Sabin became available in 1961. Both are still in use.
4 "Over the past century declining family size, improvements in household amenities, and higher standards of personal cleanliness have reduced the opportunity for cross infection in young families. This may have resulted in more widespread clinical expression of atopic disease, emerging earlier in wealthier people, as seems to have occurred for hay fever." David P. Strachan, "Hay fever, hygiene, and household size," *BMJ: British Medical Journal* 299, no. 6710 (1989): 1259.
5 Graham A. W. Rook, Roberta Martinelli, and Laura Rosa Brunet, "Innate immune responses to mycobacteria and the downregulation of atopic responses," *Current Opinion in Allergy and Clinical Immunology* 3, no. 5 (2003): 337–42.
6 Tari Haahtela, Harri Alenius, Petri Auvinen, et al., "A short history from Karelia study to biodiversity and public health interventions," *Frontiers in Allergy* 4 (2023): 1152927.
7 Lasse Ruokolainen, Nanna Fyhrquist, Tiina Laatikainen, et al., "Immune-microbiota interaction in Finnish and Russian Karelia young people with high and low allergy prevalence," *Clinical & Experimental Allergy* 50, no. 10 (2020): 1148–58.
8 "Although microbial life on Earth as such is not threatened – unlike many plant and animal species – the diversity and abundance of microorganisms in affluent urban environments has clearly declined.... Living in dense urban environments might therefore lead to an 'immune adaption syndrome' – that is, the inability of the immune system to adapt to microbe-poor environments – in a large part of the population.... Chronic inflammatory disorders can be added to the long list of reasons of why we should care for the diversity of animal, plant and microbial life on Earth." Leena von Hertzen, Ilkka Hanski, and Tari Haahtela, "Natural immunity: biodiversity loss and inflammatory diseases are two global megatrends that might be related," *EMBO reports* 12, no. 11 (2011): 1089–93.
9 Matthew M. Carter, Matthew R. Olm, Bryan D. Merrill, et al., "Ultra-deep sequencing of Hadza hunter-gatherers recovers vanishing gut microbes," *Cell* 186, no. 14 (2023): 3111–24. The human microbiome rapidly adapted itself to the industrialized environment but became increasingly disconnected from the more slowly evolving human genome. Erica D. Sonnenburg and Justin L. Sonnenburg, "The ancestral and industrialized gut microbiota and implications for human health," *Nature Reviews Microbiology* 17, no. 6 (2019): 383–90.
10 Pajau Vangay, Abigail J. Johnson, Tonya L. Ward, et al., "US immigration westernizes the human gut microbiome," *Cell* 175, no. 4 (2018): 962–72.
11 Charles Harrison Blackley, *Experimental Researches on the Causes and Nature of Catarrhus Ăstivus (hay-fever or Hay-asthma)* (London: Ballière, Tindall, & Cox, 1873).
12 Martin Blaser, "The theory of disappearing microbiota and the epidemics of chronic diseases," *Nature Reviews Immunology* 17, no. 8 (2017): 461–63.
13 Maria G. Dominguez-Bello, Dominik Steiger, Manuel Fankhauser, et al., "The microbiota vault initiative: safeguarding Earth's microbial heritage for future generations," *Nature Communications* 16, no. 1 (2025): 1–6. The project is committed to acknowledge and dismantle inequities within policies, systems, programs, and services. The original donors and collectors retain rights and sovereignty over their samples.
14 Miguel Delibes-Mateos, Isabel C Barrio, A. Marcia Bárbosa, et al., "Rewilding and the risk of creating new, unwanted ecological interactions," in *Rewilding*, eds. Nathalie Pettorelli, Sarah M. Durant, and Johan T. Du Toit (Cambridge: Cambridge University Press, 2019), 355–74.
15 Ishai Dror, Bruno Yaron, and Brian Berkowitz, "The human impact on all soil-forming factors during the anthropocene," *ACS Environmental Au* 2, no. 1 (2021): 11–19.
16 Eili Y. Klein, Isabella Impalli, Suprena Poleon, et al., "Global trends in antibiotic consumption during 2016–2023 and future projections through 2030," *Proceedings of the National Academy of Sciences* 121, no. 49 (2024): e2411919121.
17 Martin Blaser, *Missing Microbes: How the Overuse of Antibiotics is Fueling our Modern Plagues* (New York: Macmillan, 2014).
18 P. Mergaert, "Role of antimicrobial peptides in controlling symbiotic bacterial

populations," *Natural Product Reports* 35, no. 4 (2018): 336–56.

19 The antimicrobial molecules are released from the deep folds of the epithelial layer to maintain the distance of the microbial community but also by the members of that community to space themselves relative to each other. Mergaert, "Role of antimicrobial peptides," 343.

20 This mainly occurs through so-called horizontal gene transfer between microbes of the same or different species – a way of more rapidly adapting and diversifying than vertical transfers between parent and offspring. The mechanisms of horizontal gene transfer include a bacteria picking up mobile DNA, receiving DNA injected into it by a virus, and direct contact between bacteria when they exchange DNA in the form of plasmids.

21 Kudzai Hwengwere, Harisree Paramel Nair, Kevin A. Hughes, et al., "Antimicrobial resistance in Antarctica: is it still a pristine environment?," *Microbiome* 10, no. 1 (2022). 71.

22 María Mercedes Zambrano, "Interplay Between Antimicrobial Resistance and Global Environmental Change," *Annual Review of Genetics* 57, no. 1 (2023): 275–96.

23 Kathryn Winglee, Annie Green Howard, Wei Sha, et al., "Recent Urbanization in China is Correlated with a Westernized Microbiome Encoding Increased Virulence and Antibiotic Resistance Genes," *Microbiome* 5, no. 1 (2017): 121.

24 Nuohan Xu, Danyan Qiu, Zhenyan Zhang, et al., "A global atlas of marine antibiotic resistance genes and their expression," *Water Research* 244 (2023): 120488. Florent Rossi, Raphaëlle Péguilhan, Nathalie Turgeon, et al., "Quantification of Antibiotic Resistance Genes (ARGs) in Clouds at a Mountain Site (Puy de Dôme, Central France)," *Science of The Total Environment* 865 (2023): 161264.

25 Neila Gross, Johnathan Muhvich, Carly Ching, et al., "Effects of Microplastic Concentration, Composition, and Size on Escherichia Coli Biofilm-associated Antimicrobial Resistance," *Applied and Environmental Microbiology* 91, no. 4 (2025): e02282-24.

26 Yi-Fei Wang, Yan-Jie Liu, Yan-Mei Fu, et al., "Microplastic diversity increases the abundance of antibiotic resistance genes in soil," *Nature Communications* 15, no. 1 (2024): 9788.

1 The catastrophic floods of October 2024 in Valencia covered everything in bacterial-rich mud that produced a new kind of garden in a few days

What would a biotic architecture be? Probably more porous like our gut, versus the prophylactic attitude of most buildings. The immune system doesn't simply keep foreign organisms out. It curates a dynamic cosmopolitan balance. Architecture can likewise be a way of bringing others in – curating complex communities rather than narrowing them. The very idea of shelter changes from excluding danger to including it. To shelter a species means exposing it to multiple others.

BUILDING IN REVERSE

The history of antibiotic architecture, architecture opposed to more-than-human life, is as old as architectural discourse. Ever since the foundational scrolls of Vitruvius, Western architectural discourse has thought of the birth of architecture as a separation from the natural world. In the primal scene described by Vitruvius, and echoed countless times through the centuries, trees in a forest were reshaped into a simple geometric enclosure that offered some environmental protection, but more importantly a space for conversation, making sustained social entanglement possible, and thereby language, symbolic systems, and intellectual life. Sheltering the body was secondary to sheltering the collective intellect that marks an imagined human superiority over all other creatures.[1] The environment is only minimally interrupted. The building and its occupants are still in the forest, exposed to all its flows, yet also already no longer in the forest. **[1]**

This uncanny sense of detachment doesn't just represent the unique status of the human – it makes the human possible. In other words, humans don't construct architecture. Architecture constructs the human. Reshaping part of the world separates human animals from that world which is only then seen to be natural. Both humans and the materials separating them from the natural environment are from that environment but no longer of it.

The most famous image of this fantasized first house is the etching based on a drawing by Charles Eisen that was the frontispiece of the second edition of Marc-Antoine Laugier's influential *Essai sur l'Architecture* of 1755.[2] **[2]** It illustrates the structure made by "man in his primitive state" as a roof frame made of interlocking branches held up by the four living trees they have been cut from. Shelter is provided by the leaves of those trees, not the frame. As architecture emerges, tree becomes wood – living, twisting, flexing, breathing, lifeforms give way to dead geometric elements that support human life. Wood eventually becomes stone, the very image of inertness, as a testament to the species that carved it, positioned it, and lives within and around it. It is as if the newly emergent figure of the human depends on the idea that the buildings that shelter it have no life, that the very fabric of architecture has had life squeezed out of it.

This project to leave nature never simply excludes nature. On the contrary, it includes and domesticates it – whether by inviting certain species into a space and regulating their behavior or by extending the space to absorb them. On the one hand, for example, domesticated animals and plants within a building. On the other hand, external landscapes of plants and animals constrained by architectural patterns and infrastructures of gardens, parks, and fields that manifest human control.

Yet there is also a long tradition in architectural discourse that is fascinated with the loss of that control, when the line between human and more-than-human dissolves as the natural world takes over, reinfusing the built environment with bacteria, fungi, plants, insects, and animals. Think of the canonic eighteenth-century etchings of Giovanni Battista Piranesi of the ruins of Rome **[3]** sprouting an abundance of plant life, or the nineteenth-century drawings of John Ruskin lovingly detailing the staining of the aging stone buildings of Venice. More than a romantic celebration of the life flourishing in the cracks of decaying architecture, it affirms the ever-present life within building materials.

For Ruskin, the apparent degradation and spoiling of architecture is its very life. He was particularly fascinated with lichen, the hybrid colonies of bacteria and fungi whose mutual interdependence would provoke the invention of the term "symbiosis" in 1878. His earlier drawings of lichen seemingly emerging out the heart of a brick already conveyed another kind of symbiosis, that between building elements and living organisms. **[4]** The growth appears as part of the brick: on the outside but as an insider, released rather than added, free but not leaving.

This entanglement of human and more-than-human goes beyond seemingly organic materials such as the clay of the brick, stone, and wood to include seemingly artificial materials like metal. For Ruskin, iron was natural, infused everywhere in the planet and alive in nature and buildings through its constant transformation: "iron rusted is Living; but when pure or polished, Dead."[3] He describes rust stains as the "noble" evidence that metal is breathing, arguing that all building materials likewise became available for human use because they breath the same air as humans. In fact, he insists that the beauty of the diverse colors of the living earth itself is produced by the oxidation of iron.

2 Charles Eisen, frontispiece of Marc-Antoine Laugier's *Essai sur l'architecture*, 1755

3 Giovanni Battista Piranesi, *The Baths of Caracalla: Interior of the Central Hall*, from *Vedute di Roma*, 1757

4 John Ruskin, study of lichen on a piece of brick, ca. 1871

5 Selfie of Perseverance Rover taken on Mars on July 23, 2024 next to a rock with potential biosignatures of microbial life

Ruskin argues that the earth would be deadly ashen gray if it was not breathing. The iron oxide that is the very image of the vitality of rock and soil makes its way into buildings within stone and the clay that forms blocks, bricks, and tiles long before any metal structure is added. Buildings are made of the effects of breathing and keep breathing – actively sustaining the natural circuits they only appear to be detached from.

Ruskin was describing the continuous biogeochemical iron cycle that is crucial to the ecosystems of ground, oceans, and atmosphere. Some of the diverse bacteria that drive that cycle had already been identified when he was writing, but it was not until the twentieth century that the continuous dissolving and reconstitution of iron was understood as a microbially engineered flow of nutrients crucial to most other lifeforms. In reverse, the ongoing effort to find life on Mars now turns on finding metals understood to be the product of microbes. Three-and-a-half years after landing on Mars in 2021, the Perseverance Rover found colorful spots on a clay-based rock rich in oxidized iron. On analysis by the robot's instruments, these spots on the mud-stone turned out to be two iron-rich minerals that on Planet Earth are made by bacteria. **[5]** In a very Ruskinian way, the sign of life on Mars, as on Earth, is earth itself.

Decaying buildings expose the forms of life repressed within them. The love of decay, cracks, ruins, stains, and regeneration could be an ultimate version of human control, the ability to embrace the erosion of architecture as an aesthetic and intellectual delight, but it can also be a form of humility and an opening to think about microbial architectures. If humans were invented by architecture, the ruins of architecture offer a way to rethink the human.

The very image of architecture's escape from nature can be run in reverse. Think of Laugier's frontispiece in microbial terms. Architecture is personified by a woman with the professional tools of an architect sitting on a disorderly pile of some fragments of classical stone building elements in the bio-rich soil. She points to a porous structure that draws no clear line between inside and outside, ground and growth, natural and artificial, human and more-than-human. The stone fragments were supposed to be the perfected descendants of the primal wooden structure.

Yet they are already a half-buried ruin with soil and plants growing around and over them. The merging of forest and building in the primitive hut image flips from the deep past to a possible future.

SCRAPBOOK

More recent artists, architects, and designers have offered similar clues toward a biotic architecture. They experimented with works in which plants, insects, animals, bacteria, and fungi are the protagonists, even the authors, in trans-species collaborations. These works decenter the human in favor of symbiotic relationships between species and spaces.

Lina Bo Bardi drew every insect, every plant, and every animal living on the site of her Casa de Vidro of 1949 with the same precision that she drew the building. **[6]** If architecture is all about keeping the bugs out, Bo Bardi embraced a trans-species architecture where other species are not the enemy but intelligent members of the community and humans are just temporary guests. She made exhibitions and plays for children about this new understanding of community. **[7–8]** For Bo Bardi, architecture is architecture only in as much as it is dissolved by other species. Buildings are inhabited by plants, dissolved by them, and even the architect appears like a plant in a canonic photograph, embedded with the tropical plants beneath her house. **[9]**

Friedensreich Hundertwasser's "Mold Manifesto Against Rationalism in Modern Architecture" of 1958 denounced the imprisoning sterility of contemporary buildings and called for a political revolution through "creative molding."[4] **[10]** A "decomposing liquid" is to be poured over modern architecture, and life returns to buildings as they are transformed by microbes and fungi. **[11]** His *Tree Tenants* project for the 1973 Milan Triennale likewise undid the limits of buildings and human exceptionalism by giving trees the right to live inside Milan apartments filled with soil – setting up new metabolic circuits and collaborative more-than-human ethics. **[12]**

"I want to be *kabi* (bacteria)," wrote Noboru Kawazoe as a call for selflessness in the manifesto *Metabolism 1960: The Proposals*

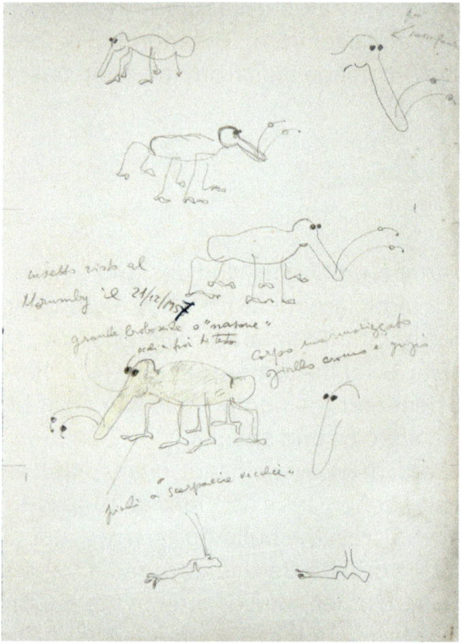

6 Lina Bo Bardi, insects seen at Morumby, the site of the Casa de Vidro, 1957

7 Lina Bo Bardi, *Entreato para crianças* (theater for children) exhibition, 1985

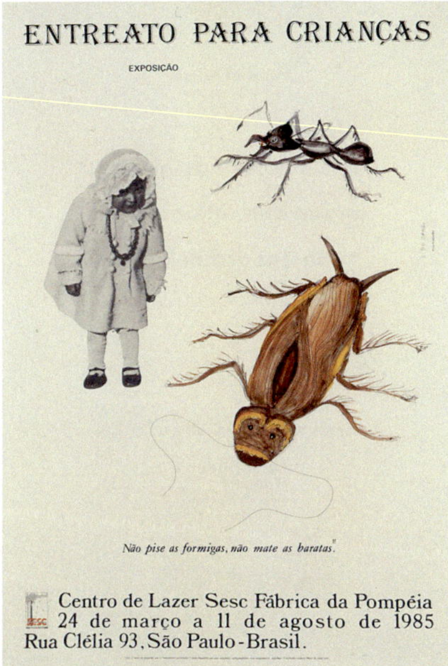

8 Lina Bo Bardi, *Entreato para crianças* exhibition poster, 1985

9 Lina Bo Bardi at Casa de Vidro, Morumby, undated

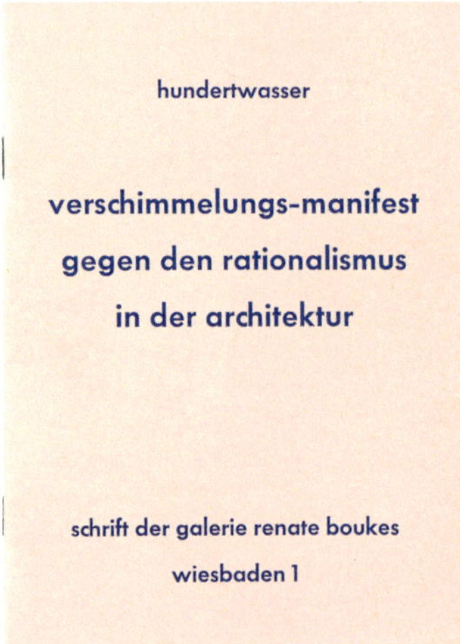

hundertwasser

verschimmelungs-manifest
gegen den rationalismus
in der architektur

schrift der galerie renate boukes
wiesbaden 1

10 Friedensreich Hundertwasser, *Moldiness Manifesto Against Rationalism in Architecture*, 1958

11 Friedensreich Hundertwasser, *Suggestion for Healing of Architecture*, 713/III, watercolor on photograph, Munich, 1971–1972

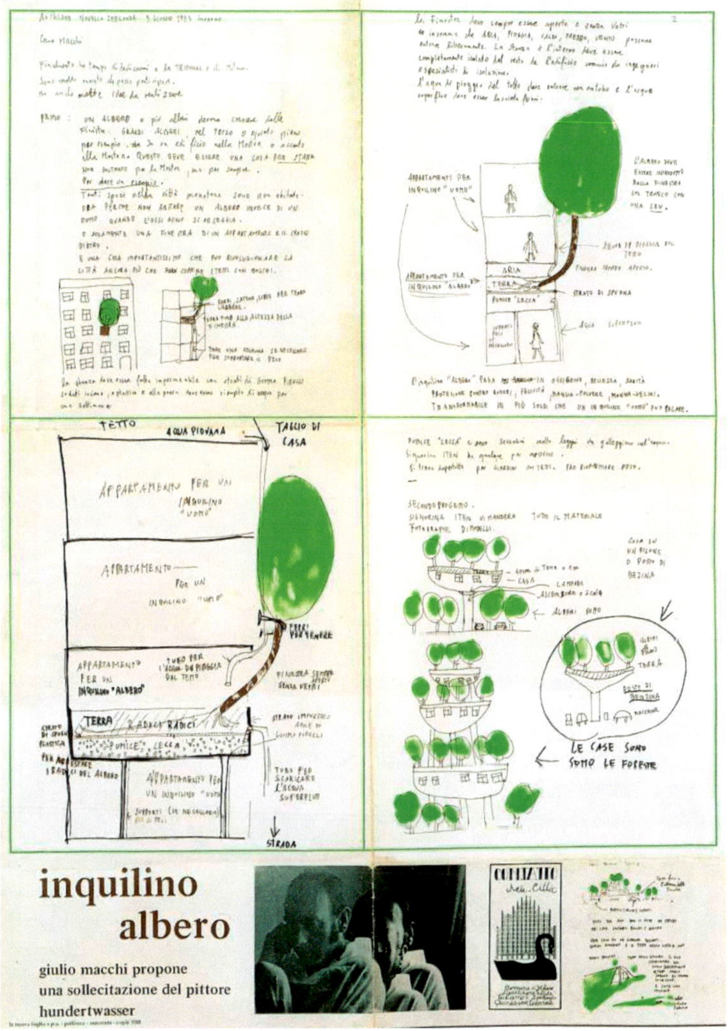

12 Poster for the exhibition organized by Giulio Macchi on Friedensreich Hundertwasser's *Tree Tenant* project, part of the 15th Milan Triennale, 1973

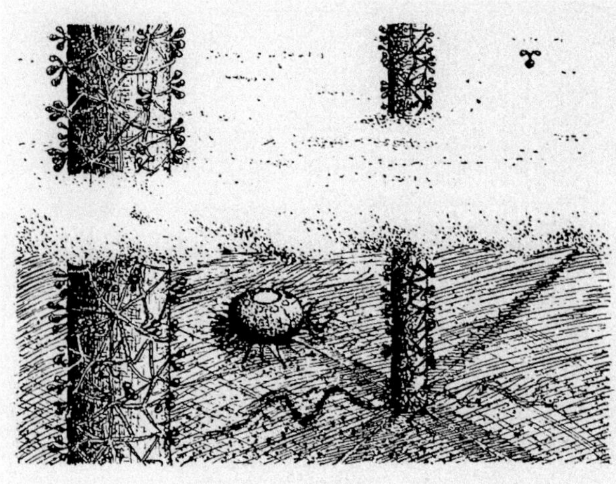

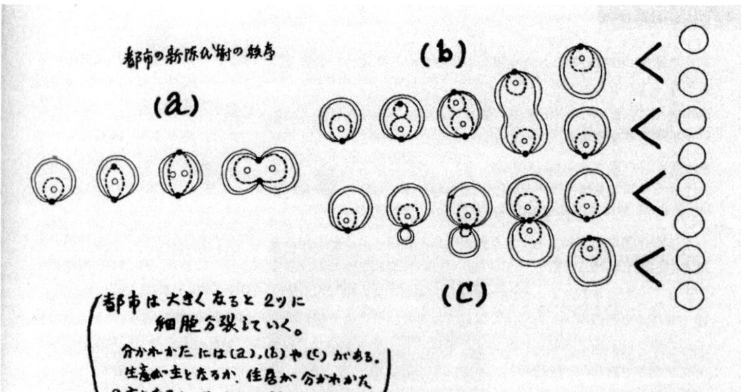

13 Yasuhiro Kawazoe, space city, from *Metabolism 1960: The Proposals for New Urbanism*

14 Kiyonori Kikutake, drawing of cell replication, from *Metabolism 1960: The Proposals for New Urbanism* *for New Urbanism*: "Now I am a cell of bacteria which is constantly propagating itself.... This means that the self-consciousness of the individual will be lost and the will of mankind will remain. It will be the same as the will of bacteria."[5] Kawazoe and his Metabolist colleagues despaired of the human future in the wake of Hiroshima and Nagasaki, and drew an urbanism of biologically inspired cells interacting as a single living entity. The accompanying drawing by Kwazoe's older brother, Yasuhiro, depicts a biotechnical "space city" as some new kind of plant reaching up through the clouds, **[13]** and Kiyonori Kikutake presented drawings of cell division to explain his floating "ocean city" that continually grows and deteriorates. **[14]**

Alan Sonfist, a pioneer of ecological art, cultivated microbial growth in a series of works between 1967 and 1971. A new kind of painting was made by laying a wet canvas in the soil or in a room to allow the microbes of those environments to become visible as colonies. **[15]** Sometimes the wall of a gallery was moistened to grow a work out of the resident microbes. A 1971 work called *Microorganism Enclosure* exhibited a complex evolving multi-colored landscape of different microbes growing in agar within a Plexiglas vitrine. **[16]** In *Breaths of Air* of 1971, gallery visitors would breathe into a jar containing agar, the medium scientists use to grow microorganisms, that was then sealed to turn "the micro content of the visitor" into the artwork forty-eight hours later. **[17]**

Gordon Matta-Clark's first works after graduating from Cornell University as an architect in 1969 were multi-colored, pungent, bacterial, and fungus-covered mini-landscapes that kept changing shape. **[18]** He cooked primeval soups with eccentric recipes of ingredients from his kitchen using agar in a large wok in his New York loft and poured them into metal pans to dry as colonies of microbes started growing. **[19]** They were exhibited suspended in vines in June 1970 at the Bykert Gallery in New York, along with a microscope in a darkened corner so visitors could look at the still-growing microbes that "were seen to be clotting, multiplying, and solidifying."[6] **[20]** Visitors were inside the work and the work was inside them as it was breathed in. Matta-Clark listed all the ingredients of his concoctions and the scientific names of the strains of bacteria and fungi they incubated. He spoke of these

15 Alan Sonfist, aging canvas, 1968

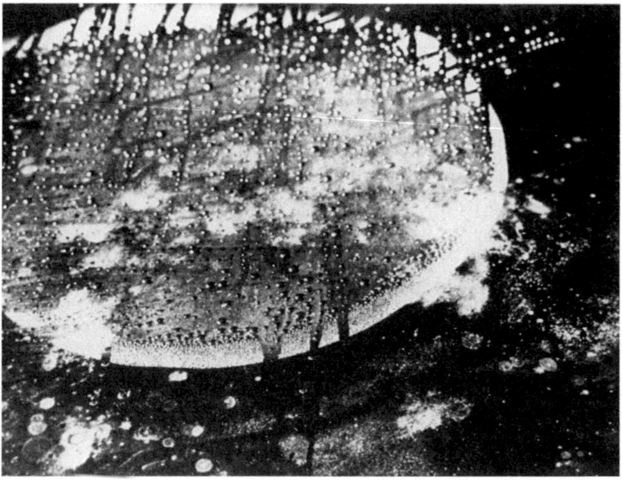

16 Alan Sonfist, *Microorganism Enclosure*, 1971, detail

17 Alan Sonfist, *Breaths of Air*, 1971

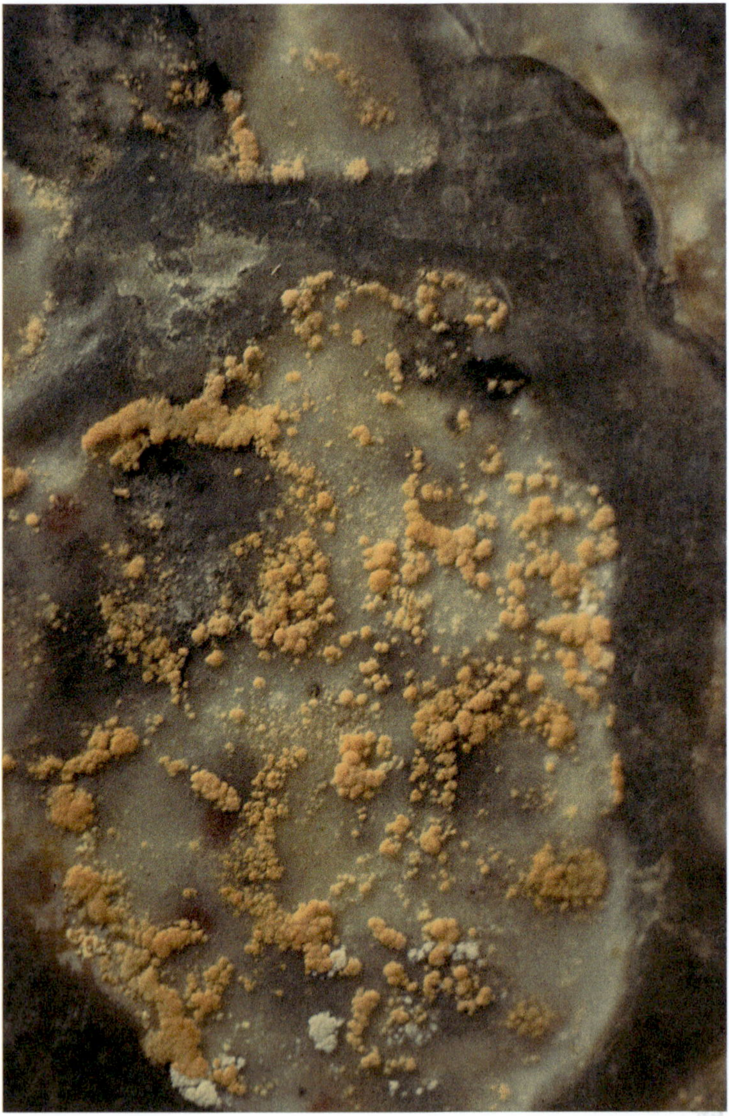

18 Gordon Matta-Clark, Agar work in production, 1969–1970

19 Gordon Matta-Clark photographed in his studio for *Vogue* magazine, August 1970

20 Gordon Matta-Clark, *Museum*, installation view, Bykert Gallery, 1970 smelly, seemingly anti-architectural organic brews as a new kind of building material, or material for a new kind of building – seeing himself heading deeper into architecture rather than leaving it behind:

> Think of it in terms of structural material, building material, which I have some project for actual housing, a living environment, in a way, putting the theme of home and garden or kitchen and garden back together again.[7]

Argentinian architect and artist Luis Fernando Benedit presented two hydroponic environments where insects, plants and bacteria "escape" anthropocentrism: *Biotron* at the Venice Biennale in 1970, and *Phytotron* at MoMA in 1972. **[21–23]** Since hydroponic systems are soilless, they have vastly different bacterial microbiota. Benedit's modular drawings of the projects, with different floor plans, elevations, and sections as if a building, envisioned an architecture for bacteria, paying utmost attention to the water pipes and deposits in which bacteria float.

The fashion designer Martin Margiela worked with the microbiologist Ad Van Egeraat in 1997 to dip white replicas of his earlier garments in agar and feed them bacteria and fungi. The microbes flourished in plastic greenhouses for seven days in the garden of the Boijmans van Beuningen Museum in Rotterdam before the garments were unveiled in a unique exhibition.[8] The microbial life was so intense that they had to be displayed outside the glass walls of the gallery. **[24–26]**

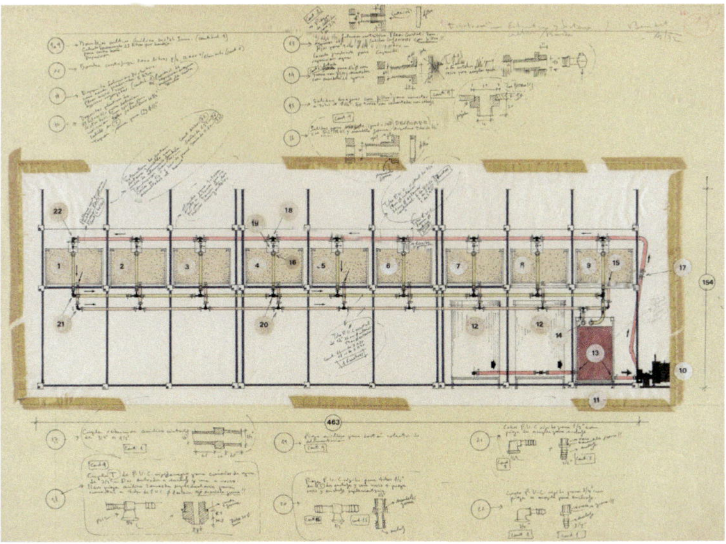

21 Luis Fernando Benedit, *Biotron*, installation view, 35th Venice Biennale, 1970

22–23 Luis Fernando Benedit, *Phytotron: Hydroponic Environment for Plants*, installation and drawing, MoMA, 1972

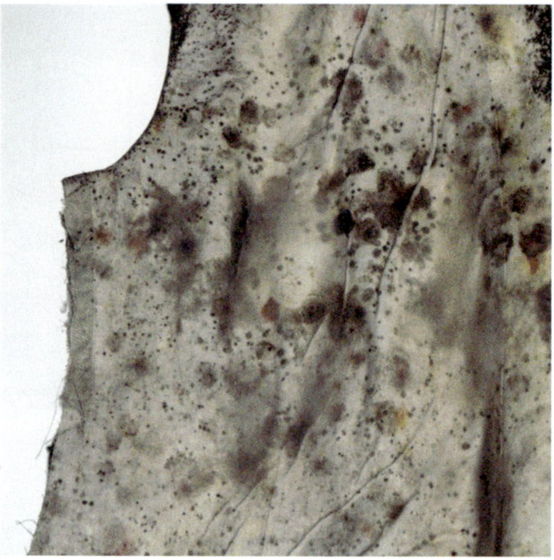

24–26 Martin Margiela, garments with microbial growth, *9/4/1615* exhibition, Boijmans van Beuningen museum, Rotterdam, 1997

CURATING MICROBES

Such examples are just a taste of a longer history culminating in the contemporary array of bioart and biodesign that depend on the uncanniness of the repressed microbial world. But microbes are no longer transgressive agents violating norms of art and architecture. They have become a crucial part of the building industry. Bacteria, fungi, and micro-algae are: growing blocks, bricks, wall systems, and substitute materials for leather and plastic; consolidating earth; generating electricity and biomass with bioreactors; remediating toxicity in ground and water, sequestering carbon dioxide, eating pollution, consuming methane, and degrading plastic; growing green layers embedded in façades; preserving deteriorating heritage buildings like the Duomo in Milan and the Alhambra in Granada; strengthening and self-healing timber and concrete; and cleaning the exteriors and interiors of buildings.[9] **[27–40]** Microbes are making, maintaining, detoxifying, and preserving the built environment – as always, but humans now offer support.

New buildings increasingly involve the cultivation of many different types of microbes in the preparation of the site, the building materials, coatings, and environmental modification and maintenance systems. Architecture has always been unconsciously made in a microbial world out of materials made and maintained by microbes for inhabitants that are themselves microbial. Contemporary architects have become curators of microbes, consciously shaping microbial communities and imagining the communities their buildings will in turn shape.

This curatorship is most evident in historic preservation. Microbial biofilms often deteriorate the surfaces of buildings they are attached to, but they are increasingly countered by applying bacteria that release enzymes to clean the buildings. Bacteria that produce calcium carbonate (the basis of the most common limestone and marble building blocks) are also sprayed or brushed onto stone buildings or applied as a paste to repair damage and fill cracks. Preserving buildings today involves doing genetic testing to determine the microbiome of the building materials. The beneficial microbes living within stone, for example, are extracted, cultivated in a lab, then reinjected into the building so that they can rebuild the stone through biomineralization – an echo of current medical immune therapy.

27 Bio-reactive algae façade converts carbon and daylight into energy-producing biomass

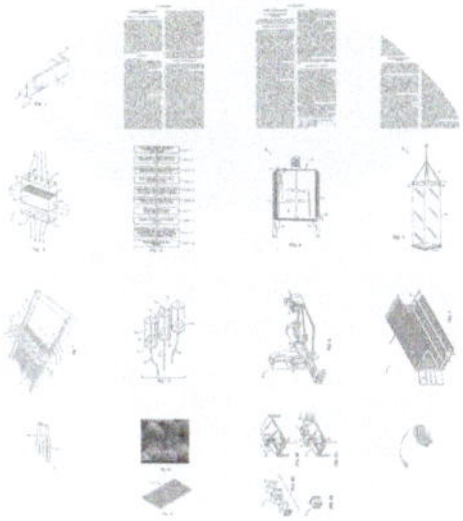

28 Mycellium networks and enzyme-producing bacteria produce load-bearing bricks

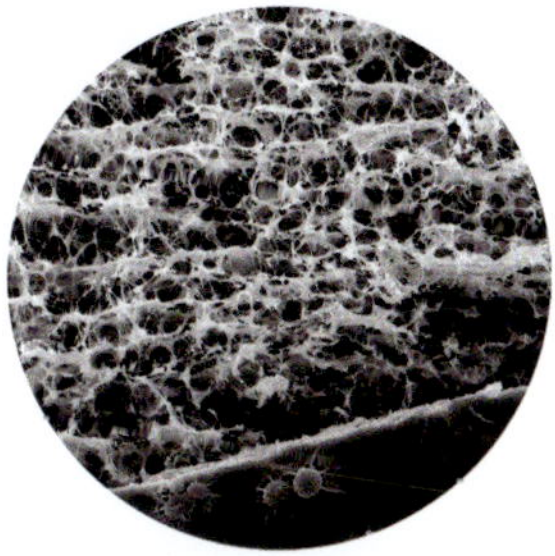

29 Bacteria ferment agricultural sugars into nanocellulose to produce alternative materials

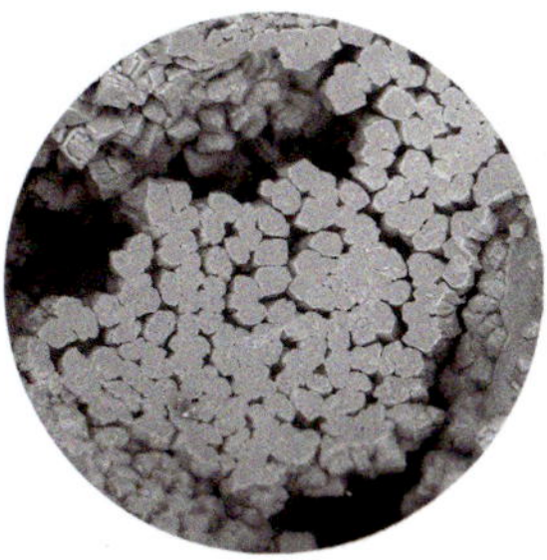

30 A solution injected into soil is consumed by indigenous bacteria which stabilize earth

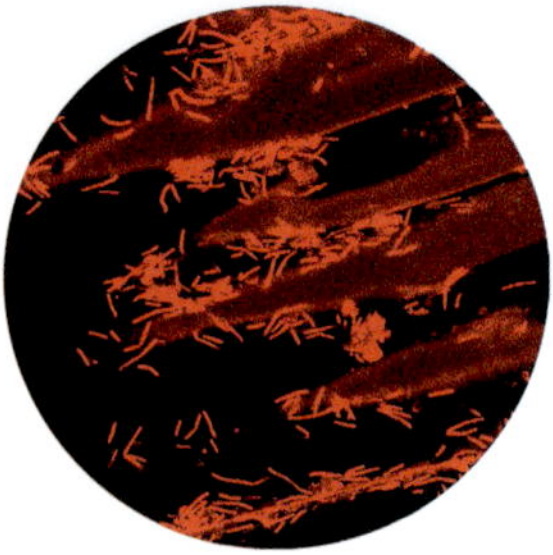

31 Microbes inoculated into timber strengthen it and enable self-healing

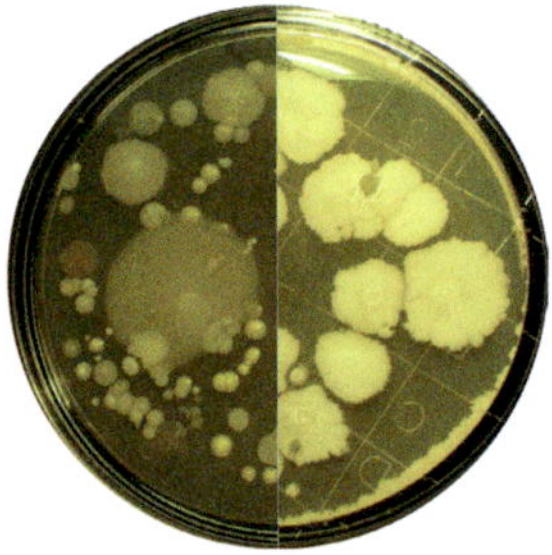

32 Probiotic cleaning spray suppresses super pathogens and antimicrobial resistance

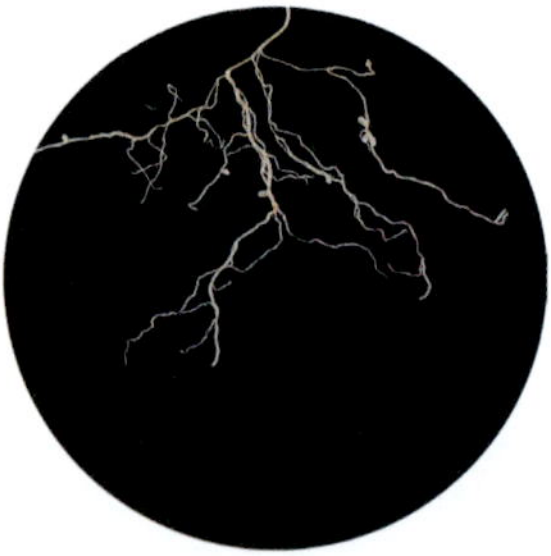

33 Biofertilizer enriched with fungi, microalgae, or rhizobacteria supports crop growth and resiliency

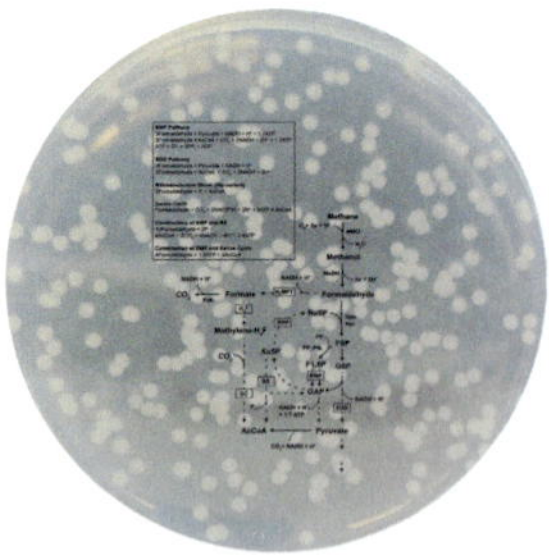

34 Trays of bacteria consume methane released by decomposing waste at landfill sites

35 Biomineralization by bacterial healing agents repairs cracks in damaged concrete

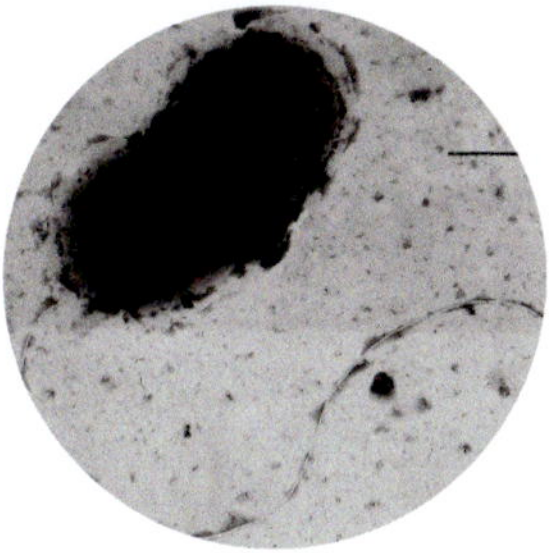

36 Microbes clean pollution-induced black gypsum crusts from marble surfaces

37 Biomineralization consolidates deteriorating rammed-earth buildings

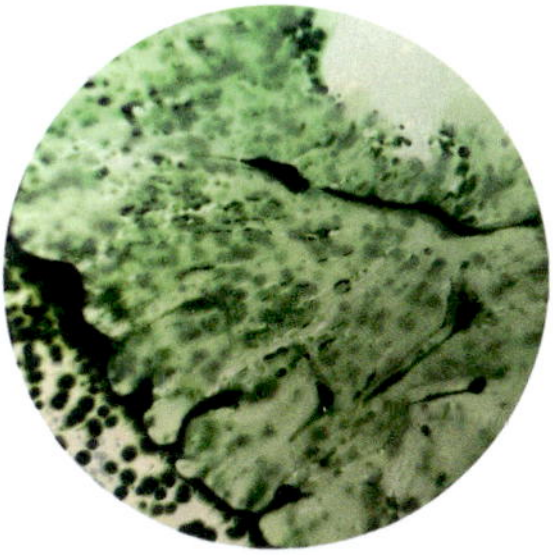

38 Carbon-fixating cyanobacteria biomineralize sand into 3D-printed scaffolds

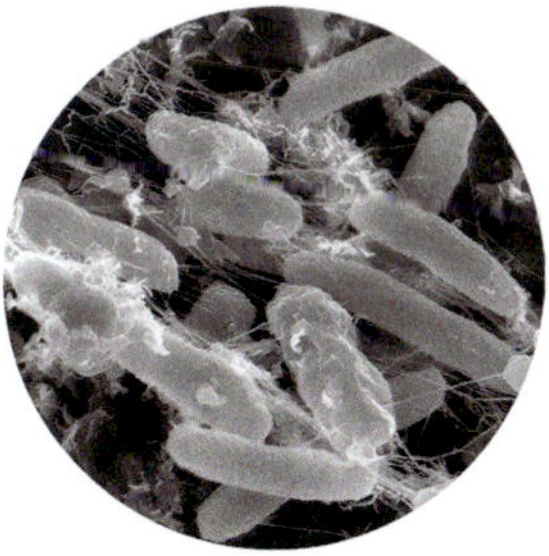

39 Bacteria produce enzymes that biodegrade discarded PET plastic

40 Injecting pressurized air into soil stimulates aerobic bacteria to break down pollutants

Curating a community of microbes within a building's structure is as important as curating microbial communities within its spaces. Stone buildings – the very image of stable, static architecture – host vibrant communities, as does wood, plaster, concrete, glass, and metal – along with the joints and gaps between them. Tending to these embedded gardens has become central to caring for buildings and their many species of occupant.

Some remarkable architectural studios are now partnering with microbiologists and microbes on building projects. The descendants of these heterogeneous projects might eventually stick to each other in a new form of urbanism, a sustainable biofilm replacing the current built environment – in the inverse of the way microbes have been turning themselves into architectural biofilms for billions of years.

Architecture as currently practiced is unlikely to survive its own effects. Regardless of the fate of humans, their massive built environment, which already weighs more than the whole biomass of the planet, will slowly but inevitably be digested by the planet – eaten by microbes. Biotic architecture hastens the process, metabolizing the deadly built environment of today into food.

1 “Because these things had been so established in the beginning, and nature had not only equipped the people with senses like all the other animals, but had also armed their minds with ideas and plans and subjected all other creatures to their power, so from the making of buildings they progressed, step by step, to the other arts and disciplines, and thus they led themselves out of a rough and brutish life into gentle humanity.” Vitruvius, “The Invention of Building, Continued,” in *Vitruvius: Ten Books on Architecture*, trans. Ingrid D. Rowland (Cambridge: Cambridge University Press, 1999), 35.

2 Marc-Antoine Laugier, *Essai sur l'Architecture* (Paris: Chez Duchesne, 1755). Each description of the supposedly singular birth of architecture has a different polemical resonance. Laugier thought Vitruvius was imprecise and inconsistent. He argued that nature is the model of rationality to be emulated not superseded, and that the appreciation of architecture is itself natural. Yet he extracted a set of unchanging principles from the flux of nature. Architecture again stands apart from the natural world it is modeled on. For Vitruvius, architecture is more beautiful and rational than nature. It is a material object produced under very particular material, political, economic, historical, and environmental conditions yet is defined by its transcendence of those conditions. It is built in a world of continuous flux yet conveys an unchanging order that supposedly resonates with the order of the cosmos that transcends time and space. These metaphysical ambitions survive today in the everyday sense that buildings should be still while life pulsates around and inside them.

3 John Ruskin, “The Work of Iron, in Nature, Art, and Policy,” in *The Two Paths: Being Lectures on Art, and its Application to Decoration and Manufacture, Delivered in 1858–9* (New York: John Wiley, 1859), 158. For Ruskin, oxidation doesn't simply happen to material. Rather, it forms material. Materials are the effect of breathing. A stone, for example, that seems so distinct from the air around it, is actually the effect of absorbing that air. The stone is thereby a living creature that actively collaborates with all other creatures, including humans: “Hence, it is impossible for you to take up the most insignificant pebble at your feet, without being able to read, if you like, this curious lesson in it. You look upon it at first as if it were earth only. Nay, it answers, ‘I am not earth – I am earth and air in one; part of that blue heaven which you love, and long for, is already in me; it is all my life – without it I should be nothing, and able for nothing; I could not minister to you, nor nourish you – I should be a cruel and helpless thing; but, because there is, according to my need and place in creation, a kind of soul in me, I have become capable of good, and helpful in the circles of vitality.’” Ruskin, “The Work of Iron,” 193.

4 Friedensreich Hundertwasser, *Verschimmelungs-Manifest gegen den Rationalismus in der Architektur* (Wiesbaden: Schrift der galerie renate boukes, 1958).

5 Noboru Kawazoe, “Material and Man,” in Noboru Kawazoe, Kiyonori Kikutake, and Kishō Kurokawa, et al., *Metabolism 1960: The Proposals for New Urbanism* (Tokyo: Bitjutu Syuppan Sha, 1960), 51.

6 Robert Pincus-Witten, “Review,” *Artforum* (September 1970): 75–76

7 Gordon Matta-Clark, interview by Cindy Nesmer, July 20 and September 1970, transcript. Cited in Tina Kukielski, “In the Spirit of the Vegetable. The Early Work of Gordon Matta-Clark (1969-71),” in *Gordon Matta-Clark: You Are the Measure*, ed. Elisabeth Sussman (New York: Yale University Press, 2007), 36.

8 *Maison Martin Margiela (9/4/1615)* (Rotterdam: Museum Boijmans van Beuningen, 1997).

9 Images 27–40 on the contemporary roles of microbes in the construction, maintenance, conservation, and remediation of the built environment were researched by Jocelyn Beausire and framed by GRACE.

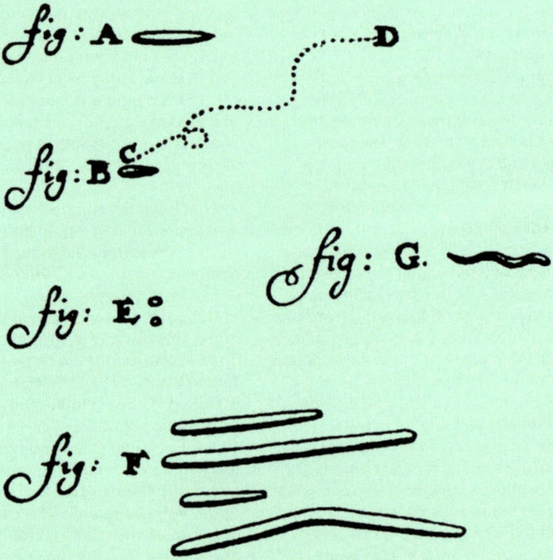

1 First published image of bacteria in a letter from Antonie van Leeuwenhoek to the Royal Society in London, dated September 17, 1683, published in 1684. It showed bacteria he had observed through a microscope in scrapings of plaque from his teeth – having first seen bacteria in 1675

All architecture is microbial. Biotic architecture is not more microbial. It just embraces the fact that microbes move, replicate, mutate, hibernate, communicate, exchange, collaborate, construct, and remember. Biotic architecture learns from microbes rather than resists them. It partners with microbes to curate microbes. Some antimicrobial protocols against pathogens remain crucial – water, sewage systems, toilets, and food preparation areas still need to be cleansed – but the main goal is to sustain the immune system by maintaining an overall background level of exposure to microbial diversity. Cleaning routines become more about adaption and invention rather than defense.

During COVID-19, for example, microbiologist Elisabetta Caselli and her colleagues applied beneficial microbes to the walls of six Italian public hospitals rather than disinfectants. The result was 90 percent fewer pathogens and reduced resistance genes, with patients contracting half the amount of typical hospital-associated illnesses, leaving earlier, and needing fewer antibiotics.[1] The most effective cleaning turns out to be to add microbes rather than remove them.

Cleaning a biotic architecture is more like gardening, tending to a living community of microorganisms by encouraging certain kinds of growth without the illusion of control. And living in a space modifies that garden and is modified by it. To inhabit a space is to be part of the garden.

No two gardens are the same. A biotic architecture is, by definition, diverse. One of the unhealthiest things about the contemporary built environment is that it is a monoculture. Buildings everywhere are increasingly built the same way from the same materials extracted from the same places. Even the simplest buildings have elements coming from all continents and closely resemble each other. An architecture that embraces biodiversity must itself be biodiverse. Biotic architecture is kaleidoscopic. It is an ever-shifting array of different kinds of buildings and different kinds of relationships within them. Biotic architecture is not uniform, but pulsates.

Biotic architecture is sticky. All the membranes that define the interior spaces of buildings and the systems that sustain them are intimately connected to the mucus-covered membranes of the guts and respiratory systems of its inhabitants. Buildings are expanded shared guts and actually part of the mucus barrier. If you look closely at buildings, they are lined with the goo that microbes exude to stick to surfaces and to each other in elaborate collaborative biofilms. Seemingly smooth empty surfaces are actually massively populated sticky cities of biofilms interacting with the biofilms sticking to our own linings. To really draw a building means tracing the intricately folded membrane that passes around, between, and through both building and body – the membrane that negotiates all exchanges. This membrane is the real home.

Architecture is not defined by impervious static walls but by ever-twisting gradients of microbes. The highest-resolution architectural drawing possible would show only the microbes in a building, which is to say the life within it. It would reveal spaces as ever-shifting clouds of microorganisms, floors as permanent sandstorms, and walls as networks of microbes glued to each other like the interlinked cities on our planet. Each inhabitant would be a spiraling dense mass radiating and absorbing microbes through its two main orifices, with a lighter cloud hovering around it like a halo. Any movement of this dense mass swirls the clouds around it and makes new clouds rise up from the floor below it. Almost everything would be moving. Yet the building, like the bodies, would be sharply etched within the drawing – every surface, crevice, and cavity: the exact geometry of the many layers of a wall, the inner spaces of an oven, the space between watch and wrist, the inner socket on a cell phone ... The flesh and structure of human bodies and the materials and frame of the building become secondary to the microbial flows within and through them. Bodies and buildings are suspended in microbial weather systems. Biotic architecture embraces the fluctuations of this internal weather over the illusion of static, sealed, hermitic shelter. To enter biotic architecture is, uncannily, to go outside.

No building can be separated from other buildings and the living networks of species, energy flows, supply chains, climate, and expanded systems of extraction and cultivation. What is outside the building is more import than what is inside. Buildings thought in terms of the life outside them enhance the life within them. Biotic architecture reconnects with the soil it is embedded in, offering itself as partner, facilitating and multiplying metabolic circuits rather than disconnecting them. It refuses any straightforward line between building and soil, plant, animal, and insect. Biotic architecture is less about lines and more about gradients, diffusion, ripples, waves, and entanglements.

This rewilding of the interior is not an attempt to recover a lost past but a wilding toward alternative futures. If wilderness is that which exceeds human control, rewilding architecture means letting go, ceding space to strangers, embracing strangeness.

Biotic architecture is not human-centric. Every aspect of building – fabrication, construction, daily life, maintenance, cleaning, energy, and preservation – is led by microbes for microbes. The human species can only survive by abdicating its self-appointed position, tuning into microbes rather than treating them as yet another site of extraction. Biotic architecture is by definition ethical – not a singular ethics, or even one that could be explicitly formulated, but ethical because of its resistance to human exceptionalism, whatever form that takes.

Human-centric architecture is unhealthy for humans and countless other species. Biotic architecture embraces human fragility and vulnerability, particularly those in the greatest need and for whom survival is always on the line. Biotic architecture is more equitable, wastes less, and is less toxic, without being virtuous. It is just less stupid.

Biotic architecture has many futures. The worlds of microorganisms that were long imagined and only became visible in 1675 are just starting to be partially understood. Biotic architecture doesn't simply apply what has been learned about microbes but contributes to this learning. It's not a specific set of practices but an ongoing project to reduce the stupidity of existing ones.

Biotic architecture is the future – perhaps the only possible future if we are to have one. The double-sided crisis of declining microbial diversity and rising antimicrobial resistance is as urgent as climate change, and inseparable from it. But the future is precisely not what can be projected from the past and present. The future is by definition surprising. The only certain thing about biotic architecture is both that it is inevitable and that it will be a surprise. It is not dependent on human agency – on the contrary, it is about letting much of that agency go. If our species stays on its suicidal path, what's left of it will only survive by adapting to become a modest part of entangled collaborative ecosystems. Architecture will necessarily evolve as human agency recedes. Biotic architecture will shape another kind of species and be shaped by it.

1 Elisabetta Caselli, Silvio Brusaferro, Maddalena Coccagna, et al., "Reducing healthcare-associated infections incidence by a probiotic-based sanitation system: A multicentre, prospective, intervention study," *PLoS One* 13, no. 7 (2018): e0199616.

ABOUT THE AUTHORS

Beatriz Colomina is the Howard Crosby Butler Professor of the History of Architecture and the founding director of the Media and Modernity program at Princeton University. She has written extensively on questions of architecture, art, sexuality, and media. Her books include *Sexuality and Space* (1992), *Privacy and Publicity: Modern Architecture as Mass Media* (1994), *Domesticity at War* (2007), *Clip/Stamp/Fold* (2010), *Are We Human? Notes on an Archaeology of Design* (2016) with Mark Wigley, *X-Ray Architecture* (2019), *Radical Pedagogies* (2022), and *Sick Architecture* (2025). Colomina was born in Madrid, studied architecture in Barcelona, and lives in New York.

Mark Wigley is a professor and dean emeritus at the Columbia Graduate School of Architecture, Planning and Preservation. As an architectural theorist and historian, Wigley explores the intersection of architecture, art, philosophy, culture, and technology. His publications include *White Walls, Designer Dresses* (1995), *Constant's New Babylon: The Hyper-Architecture of Desire* (1998), *Buckminster Fuller Inc.: Architecture in the Age of Radio* (2016), *Are We Human? Notes on an Archaeology of Design* (2016) with Beatriz Colomina, *Cutting Matta-Clark: The Anarchitecture Investigation* (2018), and *Konrad Wachsmann's Television: Post-Architectural Transmissions* (2020). Wigley was born in New Zealand, where he trained as an architect and scholar, and lives in New York.

ACKNOWLEDGMENTS

Exhibitons and books provoke new thoughts in the people that make them, and the making is always collaborative. We especially want to thank Stefano Boeri and his team at the Milan Triennale for being such supportive colleagues throughout. Ekaterina Golovatyuk and Giacomo Cantoni of GRACE, and their team, were thoughtful and inventive partners as our exhibition designers. Jonas Voegeli made brilliant exhibition graphic designs. Guillermo Sanchez Arsuaga was a remarkable assistant curator. Jocelyn Beausire, Foivos Geralis, Carter Horton, and Sergio Perdiguer Torralba did outstanding research displayed in different parts of the exhibition. Microbiologists Thomas Bosch, Roberto Kolter, Maria Gloria Dominguez-Bello, and Martin Blaser have been vital collaborators and interlocutors over the last few years. Many other scientists have been generous and inspirational in sharing their thinking. Heartfelt thanks to Monica Ponce de Leon and Andrés Jaque for the generous support to the exhibition by the Schools of Architecture at Princeton University and Columbia University. We are also very grateful for the publication support of the Barr Ferree Foundation Fund, the Graham Foundation, and Elise Jaffe + Jeffrey Brown. Thanks also to Nick Axel for his reflections on the text. Making a book with Lars Müller and his team was again a real privilege.

This book conveys our thinking when curating *We the Bacteria: Notes Toward Biotic Architecture* at the 24th Milan Triennale. It gathers the ideas that instigated the project, grew during it, and go beyond it. *We the Bacteria* is the companion of the *Are We Human? Notes on an Archaeology of Design* book we made when curating the 3rd Istanbul Design Biennale.[1] It is a set of field notes from an ongoing exploration. We had already touched on the question of the microbiome in *Are We Human?*. In the meantime, we have published on bacteria as the real clients of architecture,[2] collaborated with remarkable microbiologists, and presented joint position papers in science journals.[3] Yet the thoughts recorded here remain just the beginning, the tremors of a paradigm shift. *We the Bacteria* is both an answer to the question *Are We Human?* and a deepening of the question. More than anything, it is an urgent invitation to think again.

1 Beatriz Colomina and Mark Wigley, *Are We Human? Notes on an Archaeology of Design* (Zurich: Lars Müller Publishers, 2016).
2 Beatriz Colomina and Mark Wigley, "The Bacterial Clients of Modern Architecture," *Docomomo Journal* 62 (2020): 6–17.
3 Thomas Bosch, Mark Wigley, Beatriz Colomina, et. al., "The Potential Importance of the Built-Environment Microbiome and its Impact on Human Health," *Proceedings of the National Academy of Sciences* 121, no. 20 (2024): e2313971121.

IMAGE CREDITS

Images in the public domain are not listed. We have made every effort to identify all rightsholders. Should despite our intensive research any person entitled to rights have been overlooked, they are kindly requested to contact the publisher.

COVER

Adapted from computer-generated image of *E. coli* bacteria based on SEM imagery by Alissa Eckert, CDC

INTRODUCTION

1 Courtesy of the Department of Special Collections, Stanford University Libraries

1 WE ARE NEVER ALONE

1 Alissa Eckert, CDC
2 David Parker/Science Photo Library
3 Tasha Sturm/Cabrillo College
4 Courtesy of Gary Borisy and Steven Wilbert, © 2020
5 source: Wellcome Collection
6 © Martin Oeggerli (2012), supported by HP Marti (Swiss TPH), University Hospital Basel (Pathology) and School of Life Sciences, FHNW, Muttenz
7 Kristen Earle, Gabriel Billings, K. C. Huang, Justin Sonnenburg/Stanford University School of Medicine
8 illustration: David S. Goodsell, *The Machinery of Life* (Springer Science + Business Media New York, 1993), reproduced with permission of SNCSC
9 Illustration by David S. Goodsell, RCSB Protein Data Bank
10 Rosalinda Roberts, Courtney Walker, Charlene Farmer/University of Alabama
11 photo: Delfino Sisto Legnani – DSL Studio, courtesy of GRACE
12, 17 Steve Gschmeissner/Science Photo Library
13 Susumu Nishinaga/Science Photo Library
14 S. Schuller/Wellcome Collection
15 Dennis Kunkel Microscopy/Science Photo Library
16 Thomas Deerinck, MCMIR/Science Photo Library

2 MICROBES IN SPACE

1 source: Wellcome Collection
2 Craig Robinson/londondeposit
3 Gaetan Borgonie/Ghent University
4 photo: Tony Hisgett/Creative Commons
5 photo: © S.H. Rashedi
6 photo: Carsten Steger/Creative Commons
7 Luke Thompson from Chisholm Lab and Nikki Watson from Whitehead, MIT/Creative Commons
8 Gordon Southam and Greg Wanger
9, 15 NASA
10 Cullen Buie, Zhifei Ge, Young Soo Joun/MIT Department of Mechanical Engineering
11 Michael J Daly/Science Photo Library
12 NASA/Roscosmos
13 source: Le Muséum National d'Histoire Naturelle

3 DEEP TIME

1 source: "The Metamorphosis of Patrick Geddes," *Evergreen: Patrick Geddes and the Environment in Equlibrium*, April 13, 2018/ The University of Edinburgh
2 source: Patrick Geddes and J. Cossar Edwart, "On the Life-History of Spirillum," *Proceedings of the Royal Society of London* 27 (1878)
3 photo: Mathew R. Nitschke/Australian Institute of Marine Science
5 source: Patrick Geddes and J. Arthur Thomson, *Life, Outlines of General Biology* (New York, London: Harper, 1931), 1256
6 Formafantasma, Luisa Zanzani
7 Didier Descouens/Creative Commons
8 Dr Jacob Kegerreis, Imperial College London/Durham University
9 source: Edmund Moody, et. al., "The Nature of the Last Universal Common Ancestor and its Impact on the Early Earth System," *Nature, Ecology and Evolution* 8, (July 12, 2024)
10 AMI Images/Science Photo Library
11 Photo by Boston University Photography
12 source: Konstantin Mereschkowsky, "Theorie der zwei Plasmaarten als Grundlage der Symbiogenesis," *Biologisches Zentralblatt* 30 (1910), 366
13 source: Lynn Margulis, *Origin of Eukaryotic Cells* (New Haven: Cambridge University Press, 1970)
14 Yaxi Wang and Scott Braswell/University of Washington
15 source: Robert Altmann, *Die Elementarorganismen* (Leipzig: Veit & comp., 1890), tafel VII
16 Courtesy of Icarus Films

4 THE EXPANDED GUT

1 photo: Delfino Sisto Legnani – DSL Studio, courtesy of Triennale Milano

2 Courtesy of Everett Collection
4 source: Norman P. Kutscha, *A Compilation of Micrographs of Wood and Wood Products*, (Ruston: Forest Products Society, 2007). photo: Delfino Sisto Legnani – DSL Studio
5 source: *ScienceWise: Magazine of the ANU College of Science* 4, no. 4 (2007): 11
6 source: Krumdieck, S.P., Boichot, R., Gorthy, R. et al., "Nanostructured TiO2 anatase-rutile-carbon solid coating with visible light antimicrobial activity," *Scientific Reports* 9 (2019)/Creative Commons
7 source: Samuel R. Anderson, Mahsa Mohammadtaheri, et al., "Robust Nanostructured Silver and Copper Fabrics with Localized Surface Plasmon Resonance Property for Effective Visible Light Induced Reductive Catalysis," *Advanced Materials Interfaces* 3, no. 6 (2016)/Creative Commons
8 Power and Syred/Science Photo Library
9 Suwin Puengsamrong/Alamy
10 Courtesy of The Invisible Extinction documentary, TheInvisibleExtinction.com, © Microbe Media LLC

5 BUILDING – NETWORK – EMPIRE

1 © Martin Oeggerli (2013), supported by Institute of Veterinary Bacteriology, University of Berne, University Hospital Basel (Pathology), School of Life Sciences, FHNW, Muttenz
2 Juan José Ibáñez, and Spanish archaeological mission in Kharaysin, 2019. photo: Luis Teira
3 Juan José Ibáñez, and Spanish archaeological mission in Kharaysin, 2019. illustration: Eric S. Carlson
4 source: Nicklisch N, et al., "Rib lesions in skeletons from early neolithic sites in Central Germany: on the trail of tuberculosis at the onset of agriculture," *American Journal of Physical Anthropology* 3, no.149 (2012): 391–404. photo: Nicole Nicklisch
5 CDC Public Health Image Library
6 rendering: Dan Lewandowski
7 source: James Mellaart, "Excavations at Çatal Hüyük, 1963: Third Preliminary Report," *Anatolian Studies*, vol. 14: 39–119, reproduced with permission
8 photo: Jason Quinlan, Çatalhöyük Research Project/Creative Commons
9 source: Markman DW, et al. "Yersinia pestis Survival and Replication in Potential Ameba Reservoir," *Emerging Infectious Diseases* 42, no. 2 (2018)
10 photo: Alastair Rae/Creative Commons
11 source: Yonggang Zhu/School of Archaeology Jilin University
12 photo: Karl-Göran Sjögren, 2018

13 source: Hofmann R., et al., "Governing Tripolye: Integrative architecture in Tripolye settlements," *PLoS ONE* 14(9) (2019). Adapted in Rassmann K, et al., "High precision Tripolye settlement plans, demographic estimations and settlement organization," *Journal of Neolithic Archaeology* 16 (2014): 63–95/Creative Commons
14 source: Zhemin Zhou, et al.; "The EnteroBase user's guide," *Genome Research* 30 (2020): 138–152/Creative Commons
15 Dr Simon Carrington/University College London
16, 22 source: Wellcome Collection
17 CDC/PHANIE/Alamy
18 illustration: © Guillermo S. Arsuaga
23 Courtesy of Ancient DNA Centre, McMaster University

6 PLAGUE ARCHITECTURE

1, 5, 7–8, 13–16, 19 source: Wellcome Collection
2 KIK-IRPA, Brussels/Creative Commons
3 source: Gómez, J., Verdú, M. "Network theory may explain the vulnerability of medieval human settlements to the Black Death pandemic," *Sci Rep,* vol. 7, 43467 (2017)
4 rendering by Carter Horton
6 source: Filippo de Arrieta, *Raguaglio historico del contaggio occorso nella provincia di Bari negli anni 1690, 1691 e 1692* (1694)/ Wellcome Institute
11 Gabinetto dei Disegni, Castello Sforzesco, Milano
12 Courtesy of Daniel Savoy

7 SANITARY REFORM

1–2, 4–7, 13, 17, 21–24, 26 source: Wellcome Collection
8 Courtesy of Linda Hall Library of Science, Engineering & Technology
15 illustration: © Guillermo S. Arsuaga based on materials from the Wellcome Collection, London
16 Henry Flather/London Museum
18 London Museum
25 The National Archives (UK), ref. MH12/7489

8 THE BACTERIAL TURN

1 Courtesy of Institut Pasteur/Musée Pasteur
3, 11 source: Wellcome Collection
16 source: Library of Congress/2009630606
17 source: *A travers le monde* (January 1903)
19 Hermann Muthesius © Österreichische Nationalbibliothek

9 CURE BY DESIGN

1 akg-images/Science Source
2 VintageSpace/Alamy
3 photo: Handout/Getty Images
4 photo: Darko Vojinovic/AP Photo/Keystone
5 © SZ Photo/Scherl/Bridgeman Images
10 Reproduced with permission from Birmingham Libraries, photograph (Sutton Coldfield) Maney 15
12 source: Wellcome Collection
14, 17 source: *Deutsche Industrie und Technik bei Einrichtung und Betrieb von Sanatorien und Krankenhäusern* (Berlin: Das Rothe Kreuz, 1889).
15 source: Reinhold Ortmann, *Görbersdorf - Dr. Brehmer's Heilanstalt für Lungenkranke* (Zurich: 1880)
18 source: Philip L. Gallos, *Cure Cottages of Saranac Lake Architecture and History of a Pioneer Health Resor*t (Saranac Lake, NY: Historic Saranac Lake, 1985)
19 Courtesy of Historic Saranac Lake Collection
20 M Wanner/Creative Commons
21 piemags/LCB/Alamy
22 Courtesy of Adirondack Research Room, Saranac Lake Free Library
23 source: *Charities and The Commons*, no. 16 (Sept 1, 1906)
24 Courtesy of Barlow Respiratory Hospital
25 source: Jewish Historical Society of Southern California
26–27 source: *The Nordrach Ranch Sanatorium and Hotel Co., Colorado Springs, Colorado*, fifth edition of booklet, (Colorado Springs, 1906)
29 photo: Courtesy of the American Jewish Historical Society, New York. From the Jewish Consumptives' Relief Society (Denver, Colo.) Collection (I-333)

10 THE ARCHITECTURE OF SPIT

1, 19, 21–22, 25, 26 photo/image: Alvar Aalto Foundation
2 source: The Croatian Museum of Medicine and Pharmacy
3 Courtesy of Historic Saranac Lake Collection
5–6, 8 Dokumentationsbibliothek Davos
9 J. Compeer, Dokumentationsbbliothek Davos
10–15 source: *Tuberculosis – Monatsschrift des internationalen Centralbureaus zur Bekämpfung der Tuberkulose* 2 (1903)
16, 18 photo: © MAK – Museum für angewandte Kunst, Wien
17 source: Stadtmuseum Purkersdorf
20 photo: Gustaf Welin, Alvar Aalto Foundation, 1933
23 photo: Gustaf Welin, Alvar Aalto Foundation
24 photo: Alvar Aalto, Alvar Aalto Foundation
27 source: Alvar Aalto, "The Humanizing of Architecture," *Technology Review* 43, no. 1 (November 1940): 16

11 ARCHITECTURE TAKES THE CURE

1, 7 © 2025, ProLitteris, Zurich
2, 27 photo: ullstein bild Dtl./Getty Images
3 Süddeutsche Zeitung/SZ Photo/Keystone
4 source: Imma Forino, "The Domestic Kitchen, Between Utopias and Heterotopias of the 20th Century," *Compasses* 33 (May 2020): 33–41
5 source: *L'architecture vivante* ed. Jean Badovici (1928), 20
6, 8–9 source: Deutscher Werkbund, *Bau und Wohnung* (Stuttgart: Akad. Verlag Dr. Fr. Wedekind & Co, 1927)
10 © Thonet, Constantin Meyer
11, 25 source: Sigfried Giedion, *Befreites Wohnen* (Zurich: Lars Müller Publishers reprint, 1929)
12, 14–15, 17, 26 source: Richard Döcker, *Terrassentyp: Krankenhaus, Erholungsheim, Hotel, Bürohaus, Einfamilienhaus, Siedlungshaus, Miethaus und die Stadt* (Stuttgart: Akademischer Verlag Fritz Wedekind & Co., 1929)
13 gta Archiv/ETH Zürich, Haefeli Moser Steiger. photo: Siegfried Giedion
18 Royal Museum of Art and History, Brussels, CC BY – SA 4.0 ImageStudio RMAH Brussels
19 Royal Museum of Art and History, Brussels
21–23 © Fonds Sauvage. SIAF/Cité de l'architecture et du patrimoine/Archives d'architecture contemporaine
28 source: *L'architecture vivante*, ed. Jean Badovici (1931): 48
29 source: Alberto Sartoris, *Gli Elementi dell'Architettura Funzionali. Sintesi panoramica dell'architettura moderna* (Milan: Ulrico Hoepli, 1932)
30 © F.L.C. / 2025, ProLitteris, Zurich
31 source: *L'architecture d'aujourd'hui*, ed. André Bloc (September 1934): 78

12 ANTIBIOTIC ARCHITECTURE

1 photo: Peter Purdy/Getty Images
2 © The Trustees of the British Museum
3, 4, 5, 25 © F.L.C./2025, ProLitteris, Zurich
6 photo: Artek Collection/Alvar Aalto Foundation, circa 1932
8 source: David Gebhard, *Schindler*, (Santa Barbara Peregrine Press, 1980): 84–85 photo: JT Beals

9 source: *Das Neue Frankfurt*, no. 2 (1928): 92
10 source: *The Architectural Review*, (January 1935)
11 Los Angeles Public Library
12 source: *L'Architecture d'aujord'hui*, (June 1946): 75
13–16 source: "What is a House?," *Arts & Architecture* (July 1944)
17–20 © Courtesy of The Estate of R. Buckminster Fuller
21 DCA-30-2-4928, Design Council Archive, University of Brighton Design Archives; © Smithson Family Collection
22–23 © Smithson Family Collection
24 DCA-30-2-4090, Design Council Archive, University of Brighton Design Archives; © Smithson Family Collection

13 DYSBIOSIS

1 Deutsches Grünes Kreuz/Fixi/Creative Commons
2 photo: Bettmann/Getty Images
4 Science History Images/Alamy
5 Otis Historical Archives, National Museum of Health and Medicine/Creative Commons
6 Smith Collection/Gado/Alamy
7 © Haahtela T., et al., "A short history from Karelia study to biodiversity and public health interventions," *Front Allergy* 4 (2023), reproduced with permission
8 © Martin Oeggerli (2007), supported by Biozentrum, University Basel
9 photo: Pascale Vonaesch
10 photo: © Scott Chemileski and Roberto Kolter
11 Dennis Kunkel Microscopy/Science Photo Library
12 © Erik Zettler (NIOZ Royal Netherlands Institute for Sea Research, Texel, Netherlands. Imaged at MBL Central Microscope Facility, Woods Hole, MA, USA)

14 BIOTIC ARCHITECTURE

1 photo: © Marta Perdiguer Torralba
4 © Ashmolean Museum
5 NASA/JPL-Caltech/MSSS
6–9 Instituto Bardi/Casa de Vidro, Lina Bo Bardi/2025, ProLitteris, Zurich
10–11 © 2025 NAMIDA AG, Glarus/Schweiz
12 courtesy of Triennale Milano – Archivi
13–14 source: *Metabolism: The Proposals for New Urbanism* (Bitjutu Syuppan Sha, 1960)
15–17 Alan Sonfist, landartforward.com
18–20 Gordon Matta-Clark Estate
21–23 Collecion de Arte Amalia Lacroze de Fortabat
24–26 © Maison Margiela. photo: Bob Goedewaagen
27 photo: Ulrich Rossmann/Rudi Scheuermann, ARUP, Technische Universität Dresden
28 source: patent drawings of Mycellium Brick/MycoHAB and Enzyme Brick/BioMason
29 photo: Tom Ellis Lab/Modern Synthesis.
30 photo: Leon van Paassen/Caitlyn Hall, Nariman Mahabadi, Jean Larson, Leon van Paassen/Arizona State University
31 Robert Kindler, Edoardo Mollica, Roman Stocker, André Studart, Ingo Burgert/ ETH Zurich
32 Elisabetta Caselli, Irene Soffritti, Maria D'Accolti, Luca Lanzoni, Matteo Bisi, Antonella Volta, Sante Mazzacane, Francesca Bini, Eleonora Mazziga, Carolina Cason, Giuseppina Campisciano, Paola Toscani, Manola Comar/ University of Ferrara and Institute for Maternal and Child Health – IRCCS
33 Rinad Hamed, Shehdeh Jodeh, and Raed Alkowni/An-Najah National University
34 photo: Lian He/Mary E. Lidstrom/ University of Washington
35 Nele De Belie and Elke Gruyaert/ Magnel-Vandepitte Laboratory for Structural Engineering and Building Materials, Ghent University
36 photo: Graham Bradley/Francesca Cappitelli, University of Milan. Federica Troiano, Annalisa Balloi, Maurizio Zangrossi, Alberto Gnesutta
37 Photo of Alhambra: Øyvind Holmstad/ Kerstin Elert, University of Granada; Carlos Rodriguez Navarro, University of Granada; Davide Gulotta, Getty Institute
38 Photo of cyanobacteria: Lubov Iliassafov, Yechezkel Kashi/Laboratory of Applied Genomics and Food Microbiology/Shany Barath, Porla Armaly, Yuval-Pesach Berger, Disrupt.Design Research Laboratory, Technion IIT
39 photo: Kohei Oda/Shosuke Yoshida, Kazumi Hiraga, Toshihiko Takehana, Ikuo Taniguchi, Hironao Yamaji, Yasuhito Maeda, Kiyotsuna Toyohara, Kenji Miyamoto, Yoshiharu Kimura, and Kohei Oda
40 photo: Rebecca McWatters Australian Antarctic Division

TOWARD BIOTIC ARCHITECTURE

1 source: *Philosophical Transactions of the Royal Society* (May 20, 1684)

WE THE BACTERIA
Notes Toward Biotic Architecture

Authors: Beatriz Colomina, Mark Wigley
Copyediting: Nick Axel
Proofreading: Ian McDonald
Editorial coordination: Hester van den Bold, Emilia Maier
Design: Lars Müller Publishers / Lars Müller and Esther Butterworth
Production: Esther Butterworth
Lithography: Gundula Seraphin, Bad Münstereifel, Germany
Printing and binding: Graspo, Zlín, Czech Republic
Paper: G-Print Vol 1.0, 90 g/m²

Lars Müller Publishers is supported by the Swiss Federal Office of Culture with a structural contribution for the years 2021–2025.

Lars Müller Publishers
Pfingstweidstrasse 6
8005 Zurich
Switzerland
+41 44 274 37 40
info@lars-mueller-publishers.com
www.lars-mueller-publishers.com

Product safety
Producer: Lars Müller Publishers GmbH
Responsible person in accordance with EU Regulation 2023/988 (GPSR): Michael Klein, sales representative, Hub 1, DE-84149 Velden
+49 8742 964 552 2
gpsr@lars-mueller-publishers.com

ISBN 978-3-03778-783-0

Distributed in North America, Latin America and the Caribbean by ARTBOOK | D.A.P.
www.artbook.com

Printed in the Czech Republic

This publication is made possible with support from:

The Barr Ferree Foundation Fund for Publications, Department of Art and Archaeology, Princeton University

The Graham Foundation for Advanced Studies in the Fine Arts

Elise Jaffe + Jeffrey Brown